DAYS OF THE WEST

DAYS OF THE WEST

Mike Flanagan

RENAISSANCE HOUSE

A Division of Jende-Hagan, Inc.
541 Oak Street • P.O. Box 177
Frederick, CO 80530

Copyright © 1987 by Mike Flanagan. Printed in the United States of America. All rights reserved. This book or any parts thereof, may not be reproduced in any manner whatsoever without written permission of the publisher:

RENAISSANCE HOUSE PUBLISHERS
A Division of Jende-Hagan, Inc.
541 Oak Street * P.O. Box 177
Frederick, CO 80530

Library of Congress Cataloging in Publication Data:

Flanagan, Mike.
  Days of the West.

  Bibliography: p.
  Includes index.
  1. West (U.S.)--History--Chronology. I. Title.
F591.F53 1987   978'.002'02   87-26542
ISBN 0-939650-14-2

Cover illustration by Vaughn Reichelderfer

Acknowledgements

Many have contributed to this project, in person and in spirit. The staff at the Western History Department of the Denver Public Library never ceases to amaze me with its knowledge, expertise, and determination to resolve an issue. Their guidance through stacks of yellowed newspapers, dusty dime novels, and rare books from the frontier was invaluable. That, combined with more than 50 years of their collecting skills, made this book a reality.

My thanks to *The Denver Post* for the opportunity to explore this fascinating ground on a regular basis, and to the readers of my "Out West" column who contribute with their comments and suggestions.

For this project specifically, thanks to the staff at Renaissance House, to Warren Onken for double checking facts, and to Bruce Cousins for transmitting the manuscript on his modem.

Most of all, I would like to thank my wife, Nancy Flanagan, who reads and rereads with patience, understanding, and style.

For the information, thanks to the journalists, western history writers, diary keepers, any and all who took notes on the West and thought enough to jot a date next to them. To chronicle such a vast and varied national experience was a major undertaking, accomplished by thousands. People lived and died here, which is what *Days of the West* is all about.

For my parents, who filled my days with wonder.

"Had you left New York or San Francisco at ten o'clock this morning, by noon the day after tomorrow you could step out at Cheyenne. There you would stand at the heart of the world that is the subject of my picture, yet you would look around you in vain for the reality. It is a vanished world. No journeys, save those which memory can take, will bring you to it now. The mountains are there, far and shining, and the sunlight, and the infinite earth, and the air that seems forever the true fountain of youth, ~ but where is the buffalo, and the wild antelope, and where the horseman with his pasturing thousands? So like its old self does the sage-brush seem when revisited, that you wait for the horseman to appear."

--Owen Wister

On my first visit to Denver in 1974, I was overwhelmed by the West. I had always lived there, in Oklahoma where the wind comes sweeping down the plain. Being "Out West" was no big deal, really. Cowboys and Indians were an everyday occurrence in my hometown, at least the 1950s version of them. Instead of shooting guns and arrows at each other, they worked the oilfields, ran the grocery stores, taught the schools, played baseball in the summer and football in the winter. They were direct descendants of the aftermath of the Old West, the struggles of the pioneer days having given way to more modern predicaments.

In considering Denver as a place to live, I was being a good tourist. I had always been in love with the past, and a visit to the Buffalo Bill museum on Lookout Mountain west of the city had more than filled my nostalgia cup. Inside were glass-encased fragments from the wild and woolly showbiz West. Here was Bill's gun, over there his hunting knife. On the wall an elephantine poster shouted in Victorian red letters BUFFALO BILL'S WILD WEST. All the fringed memorabilia was there, the bureau drawer of a buckskin superstar who for two decades before the movies kept the romance and the dream of the West alive.

The day faded into one of those Colorado summer nights, rain fresh from afternoon showers and crystal clear. Off one edge of the mountain was another story from the West, the brewery Adolph Coors built to sell his improved Rocky Mountain springwater. Then, to the east, Denver began turning on her night lights. Slowly, the sea plain glistened here and there, little pins of light spreading for miles. All the cars moved, everybody had his own little story going. Not that long ago, the days had been so different, right in that same location.

So much had happened down there ~ the roaming buffalo herds, the gold crazy prospectors, the gamblers, the whores, the dreamers, the failures ~ so much had gone into this city, the largest commercial center between St. Louis and the Pacific. The ghosts of Bat Masterson and Jack Kerouac were right at home. Like the spellbound inventor in H.G. Wells' time machine, the gears of history seemed to whir before my eyes. The heart of the West was still beating.

Like the first inhabitants of earth to whom they were so closely connected, the Indians had conveyed their greatest achievements in art. On tanned buffalo skins, tipi walls, in the sand, they had sketched their heroes and villains. The stories were handed down with love and wonder. All time suspended itself in a region just beyond a grandfather's earliest memory. On a glorious field a battle was won, a great bear was slain, a drought ended with the sound of thunder walking.

We document ourselves in ways that are surprisingly similar to the first Americans. Newspapers and history books have taken the place of cave walls and tipi drawings, but we still tell stories about what goes on around us. We record deeds, great and otherwise, reward progress and regret lunacy. Each moment is tagged in time by the date on which it occurred.

The American West is our wonderful folk adventure. For so long, the land was the great unknown, a vast, wild region populated with fierce Indians and even fiercer weather. The thinking about the West in colonial times was simple: no one in his right mind would go there. Still, there was that aura of adventure that Lewis and Clark had turned into a national fascination. The Indians had been friendly, the country was spectacular. Perhaps, people began thinking, the West wasn't so bad after all. By the 1840s, wagon trains were creaking slowly toward a land of plenty, yours for the breaking of your back. The discovery of gold opened the flood gates and across the frontier, countless dramas filled the days.

Seeking the information for this book was like panning for gold. Recovering nuggets from history is great fun, but you always have that feeling that there is more in the stream. In an attempt to present as broad a cross section as possible, there is the chance that someone's favorite tidbit might have been omitted. No malice was intended. It would take volumes to give you every incident in the history of the West. If your curiosity is piqued enough to dig deeper, then this project will have served its purpose.

Days of the West is a simultaneous look at the old and new West, a collection of highlights, lowlights, birth dates, death dates, discoveries, losses, matters important and trivial. The notations for each date, from January 1 to December 31, are arranged chronologically by year. Events will always occur in order for a certain day, but remember that some things took time to unfold. For example, the revenge over the incident at the OK Corral was still going on in March of 1882 after the gunfight itself took place in October, 1881. For that reason, in this book, the aftermath might be noted before the main action. Every effort had been made to verify each entry but, as with any kind of history, precise dates are sometimes recalled differently. In instances where dates conflicted, the more reliable source was used.

Here are the paths of the explorers, the cattle trails, the discoveries of wealth, the loss of life, the battles, and the results, all from the region that gave you the Eskimo Pie and the atomic bomb. Rails are joined, houses are burned, war is declared, a peace is signed, all in the warmth of a 118 degree day or a 249 inch snow. From stagecoaches, Pony Express, transcontinental railroads, newspapers, telegraph wires, telephones, radios, and televisions, come the moments of our Western cornucopia. Our setting is the Rocky Mountains, the Great American Desert, and the Great Plains from the Mississippi to the Pacific. Our destination is set for those thrilling days of yesteryear.

-- Mike Flanagan
January, 1987

January

JANUARY 1

1821: Davy Crockett resigns as town commissioner of Lawrenceburg to run for the Tennessee legislature.

1833: Antonio Lopez de Santa Anna begins his term as President of Mexico.

1863: Confederates win the battle of Galveston, Texas during the Civil War.

1863: Daniel Freeman files the first claim under the Homestead Act near Beatrice, Nebraska.

1877: Gen. Nelson Miles begins an eight-day running fight with Sioux and Cheyennes.

1896: The Leadville Ice Palace, a 450 by 350-foot castle made of blocks of ice, weighing a total of 5,000 tons, opens with 2,500 attending chilly ceremonies. Town fathers had come up with the idea to bolster community coffers; however, an early thaw leaves them with a beautiful but financially disastrous memory.

1909: Future Sen. Barry M. Goldwater born in Phoenix, Arizona.

1913: First parcel post package leaves Denver ~ limburger cheese en route to Boston.

1916: Prohibition goes into effect in Colorado. Adolph Coors watches as 17,931 gallons of his finest beer are dumped into the waters of Clear Creek in Golden, Colorado.

1917: Simon Bamberger becomes the first non-Mormon governor of Utah.

1923: Evangelist Aimee Semple McPherson dedicates her grandiose Angelus Temple in Los Angeles. It will be headquarters for her Foursquare Gospel Creed.

1942: Mine explosion at Mount Harris, Colorado, kills 34.

1953: Country-western legend Hank Williams Sr., aged 29, dies of a heart attack brought on by excessive drinking.

1955: *Bad Day at Black Rock* with Spencer Tracy and Robert Ryan released by MGM.

1955: *Destry* with Audie Murphy released by Universal.

1979: Maybell, Colorado registers -60 degrees, equalling the state's record low.

JANUARY 2

1777: Expedition of Fathers Dominguez and Escalante ends in Santa Fe, New Mexico. Although failing in their quests to find new routes to the California missions, they did explore much of the previously uncharted southwest.

1850: First public sale of beach and water property in San Francisco.

1853: U.S. Land Commission begins hearings in San Francisco to examine claims under old "Spanish grants."

1871: City of Golden, Colorado incorporated.

1907: Head-on train collision at Volland, Kansas claims 32 lives.

1913: Singer Roger Miller ("King of the Road") born in Fort Worth, Texas.

1923: Interior Secretary Albert Bacon Fall resigns in the wake of the Teapot Dome affair.

1982: Cartoonist Fred Harman ("Red Ryder") dies at age 79 in Phoenix, Arizona.

JANUARY 3

1823: Mexican Congress agrees to admit colonizers into Texas, provided they are Roman Catholics.

1834: Stephen F. Austin is arrested by Mexican authorities for inciting Texans to rebel. His wish for Texas to be separate from Coahuila will get him eight months in prison.

1846: The term "Manifest Destiny" is first used in Congress by Massachusetts representative Robert Winthrop.

1911: Hiram Johnson becomes governor of California. After serving two terms, he will serve four successive terms as a U.S. Senator.

1933: First woman speaker of a state house of representatives, M.D. Craig, is elected in North Dakota.

1961: Nuclear accident in Idaho Falls, Idaho kills three atomic reactor technicians.

1967: Jack Ruby, awaiting a second trial for the slaying of accused Presidential assassin Lee Harvey Oswald, dies at age 65.

1979: Hotel magnate Conrad Hilton dies at age 91 in Los Angeles.

JANUARY 4

1806: Fire in Zebulon Pike's camp destroys clothing and a tent during the northern expedition.

1847: U.S. government buys 1,000 Colt revolvers.

1880: Pat Garrett marries his late wife's sister, Apolinaria Gutierrez.

1896: Utah becomes the 45th state.

1915: Moses Alexander becomes the first Jewish governor of Idaho.

1948: Benedum and Slick strike oil in Upton County, Texas.

JANUARY 5

ZEBULON PIKE

1779: Zebulon Pike born in Lamberton, New Jersey. An intrepid if somewhat misguided explorer, his mission to the West will remain a controversy throughout history. Nevertheless, he will blaze a trail across the plains of Kansas, then explore the Rockies in the dead of winter, where he will enjoy a close encounter with the mountain ultimately named for him.

> **ZEBULON PIKE**
> **Born:** January 5, 1779
> **Died:** April 17, 1813
> **Explorer, military leader**
>
> **1805:** Sets out on northern voyage to locate the source of the Mississippi River.
> **1806:** Returns to St. Louis from Mississippi exploration. Begins western expedition from Fort Belle Fountaine, near St. Louis. Proceeds overland through Kansas to Colorado. "Discovers" Pikes Peak in Colorado Springs.
> **1807:** Arrested by Spanish dragoons near Alamosa, Colorado on suspicion of spying. Tells them he is lost. Escorted to Chihuahua for interrogation. Released at Natchitoches, Louisiana July 1.
> **1813:** Killed while leading troops in the Battle of York during the War of 1812.

1807: On his birthday, Lt. Zebulon Pike, camped at the upper end of the Royal Gorge in the dead of winter, writes: "Most fervently did I hope never to pass another so miserably."

1833: *Life and Adventures of Colonel David Crockett of West Tennessee* by Mathew St. Clair Clarke is deposited for copyright.

1848: Western speedster Francis X. Aubry arrives in Independence, Missouri after, a 14-day horse ride from Santa Fe, New Mexico.

1850: California Exchange opens in San Francisco, ready to handle the latest gold discoveries.

1852: Margaret Emma Custer, sister of George Armstrong Custer, born.

1874: Physiologist Joseph Erlanger born in San Francisco, California. He will win the 1944 Nobel Prize for his studies of nerve impulses.

1879: Rations for Dull Knife's captive Cheyennes at Fort Robinson, Nebraska, are cut off.

1886: Snows from Omaha to North Platte, Nebraska, cause six-foot drifts.

1925: In Wyoming, Nellie Tayloe Ross, is sworn in as the first woman governor in history.

1930: *The Lone Star Ranger* is released by 20th Century Fox.

1933: Construction begins on San Francisco's Golden Gate Bridge.

> **1943: Agricultural chemist George Washington Carver dies** at age 79. Born on an unknown date in 1864, Diamond Grove, Missouri, he earned a masters degree in science from Iowa State Agricultural College before becoming head of the Agriculture department at Tuskegee Institute in Alabama. His revolutionary experiments with peanuts and sweet potatoes lead to over 400 by-products. His major concern was helping the downtrodden farmer. In his lifetime, he refused profit from his discoveries and rejected offers to work for Thomas Edison and in the Soviet Union.

1982: Federal judge in Little Rock, Arkansas declares a state law that requires a balance between the teaching of creationism and the theory of evolution to be unconstitutional.

JANUARY 6

1799: Jedediah Strong Smith born in Bainbridge, (then known as Jericho) New York. One of the most notable mountain men, he will lead the first party overland from the Great Salt

Lake to California.

> **JEDEDIAH SMITH**
> Born: January 6, 1799
> Died: May 27, 1831
> Trapper, explorer
>
> 1822: Joins Ashley's expedition to fur trap the Missouri River.
> 1823: Leads overland party to the Black Hills.
> 1825: Partners with Ashley.
> 1826: Sets out on the first expedition overland from Utah to California.
> 1827: Returns with three of his original party to the Great Salt Lake.
> 1828: Party reaches Oregon's Umpqua River. Kelawatset Indians attack his trappers; 15 are killed.
> 1830: Enters the Santa Fe trade.
> 1831: Killed by Comanches on the Cimarron River.

1869: Outlaw Cullen Baker is tracked down and killed by Thomas Orr, a schoolteacher he had picked on once too often.

1880: Cowboy movie idol Tom Mix born in Driftwood, Pennsylvania.

1882: Sam Rayburn born in Tennessee. At age five he moves to Texas, where an illustrious political career will follow. He is elected Speaker of the House in 1940, and serves that seat's longest term, 17 non-consecutive years.

1882: Pony Deal and two others hold up the Tombstone-Bisbee stage.

1891: Last attack on a wagon train by a band of Sioux, in the days following the Wounded Knee massacre.

1900: Bob Curry sells his saloon in Harlem, Montana, as the law closes in on him.

1905: Humble Oil Field discovered in Texas.

1912: New Mexico (pop. 325,000) becomes the 47th state.

1912: Frederick Manfred author of *Lord Grizzly* and *Conquering Horse* born in Doon, Iowa.

1913: Actress Loretta Young born in Salt Lake City, Utah.

1923: Body of U.S. Mint robber found in a Denver garage.

JANUARY 7

1830: Landscapist Albert Bierstadt born near Duesseldorf, Germany. His massive panoramas will become world famous, portraying the unspoiled West as an Eden with Rocky Mountains.

1860: Animal trainer Grizzly Adams and his menagerie, which includes bears and mountain lions, set sail from San Francisco, around the tip of South America to New York, where he will work for P.T. Barnum.

1865: Cheyenne and Sioux forces attack Julesburg, Colorado during a march to Powder River country. The raid on the stagecoach station there is in retaliation for the Sand Creek Massacre.

1874: Clay Allison and Chunk Colbert tie in a horse race in New Mexico. At a dinner following the race, the two go for their guns. Allison shoots Colbert dead.

1892: Krebs, Oklahoma mine explosion kills 100.

1899: Texas Ranger Bigfoot Wallace dies at age 82.

1901: Alfred Packer, confessed cannibal who was convicted of manslaughter, is paroled after a vigorous promotional campaign by *The Denver Post*.

PACKER PARTY VICTIMS

1929: Notorious madame Mattie Silks dies at age 81 at Denver General Hospital.

1950: Fire at Davenport, Iowa's Mercy Hospital kills 40.

1961: Thomas Hotel fire in San Francisco kills 20.

1971: Coldest temperature ever recorded in Arizona is -40 degrees at Hawley Lake.

JANUARY 8

1815: Gen. Andrew Jackson's troops inflict 2,000 enemy casualties during the defense and Battle of New Orleans. Unfortunately, neither side is aware that the war had ended on December 24, 1814.

1818: First petition for Missouri statehood is received by Congress.

1856: D. John Veatch discovers the first borax in the United States at a spring in California.

1859: Jim Sanders, Denver's only postal service, returns with mail from Wyoming, Christmas cards and all.

1865: En route to Mexico, a band of 1,400 Kickapoo Indians under Chief No-Ko-Wat defeats 370 militia men on Dove Creek near San Angelo, Texas.

1877: Forces under Col. Nelson A. Miles clash with a combined Sioux and Cheyenne war party under Crazy Horse at the Battle of Wolf Mountain on Montana's Tongue River. Miles turns back the attack.

1881: Historian John G. Neihardt, author of *Black Elk Speaks*, born in Illinois.

1884: Texas legislature meets to discuss the Fence Cutter War, a bloody conflict between cattlemen who are fencing their lands with barbed wired and those who prefer the open range.

1886: During the terrible winter of

'86, the *Clark County Chief* in Kansas reports: "Blessed is he who has plenty of shelter and feed for his stock and coal for fuel these times, but woe unto him that hath them not."

1892: McAllister, Oklahoma coal mine explosion kills 100.

1894: Idaho's Albion Normal School opens.

1981: Environmentalists go into an uproar when President-elect Reagan picks James Watt to head the Department of the Interior.

JANUARY 9

1789: The Treaty of Fort Harmar establishes payment principles for land with the Ohio Indians.

1802: Western University, now known as Ohio University, is chartered at Athens, Ohio.

1847: San Francisco's first newspaper, *The California Star*, publishes first issue.

1847: Last battle of Mexican "rebellion" won by American forces. Four days later, articles of capitulation will be signed at Rancho Cahuenga, making it the last battle of the Mexican War.

1848: First commercial bank is established in San Francisco.

1858: Texas politician Anson Jones commits suicide after failing to tally a single vote in the 1857 senatorial election.

1879: Starved after four days with no food, captive Cheyenne under Dull Knife at Fort Robinson, Nebraska, crash their barracks. Soldiers shoot and club to death 50 Indians, mostly women and children.

1886: Noon temperature in Fargo, North Dakota is -27 degrees. Bismarck records -35 degrees.

1887: During the "Great Die-Up" ("the worst winter in the West," that kills millions of cattle on the open range), inch-an-hour snow falls for 16 hours.

1903: Wind Cave, South Dakota, known for limestone caverns and wildlife, is designated a national park.

1908: California's Muir Woods designated a national monument.

1913: Richard Milhous Nixon, 37th U.S. President, born in Yorba Linda, California.

1925: Actor Lee Van Cleef, western movie bad guy, born in Somerville, New Jersey.

1944: Lawman Chris Madsen, 93, dies after a fall in Guthrie, Oklahoma.

1975: The grizzly bear is placed on the "threatened" list by the Department of the Interior.

JANUARY 10

1807: President Thomas Jefferson receives the first report from Lewis and Clark.

> **1843: Outlaw Frank James born** in Clay County, Missouri. With brother Jesse he will rob trains and banks, but after his sibling's assassination, (for a paltry reward) he will see the error of his ways. He will serve a brief prison sentence, receive a pardon, and work straight, odd jobs, the rest of his days.

1847: During the Mexican War, Los Angeles is recaptured from Mexican rebels by Commodore Robert F. Stockton and Gen. Stephen Kearny. Fighting ceases in California.

1862: Samuel Colt, 47, dies at his mansion, Armsmear. His estate is estimated at $15 million.

FRANK JAMES

1863: Union gunboats fire on Galveston, Texas, during the Civil War.

1889: Artist John Held Jr., who will capture the Roaring Twenties with his round-headed men and leggy flappers, is born to Mormon parents in Salt Lake City, Utah.

1893: Como Mine in King, Colorado explodes killing 27.

1901: Alfred Packer, fresh from his parole from prison, pays a visit to the offices of *The Denver Post* to thank them for bringing his case to the public's attention.

> **1901: First oil discovered in Texas.** Curt and Al Hamill and Peck Byrd make the big strike on the claim of Anthony F. Lucas at Spindletop in Beaumont, Texas.

1911: Temperatures drop an incredible 47 degrees in 15 minutes at Rapid City, South Dakota.

1914: Salt Lake City grocer John Morrison and his son Arling are slain by two masked gunmen who enter his store at closing time. Labor activist Joe Hill will be arrested, convicted, and executed for the deed, although he may have been innocent. Hill will become a martyr for the labor cause.

1917: William F. Cody, Buffalo Bill, dies at age 71 in Denver. Wyoming and Nebraska both want the body to be laid to rest there, but *The Denver Post* has other ideas. After much maneuvering within the family, a huge promotional funeral is held and Cody is entombed on Lookout Mountain, just west of that city. As a precaution against graverobbers, the casket is encased in tons of cement.

1925: The wife of impeached Texas Gov. James Ferguson is inaugurated governor of the state.

1949: Second and last snow seen to date in San Diego, California.

JANUARY 11

1854: Fort Bliss established near El Paso, Texas.

1872: Royal party of Russia's Grand Duke Alexis leaves St. Louis for a western buffalo hunt.

1874: Gail Borden Jr., the man who developed a way to process condensed milk in a vacuum, dies in Bordenville, Texas.

1890: Western actor Monte Blue, star of silents and talkies such as *Geronimo* (1940) and *Cheyenne* (1947), born.

1892: Pecos Forest Reserve created in New Mexico.

1897: Bernard Augustine DeVoto, editor of *The Journals of Lewis and Clark; The Course of Empire; Across the Wide Missouri*, born in Ogden, Utah.

1908: Grand Canyon becomes a national monument.

1914: Mother Jones, 84, is arrested for being an inciting force at a miners' strike in Trinidad, Colorado.

JACK LONDON

1922: Montana declares its "bachelor tax law," a poll tax on 21 to 60-year-old males.

1935: Amelia Earhart takes off from Honolulu on a flight that will make her the first person to fly from Hawaii to California.

JANUARY 12

1777: Mission Santa Clara de Asis founded in California.

1812: The steamboat *New Orleans* becomes the first to make the Pittsburgh/New Orleans run. To do so, she had to survive the New Madrid Earthquake of December 16, 1811.

1838: Following the failure of a Mormon bank, Joseph Smith leaves Kirtland, Ohio to avoid arrest and seek a new future in Missouri.

1853: Willamette University chartered in Salem, Oregon. It opened as the Oregon Institute in 1844 and was the first college on the Pacific coast.

1872: Grand Duke Alexis and his entourage are met at the train depot in Omaha by George Armstrong Custer.

1876: Author Jack London (*The Call of the Wild, White Fang*) born in San Francisco.

1884: Night club personality Texas Guinan born in Waco, Texas. During the heyday of the speakeasy, her famous salutation is "Hello, Sucker!"

1886: Explosion at Almy mine No. 2 in Wyoming kills 13.

1904: Mounties apprehend outlaw Ernie Cashel.

1906: Actor-singer Woodward Maurice "Tex" Ritter born in Murvaul, Texas. In addition to 80 film credits, his recorded hits will include the theme from *High Noon*, better known as "Do Not Forsake Me Oh My Darling." Inducted into the Country Music Hall of Fame, 1964.

1920: Civil rights leader James Farmer born in Marshall, Texas.

JANUARY 13

1846: President Polk sends Gen. Zachary Taylor and 4,000 troops into the disputed area between the Nueces River and the Rio Grande, near the present Texas/Mexico border.

1847: Forces under Andres Pico surrender to John C. Fremont. The Treaty of Cahuenga is signed in the San Fernando Valley.

1879: A court of inquiry, requested by Maj. Marcus Reno and ordered by President Hayes, meets in Chicago. Reno will be cleared of any blame in the Custer debacle at the Little Bighorn.

1901: Author A.B. Guthrie, Jr. (*The Big Sky, The Way West*) is born in Bedford, Indiana. Awarded Pulitzer Prize in 1950.

1926: Mine explosion in Wilburton, Oklahoma kills 92.

1929: Wyatt Earp dies at age 80 at his home at 4004 West 17th Street in Los Angeles. He is buried in

Colma, California.

1937: *The Plainsman* with Gary Cooper as Wild Bill Hickok is released.

1939: *Jesse James* with Tyrone Power is released.

1985: Major snows hit Texas; San Antonio receives 13.5 inches.

JANUARY 14

1864: Highwayman Jack Gallagher is hanged by vigilantes.

1872: Celebrating his 21st birthday with a buffalo hunt in the West, Grand Duke Alexis gets his first kill. After six wild shots, his guide, Buffalo Bill Cody, hands him the famed "Lucretia Borgia" .50 caliber rifle. Alexis gets within ten feet of his mark and scores a bull's-eye.

1882: First snow seen in San Diego, California.

1891: Gen. Nelson Miles, in the days following the Wounded Knee massacre, reports that Sioux Indians are returning to the reservation.

1963: A 630-acre tract of land is deeded from the state of Texas back to Mexico. It had been created when the Rio Grande changed course in 1864.

1967: A "Human Be-In" held in San Francisco's Haight-Ashbury district, where 20,000 hear music by Quicksilver Messenger Service, Jefferson Airplane, and the Grateful Dead.

1985: Legal action against actor Clayton Moore, to prevent him from wearing the Lone Ranger mask he made famous in the 50s, is dropped by the Wrather Corporation.

JANUARY 15

1844: Outlaw Cole(man) Younger born near Lee's Summit, Missouri. He will ride with Quantrill during the Civil War, then with relatives Frank and Jesse James. During the raid on Northfield in 1876 he will be severely wounded, surviving to do 25 years in the slammer. He then will spend his retirement in show business.

1848: Outlaw Jim Younger born near Lee's Summit, Missouri. His career as a badman will parallel brother Cole's, but a few months after release from his 25-year prison term, he will commit suicide.

1852: In San Francisco, Charles Pickett begins publishing his weekly newspaper, the *Western American*.

1856: Kansas free-soilers elect Charles Robinson governor. President Pierce calls it an act of rebellion, since slavery has already been approved in the area.

1864: Stephen Marshland, member of Henry Plummer's gang "Innocents" is lynched by vigilantes at Big Hole, Wyoming.

1874: Frank and Jesse James, Cole and Jim Younger, and Clell Miller hold up the Concord Stage at Malvein, Arkansas, netting $4,000 in jewelry and money.

1896: Photographer Mathew B. Brady (born in 1823) dies in New York. Best-known for his Civil War portraits, he also took his lens out West.

1897: John Duval, longest surviving member of Fannin's Army, dies in Fort Worth.

1909: Denver and Rio Grande trains collide near Dotsero, Colorado, killing 20.

1923: *Donnegan* by George Owen Baxter published by Chelsea House.

1932: Heaviest Los Angeles snowfall in history dumps two inches.

JANUARY 16

1847: John C. Fremont appointed governor of California.

1850: Eagle Theater and Washington Hall, some of the city's first theaters, open in San Francisco.

1855: First territorial legislature in Nebraska meets at Omaha City.

1869: Lincoln County, New Mexico established.

1892: All mines in Coeur d'Alene, Idaho are shut down due to high freight charges and low silver prices.

1908: Pinnacles National Monument established in California.

1919: Nebraska is the 36th state to ratify the 18th Amendment. With this action, all alcoholic beverages become illegal in the United States.

1929: Pall bearers at Wyatt Earp's funeral include William S. Hart and Tom Mix.

1934: Clyde Barrow springs Raymond Hamilton from the Eastham Prison Farm in Huntsville, Texas.

1935: Outlaw Kate "Ma" Barker dies at age 62, killed in a gun battle with FBI agents in Oklawaha, Florida.

1935: Auto racer A.J. Foyt born in Houston, Texas.

1964: Record Dallas snowfall drops 12 inches.

1973: Newspaperman Harold Pullman Coffin of Reno, Nevada creates National Nothing Day.

1973: Last telecast of "Bonanza" after 14 seasons (NBC).

JANUARY 17

JOHN JACOB ASTOR
Born: January 17, 1763
Died: 1848
Early fur trading tycoon

1783: Arrives penniless in New York from native Germany.
1808: Organizes American Fur Trading Company, a series of trading posts that will carry his name and reputation across the frontier.
1811: Representatives of his company found Astoria, first permanent settlement in Pacific Northwest.
1812: Following War of 1812, he establishes Second Bank of the United States.
1821: Astoria absorbed by Hudson Bay Company.
1834: Leaves fur business for real estate ventures.
1848: America's first millionaire dies, leaving a $20 million estate.

1821: Moses Austin obtains Mexican permission to bring 300 colonizers into Texas.

1859: Benjamin Franklin, favorite bear of Grizzly Adams, dies of a mysterious illness in San Francisco.

1863: Apache chief Mangas Coloradas is murdered in his sleep by Col. J.R. West. At the time, he was in peace negotiations at an army camp near Fort McLean, in present-day New Mexico. Some believe Mangas was captured treacherously by gold-seeking members of the Joseph R. Walker party, turned over to California Volunteers, and shot while trying to escape when he protested his guards' burning his legs and feet with heated bayonets.

1871: First cable streetcar patented in San Francisco.

1886: Aircraft designer Glenn Luther Martin born in Macksburg, Iowa. He will establish one of the first airplane factories in the U.S., and make the first flight over water in this country, in 1912. Other firsts will include the twin-engine bomber and the first armored bomber.

1922: Clackama, Umpqua, and Rogue River tribes meet in Portland, Oregon to sue the United States for $12.5 million over tribal lands that were taken without payment.

1972: Montana sets record for a single snowfall with 77.5 inches at Summit.

1977: Convicted murderer Gary Gilmore is executed by a firing squad at Utah State Prison. This is the first capital punishment in the U.S. in the past ten years.

JANUARY 18

1803: President Thomas Jefferson tells Congress of his wish to explore the West recently acquired in the Louisiana Purchase, "even to the Western ocean." Congress will grant his request for $2,500 to fund a major expedition.

1836: Jim Bowie arrives at the Alamo.

1892: Rodeo champion Chester Byers born in Knoxville, Illinois.

1931: *The Painted Desert* with William Boyd released by RKO/Pathe.

1933: White Sands, New Mexico becomes a national monument.

1935: Baseball outfielder Curt Flood born in Houston, Texas. From 1965-67 he will play in 226 consecutive games without an error.

1969: A week of heavy rains begins in California. The result will be massive mudslides that will wreck thousands of homes, kill 100, and cause $138 million in damage.

1982: Worst accident in the history of the popular Thunderbirds occurs near Las Vegas, Nevada as four jets crash, killing four pilots.

1987: With the closing of the Capri and the Cinema, Utah becomes the only state without an X-rated, adult movie house.

JANUARY 19

1847: Sister Arsene Blin and six nuns arrive at Port of Galveston, Texas, to set up Catholic schools.

1847: Shortly after dawn, New Mexico Gov. Charles Bent is slain by Mexican rebels at Taos.

1897: Miners' strike in Colorado ends after seven months; owners increase wages.

1905: Oveta Culp Hobby, first Secretary of Health, Education, and Welfare (1953-55) born in Killeen, Texas.

1922: Actor Guy Madison, TV's "Wild Bill Hickok," is born Robert Moseley in Bakersfield, California.

1922: Idaho Sen. William E. Borah introduces a resolution to ban war.

1940: Idaho Sen. William E. Borah dies after 33 years of service.

1943: Singer Janis Joplin born in Port Arthur, Texas.

1946: Singer Dolly Parton born on a farm in Locust Ridge, Tennessee. Her first number one hit is "Joshua" (1970).

JANUARY 20

1874: Welterweight boxing champ Jim Ferns, The Kansas Rube, born in Pittsburg, Kansas.

1891: Hawaiian King Kalakaua dies in San Francisco, where he had gone in 1890 to improve his health.

1891: James S. Hogg sworn in as first native-born Texas governor.

MOTHER JONES

1914: A thousand women, protesting the illegal incarceration of labor sympathizer Mother Jones in Trinidad, Colorado, are charged by National Guard forces on horseback.

1929: *In Old Arizona* released by Fox.

1932: *The Fighting Fool* with Tim McCoy released.

1943: Temperatures of 52 degrees and -16 degrees are reported at Lead and Deadwood, South Dakota. They are only two miles apart.

1965: President Lyndon Baines Johnson takes the oath of office amidst tight security.

1981: Former "Death Valley Days" host and California Gov. Ronald Reagan is sworn in as the nation's 40th President.

JANUARY 21

1785: With the Treaty of Fort McIntosh, Chippewa, Delaware, Ottawa, and Wyandots cede nearly all of present Ohio to the United States.

1813: Explorer John Charles Fremont born in Savannah, Georgia. He will map the Oregon Trail in 1842, reach California in 1845, and become one of the first U.S. Senators from that state, as well as the first Presidential nominee of the Republican Party in 1856, and territorial governor of Arizona from 1878-81.

JOHN CHARLES FREMONT
Born: January 21, 1813
Died: January 13, 1890
Explorer, politician, soldier

1831: Dismissed from college in South Carolina.
1836: Works on railroad survey crews for Charleston and Cincinnati railroad.
1838: Explores Minnesota.
1842: Rocky Mountain expedition.
1844: Second expedition west, this time to California.
1846: Reaches Monterey; Bear Flag Revolt.
1847: Forces under Andres Pico surrender; appointed governor of California.
1848: Found guilty of mutiny.
1861: Declares martial law in Missouri.
1890: Dies at 77.

1855: Gun designer John Moses Browning born in Ogden, Utah. He will obtain patent on the breech-loading single shot rifle in 1879, and will invent the Browning automatic pistol in 1911, the Browning machine gun in 1917, and the Browning automatic rifle in 1918.

1861: Sam Houston submits the Texas resolution of secession to the legislature, although he himself opposes the measure.

1874: Alfred Packer's ill-fated expedition enters the valley of the Uncompahgre in southwestern Colorado.

1885: Bluesman Huddie Ledbetter born.

1924: Mount Hood National Forest created out of Oregon National Forest.

1945: Four-time national calf-roping champ Clyde Burk is killed during a steer wrestling event at Denver's National Western Stock Show.

1962: A massive avalanche at Twin Lakes, Colorado destroys several homes, killing seven.

JANUARY 22

1807: President Jefferson informs Congress of Aaron Burr's alleged plot to form a separate country in the Southwest.

1822: Black western entrepreneur Barney Ford is born a slave in Stafford, Virginia. Ford will make his fortune in the restaurant and hotel business in Denver and Cheyenne.

1850: The first daily newspaper in California is San Francisco's *Alta California*.

1879: Last of the fights in the Dull Knife outbreak. Dull Knife will surrender at the Pine Ridge Reservation in early February.

1890: Vigilante John X. Beidler dies in Helena, Montana, at age 58.

1911: Actress Ann Sothern born in Valley City, North Dakota.

1934: *The Lucky Texan* with John Wayne is released by Lone Star/Monogram.

JANUARY 23

> **1870: The Baker Massacre ~** Col. Eugene M. Baker, on the trail of Blackfoot killers of a fur trader, happens upon an encampment of Indian smallpox victims. He orders a charge and slaughters 170 men, women, and children. At his court martial, he is cleared of any wrongdoing.

1875: Molly Wright born in Bell County, Texas. As Dr. Molly Armstrong, she will become the first female optometrist in Texas, second in the nation.

1903: Actor Randolph Scott born in Orange County, Virginia. His movies will include *Abilene Town* (1945) and *Comanche Station* (1960).

1907: Charles Curtis of Kansas, first American Indian senator, is sworn in.

1907: Primero, Colorado mine explosion kills 24.

1964: South Dakota ratifies the 24th amendment banning payment of poll taxes in federal elections, giving it the necessary two-thirds majority to become law.

1974: Government authorization is granted for the Alaska pipeline.

JANUARY 24

> **1848: Gold discovered in California** ~ While erecting a sawmill for John Sutter on the American River, James Wilson Marshall, a New Jersey mechanic, discovers the gold that will change the face of the West.

1876: In a saloon fight in Mobeetie, Texas, Molly Brennan is killed by a stray bullet fired by one of two men fighting over her, a Cpl. Melvin A. King and Bat Masterson. King is also slain, by Masterson. Bat is wounded and from this day forth, he will walk with a cane.

1902: Mine disaster at Oskaloosa, Iowa, kills 20.

1918: Evangelist Oral Roberts born in Ada, Oklahoma.

1922: Lehman Caves, Nevada, is designated a national monument.

1922: Christian K. Nelson patents the "Eskimo Pie," ice cream in a chocolate shell, in Onawa, Iowa. He is soon partnered with future candy tycoon Russell Stover, who has renamed the confection from Nelson's original "I Scream Bar." Already, 1,500 have signed up to manufacture the treat.

1923: New Mexico's Aztec Ruins designated a national monument.

1924: Oilman Edward Doheny admits "lending" $100,000 to former Secretary of the Interior Albert Bacon Fall during the Teapot Dome scandal.

1925: Native American Prima Ballerina Maria Tallchief born in Fairfax, Oklahoma.

1931: Denver vice cops arrest 29 bootleggers in a raid on one Italian restaurant.

1974: Shirley Plume becomes the first Native American to be appointed superintendent of the Bureau of Indian Affairs.

JANUARY 25

1839: The newly formed Republic of Texas adopts a flag.

1845: House of Representatives votes to annex Texas.

1860: Charles Curtis born in Topeka, Kansas. In addition to being the first American Indian Senator (1907-1913; 1915-1929) he will become the 31st Vice-President of the United States under Herbert Hoover.

1869: Following a futile estate fight, 18-year-old Pat Garrett leaves his Claiborne Parish, Louisiana home for the West.

1899: Leadville, Colorado gets the first of 38 straight days of snow.

1915: The first transcontinental telephone hookup connects two of the great electronic conversationalists of the time, Alexander Graham Bell in New York and Thomas Watson in San Francisco.

1934: Public enemy John Dillinger is arrested in Tucson, Arizona.

1965: Utah's greatest snowstorm dumps 105 inches on Alta.

1971: Highest recorded winds in Colorado reach 147 MPH in Boulder.

JANUARY 26

1875: In an attempt to destroy Jesse James, Pinkerton agents and railroad operatives toss a bomb into the home of his mother, Zerelda. Jesse's 8-year-old half-brother Archie Samuel is killed. His mother loses an arm. Jesse is nowhere around at the time.

1915: Rocky Mountain National Park is established in Colorado. It claims 65 peaks over 10,000 feet.

1923: *Alcatraz* by Max Brand published by Putnam.

1925: Actor Paul Newman, who will play Billy the Kid and Butch Cassidy during a celebrated film career, is born in Cleveland, Ohio.

1945: Texan Audie Murphy, 20, kills or wounds 50 Nazi soldiers in battle near Holtzwihr, France. World War II's most decorated soldier, he will win the Medal of Honor for his actions.

1955: Walt Disney airs the second part of his frontier adventure, "Davy Crockett Goes to Congress."

1971: Charles Manson and three members of his "family" found guilty for the 1969 murders of Sharon Tate and six others.

1982: Oglala Sioux in South Dakota file a $6 billion suit against Homestake Mining Co. for running a gold mine in the Black Hills, their tribal home, for over a century.

JANUARY 27

1807: Zebulon Pike party crosses the Sangre de Cristo Range in southern Colorado.

1825: Congress approves an Indian Territory, a place to relocate eastern tribes, in present Kansas and Oklahoma.

1846: John Charles Fremont and his party reach Monterey, California on an exploratory mission. Historians have since wondered if Fremont were under government orders to prepare the region for U.S. acquisition.

1870: U.S. troops destroy the camp of Apache leader Cochise in Arizona.

1955: Denver-born director Robert McGowan ("The Little Rascals") dies in Santa Monica, California.

JANUARY 28

1842: Kit Carson converts to Catholicism in Taos so he may marry the beautiful Josefa Jaramillo. They are married the following year.

1878: Sheriff Bat Masterson and posse capture outlaw Dave Rudabaugh, 24 hours after his gang robs a pay train near Kinsley, Kansas.

1890: Author Harvey Fergusson (*The Blood of the Conquerers*, *Rio Grande*, and *Wolf Song*) born in Albuquerque, New Mexico.

1912: Artist Jackson Pollock born in Cody, Wyoming.

1914: The city of Beverly Hills, California is formally incorporated.

1917: After nearly a year of failing to find Pancho Villa in the mountains of Mexico, Gen. John J. Pershing is ordered back home.

1960: Texas millionaires Bedford Wynne and Clint Murchison are granted the NFL franchise for a team that will become the Dallas Cowboys.

1969: An oil well blowout in California's Santa Barbara Channel results in hundreds of thousands of gallons of oil leaking into the Pacific.

JANUARY 29

> **1850: The Compromise of 1850** – Henry Clay moves that California be admitted as a free state and that territorial governments be organized in lands newly acquired from Mexico, specifically New Mexico and Utah, with no mention of slavery. Texas boundaries are changed. That state's public debt is assumed by the United States.

1861: Kansas enters the Union as the 34th state.

1881: Fifteen Texas Rangers surprise 12 Apache warriors and eight women and children, killing them all. This, the last Indian fight in Texas, takes place at Sierra Diablo.

1905: Arizona trunk murderess Winnie Ruth Judd born in Oxford, Indiana.

1906: First National Western Stock Show held in Denver.

1927: Author Edward Abbey (*Desert Solitaire, The Monkey Wrench Gang*) born in Home, Pennsylvania.

1964: Actor Alan Ladd dies.

JANUARY 30

1807: Zebulon Pike reaches the Rio Grande near present Alamosa, Colorado, and begins building a stockade. In Spanish territory, he flies the American flag.

1847: Yerba Buena is renamed San Francisco.

1885: Interior secretary Henry M. Teller proposes that lands set aside as Indian Territory in present Oklahoma be opened to settlers.

1890: World War I hero Louis John Jordan is born in Fredericksburg, Texas.

1895: Outlaw Cherokee Bill is captured by authorities near Nowata, Oklahoma following the treachery of Ike Rogers.

1933: "The Lone Ranger" debuts over Detroit's WXYZ radio. For the leading man, writer Fran Striker has created a mask, silver bullets, a white horse named Silver, and an Indian companion named Tonto.

JANUARY 31

1848: John Charles Fremont found guilty of mutiny, disobedience, and prejudicial conduct, is dismissed from the Army. He is later restored.

1872: Western author Zane Grey is born Pearl Zane Gray in a town founded by his ancestors, Zanesville, Ohio. A disgruntled dentist, he will eventually change the spelling of his last name and drop his first name after a fan writes, "Dear Miss Grey...."

1874: The James Gang robs the Little Rock express train of $22,000 near Gadshill, Missouri.

1876: The deadline established by the U.S. Army for all Sioux to be on reservations. War begins when the Indians refuse to comply.

1896: Judge Albert J. Fountain and

his 8-year-old son disappear en route by wagon from Lincoln, Nebraska to Las Cruces, New Mexico. Despite the efforts of Sheriff Pat Garrett, the mystery is never solved.

1909: Only one of 150 miners is saved from a disaster at Primero, Colorado.

1927: The mockingbird becomes the Texas state bird.

1931: Tombstone lawman William "Billy" Breakenridge dies peacefully at age 84 in a Tucson hospital.

1931: Chicago Cub great Ernie Banks born in Dallas, Texas.

1938: Future Secretary of the Interior James Watt born.

1947: Baseball pitcher Nolan Ryan born in Refugio, Texas.

ZANE GREY
Born: January 31, 1875
Died: October 21, 1939
Western Author

1889: His father rips up his first story, "Jim of the Cave".
1896: Sets up a dental practice in New York City.
1903: First book, *Betty Zane*, is self-published with $200 of his wife's inheritance.
1907: Career not going well, takes his first trip to the West.
1909: Year's income totals $423
1912: *Riders of the Purple Sage* published.
1913: *Desert Gold* released, income $100,000 a year.
1918: *The U.P. Trail* is this year's #1 best seller.
1920: *The Man of the Forest* sells 714,500 copies (by contrast, F. Scott Fitzgerald sells 35,000 of *This Side of Paradise*).
1920s: First of more than 130 films to be made from his works is shot.
1939: Dies of a heart attack. Sixty-six novels are in print; another 26 will be published posthumously.
1975: On the 100th anniversary of his birth, estimates of total book sales reach 50 million.

COWBOY MOVIE IDOL TOM MIX

February

FEBRUARY 1

1845: The University of Waco is chartered in Texas. In 1886, the name will be changed to Baylor University.

1859: First hotel in Denver opens, the Eldorado.

1861: Legislators in Texas vote 167-7 to secede from the Union. An angry Sam Houston storms out of the session.

1864: A gang of horse thieves led by Nevada's John Daly kills law-abiding William Johnson in retaliation for Johnson's shooting of Jim Sears, a horse thief.

1876: Interior Secretary Chandler turns Sitting Bull's Sioux over to the War Department "for such action ...as you may deem proper under the circumstances."

1885: Mormon Church president John Taylor begins conducting church business from several hidden locations in Salt Lake City because of the government's attitude toward Mormons and increased religious persecution. He will escape all attempts at arrest.

1895: Acclaimed Western director John Ford (*Stagecoach*, *My Darling Clementine*, *Fort Apache*, *The Searchers*) born as Sean Aloysius O'Feeney in Portland, Maine.

1910: Louis Paulhan flies the first airplane in the skies above Denver from Overland Park.

1935: Gates close at Boulder Dam, officially beginning the storage of Colorado River water for California.

1935: Film version of Zane Grey's *Home on the Range* released by Paramount.

1935: *Texas Terror* with John Wayne released by Lone Star/Monogram.

1951: Coldest temperature so far in Colorado is -60 degrees at Taylor Park, near Aspen, Colorado.

1958: Airliners collide over Los Angeles killing 48.

1985: Lowest Colorado temperature ever recorded is -61 degrees at Maybell.

FEBRUARY 2

1811: Russian settlers establish Fort Ross on Bodega Bay, just north of San Francisco.

1848: The Treaty of Guadalupe Hidalgo formally ends the Mexican War. As conquerors, the United States obtains California, New Mexico, Utah, Nevada, most of Arizona, and a portion of Colorado ~ some 1,193,061 square miles. The United States pays $15 million for the land.

1848: The first shipload of Chinese

arrives in San Francisco on the brig *Eagle*.

1858: President Buchanan asks Congress to admit Kansas as a slave state.

1865: Sioux, Cheyenne, and Arapaho Indians set out for the Powder River Country. On the way, a thousand warriors raid Julesburg again.

1869: James Oliver patents a plow that can bust western sod without clogging.

1870: Territory of Utah follows Wyoming's lead, becoming the second state to grant women's suffrage.

1883: Six coal miners are killed near Crested Butte, Colorado when their shack is buried by an avalanche.

1904: Wyoming outlaw Ernie Cashel is hanged in Canada.

1925: Gunnar Kasson arrives in Nome on a dogsled, the last leg in a frantic relay to get anti-diphtheria medicine to battle an epidemic.

1927: *Rio Rita*, a musical comedy about a Texas Ranger and a lovely senorita, opens on Broadway.

1931: Martha Graham stages *Primitive Mysteries* in New York, based on southwestern Indian and Spanish rites.

1933: *The Denver Post* editor and founder, F.G. Bonfils dies.

1934: *West of the Divide* with John Wayne released by Lone Star/Monogram.

1947: Actress Farrah Fawcett born in Corpus Christi, Texas.

1952: Trunk murderess Winnie Ruth Judd pulls her fifth escape from the Arizona State Insane Hospital.

FEBRUARY 3

1811: Journalist Horace Greeley born at Amherst, New Hampshire. His most famous quote, "Go West, young man, go West," will be one he picks up from *Terre Haute Express* editor John Babson Lane Souile. In 1859, he will take the advice himself, giving his readers one of their first accounts of the new region.

1843: The Oregon Bill, designed to promote migration there, passes the Senate. It will die in the House.

1845: The House of Representatives passes a bill that would set up government in Oregon with a northern border of 54 degrees 40 minutes. The Senate will not consider it because slavery is prohibited.

1846: Gen. Zachary Taylor ordered to the Rio Grande in the Mexican War.

1883: Author Clarence Edward Mulford, who will produce such popular favorites as *Hopalong Cassidy* and *Bar-20*, is born.

BELLE STARR

1889: Belle Starr murdered near Eufala, Oklahoma. As she rides her horse home, an unknown gunman fells her with a shotgun blast to the back. Her tombstone will read: "Shed not for her the bitter tear, Nor give the heart to vain regret. 'Tis but the casket that lies here, The gem that filled it sparkles yet."

1904: Charles Arthur "Pretty Boy" Floyd is born in Bartow County,

Georgia. As an infant, he will move with his family to Oklahoma, where he will grow into a bloodthirsty Robin Hood figure. This reputation comes from his habit of tearing up mortgages during Depression-era bank holdups. In reality he is a cold-blooded cop killer.

1923: Following two earthquakes in the Pacific, Lassen Peak in California erupts for 12 hours.

> **1959: The Day the Music Died** ~ After a performance in Clear Lake, Iowa, Texas rocker Buddy Holly, along with Ritchie Valens and the Big Bopper (J.P. Richardson), die in a plane crash *en route* to their next performance. Holly is 22.

1965: One hundred five cadets resign from the Air Force Academy in Colorado Springs after they are caught cheating.

1980: Authorities recapture state prison at Santa Fe, ending one of the nation's bloodiest prison riots that leaves 33 dead and 89 wounded.

FEBRUARY 4

1847: American forces recapture Taos from Mexican insurgents.

1847: Colorado brewer Adolph Coors born in Barmen, Prussia, present Wuppertal, West Germany.

1848: Myra Maybelle Shirley, who will grow up to be "Bandit Queen" Belle Starr, born near Medoc, Missouri.

1889: Harry Longabaugh, the Sundance Kid, paroled in Wyoming.

1894: The Basket Maker Culture is discovered by Richard Wetherill in present Mesa Verde National Park, Colorado.

1906: Clyde Tombaugh, who will become the only person thus far in the 20th century to discover a planet (Pluto), born in Streator, Illinois.

1920: United States Mint employee Orville Harrington arrested in Denver after it is discovered he has been taking home gold bars in his wooden leg.

> **BELLE STARR**
> **Born**: February 4, 1848
> **Died**: February 2, 1889
> **Bandit queen**
>
> **1866**: Meets Cole Younger in Texas after family relocates from Missouri. Has a daughter, Pearl, by him. Marries James Reed that November. Deals cards in a Dallas saloon.
> **1871**: Relocates to California, has a child. Moves back to Texas, sells stolen horses.
> **1872**: Rumored to be involved in various rustlings and robberies.
> **1874**: Reed killed by bounty hunter. Reward goes unpaid when Belle refuses to identify the body. Six common-law marriages follow.
> **1880**: Marries Sam Starr. Moves to Eufala, Oklahoma.
> **1882**: Arrested for stealing a horse.
> **1885**: Affair with murderer John Middleton.
> **1886**: Sam and lawman Frank West shoot each other dead. Enters into common-law marriage with Bill July who she renames Bill July Starr.
> **1889**: Shot in the back and killed, possibly by a neighbor.

1961: *The Misfits*, a modern western and the last film for Marilyn Monroe and Clark Gable, is released by United Artists.

1974: Newspaper heiress Patricia Hearst is kidnapped by the Symbionese Liberation Army in Berkeley, California.

FEBRUARY 5

1883: The Southern Pacific railroad

February   21

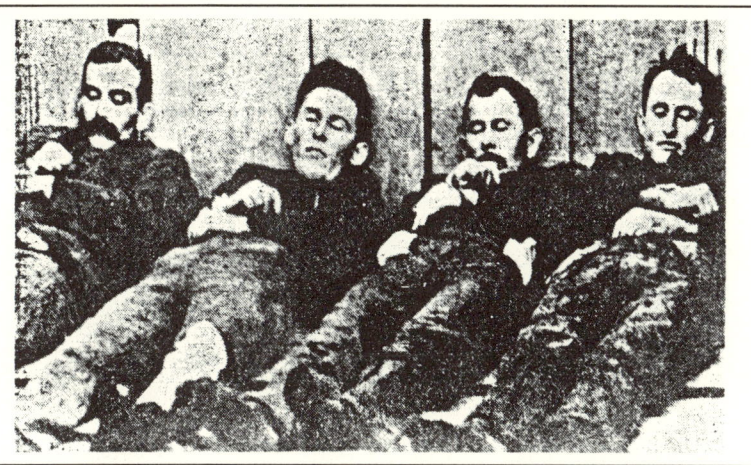
DEAD DALTONS IN THE STREETS OF COFFEYVILLE

completes the "Sunset Route" building east from New Mexico to New Orleans.

1887: San Francisco reports a record 3.7 inches of snow.

1918: Cowboy actor Tim Holt born. His film career will begin in 1937, and will include such matinee favorites as *The Law West of Tombstone* and *Stagecoach*.

1936: National Wildlife Federation established.

1969: Actress Thelma Ritter dies.

FEBRUARY 6

1832: *The Emigrant* of Ann Arbor, Michigan becomes the first publication to suggest a transcontinental railroad.

1878: Robert Frank James, only child of outlaw Frank James, is born.

1891: The first crime committed by the Dalton Gang is a train robbery in Alila, California.

1897: A Texas posse catches up with remnants of the Dalton Gang, kills two and takes one prisoner in Menard County.

1899: Record low temperature in Utah, -50 degrees at Woodruff.

1915: The San Francisco Panama-Pacific International Exposition opens to honor the building of the Panama Canal. This is the city's opportunity to show the world the remarkable rebuilding that has been done since the devastating earthquake of 1906.

1919: A general strike paralyzes Seattle as 60,000 stay home from work.

1930: Standardville, Utah mine accident kills 23.

1933: Mamie Van Doren born in Rowena, South Dakota.

FEBRUARY 7

1778: Daniel Boone is captured by Shawnees near Blue Ticks (northern Kentucky). He will be adopted in captivity by Chief Blue Fish and named Big Turtle. He escapes five months later.

1854: Mountain man/Indian agent Thomas Fitzpatrick dies at age 55 in Washington, D.C.

1855: Charles Siringo, author of the

classic *A Texas Cowboy*, born on the Matagorda Peninsula in Texas.

1886: Anti-Chinese riots rock Seattle; 400 are left homeless.

1895: 6,522 rabbits are caught in a Las Animas, Colorado community rabbit hunt.

1902: "The James Boys in Peril" published in *The James Boys* weekly.

1908: Fred Gipson, author of *Old Yeller*, born in Mason, Texas.

1908: Actor Buster Crabbe, one of the screen's many Billy the Kids, born in Oakland, California.

1919: Actor Jock Mahoney, TV's Yancy Derringer, born.

1952: Trunk murderess Winnie Ruth Judd is recaptured.

1984: The "boy in the bubble" in Houston, known only as David, is taken out of his sterile plastic bubble for the first time in his 12-year life. The environment was required because of a rare immune deficiency syndrome that could make a common cold fatal. He kisses his mother for the first time.

FEBRUARY 8

1836: Davy Crockett and a group of hunting cohorts from Tennessee arrive at the Alamo.

1864: Jim Daly and three members of his gang are hanged in Aurora, Nevada for the murder of William Johnson.

1887: By signing the Dawes Severality Act, President Cleveland dissolves Indian tribes as legal entities and assumes the power to divide tribal lands, giving heads of households 160 acres. The catch is that the land will be held in trust by the United States government for 25 years, after which full ownership will be granted.

1895: Director King Vidor born in Galveston, Texas.

1920: Actress Lana Turner born in Wallace, Idaho.

1923: Explosion at the Stagg mine in Dawson, New Mexico kills 120.

1924: Gee Jon is the first person in history to be executed by lethal gas, at Carson City, Nevada. He was accused of a gangland murder.

1931: Amelia Earhart marries publisher George Putnam.

1931: Actor James Dean, who will strike the classic modern west pose in *Giant*, is born in Fairmont, Indiana.

1936: First Indian senator and former Vice-President Charles Curtis of Kansas dies.

1936: Denver reaches record low temperature of -30 degrees.

1981: Fire at the Las Vegas Hilton claims four, injures 200.

FEBRUARY 9

1822: American Indian Society is organized.

1864: George Armstrong Custer marries Elizabeth Bacon in the Presbyterian Church at Monroe, Michigan.

1874: Alfred Packer and five members of his ill-fated party leave the safety of a Ute Camp to plunge headlong into a blizzard in search of gold. Chief Ouray notes they have few provisions.

1902: Artist Fred Harman, creator of "Red Ryder," born in St. Joseph, Missouri.

1911: Cokedale mine disaster at Trinidad, Colorado kills 17.

1914: Singer Ernest Dale Tubb born

in Texas. The "Texas Troubadour" will sell over three million copies of "Walking the Floor Over You," and be elected to the Country Music Hall of Fame in 1965.

1931: *Cimarron*, the only Western to win a best picture Oscar, released by RKO/Radio.

1933: Wyoming record low reached at Moran as the mercury hits -63 degrees.

1960: Brewing executive Adolph Coors III is kidnapped and murdered on his way to work in Golden, Colorado.

1969: Western sidekick Gabby Hayes dies. In over 80 films, he has provided comic relief for William Boyd and Roy Rogers and has been among the top-grossing cowboy stars for a decade.

1971: Southern California earthquake kills 62 and does $1 billion damage in Los Angeles.

1981: Rock singer Bill Haley ("Rock Around the Clock") dies.

FEBRUARY 10

1846: The Mormon exodus begins, led westward by Brigham Young from Nauvoo, Illinois.

1850: The first railroad in Texas, the Buffalo Bayou, Brazos, and Colorado, obtains its charter.

1876: Brig. Gen. Alfred Terry receives his orders to take action against Sioux and Cheyenne tribes in Dakota Territory. Among the measures he takes will be to send George Armstrong Custer and the 7th Cavalry into Montana Territory, a campaign which will end at the Battle of the Little Bighorn.

1879: First electric arc lights are used in the California Theater in San Francisco.

1907: Workers complete a 52-day project to divert the Colorado River to its original channel so that it will empty into the Gulf of Mexico.

1915: Pitcher Allie Reynolds, who will lead the American League in 1952 with 160 strike-outs, born in Bethany, Oklahoma.

1937: Scaffold falls from Golden Gate Bridge, killing ten workers.

FEBRUARY 11

1805: Lewis and Clark's 16-year-old Shoshone guide, Sacajawea, gives birth at a Mandan village near present Bismarck, North Dakota. The father is Toussaint Charbonneau; the baby boy is named Jean Baptiste Charbonneau. Meriwether Lewis acts as a midwife. Sacajawea greatly assists the explorers by obtaining horses and supplies from her brother's band of Shoshonis. The presence of a woman also indicates to other Indian tribes the expedition's peaceful intentions.

1836: Lt. Col. James C. Neill departs from the Alamo for "family reasons."

1839: University of Missouri chartered at Columbia.

1842: Crew members aboard the *San Antonio* stage the only mutiny ever held in Texas.

1866: Jacob Moses, father of five-year-old Annie Oakley, dies of pneumonia.

1881: Phoenix, Arizona is incorporated.

1890: Half of the Great Sioux Reservation covering 22 million acres in the Black Hills regions of the Dakotas is opened for white settlement by President Harrison.

1909: Max Baer, 1934 heavyweight boxing champion, born in Omaha.

1911: Zerelda James, mother of Frank and Jesse, dies at age 87 in Missouri.

1916: Bandelier National Monument established in New Mexico.

1933: Death Valley in California becomes a national monument. With 2,067,627.68 acres, it is the nation's largest.

FEBRUARY 12

1806: Zebulon Pike incorrectly identifies Lake Cass as the source of the Mississippi.

1825: Creek Indians cede all their Georgia lands to the United States, and agree to get out in 17 months. Many in the tribe disagree, but the treaty is considered binding for all.

1836: Santa Anna's troops cross the Rio Grande en route to the Alamo.

1849: C.B.&Q. (Chicago, Burlington, and Quincy) railroad is incorporated.

1873: Gold dollar becomes the American standard of currency.

1880: President Hayes threatens to get tough with illegal settlers squatting on lands in Indian Territory in present-day Oklahoma by issuing an official warning.

1899: Temperature at Tulia, Texas drops to -23 degrees.

1899: Record Nebraska low, -47 degrees, reached at Camp Clarke.

1899: Ten die as two nearly simultaneous snowslides occur near Silver Plume, Colorado.

1904: "Amateur Hour" host Ted Mack born in Denver.

1915: Actor Lorne Greene, best known for his Ben Cartwright role on TV's "Bonanza" born in Ottawa, Ontario, Canada.

1926: Baseball catcher / commentator Joe Garagiola born in St. Louis, Missouri.

1933: Wealthy Denverite Charles Boettcher kidnapped. He will be released after a $60,000 ransom is paid.

1971: Merchant J.C. Penney dies at age 95, after nearly seven decades in the dry goods business.

FEBRUARY 13

1819: The Missouri Bill, designed to permit the people of that territory to make preparations for statehood, is introduced in Congress.

1822: Missouri Lt. Gov. William Ashley places his famous ad in the *Missouri Gazette and Public Advisor* seeking a hundred "enterprising young men" to trap the Missouri River. The ad is answered by Jedediah Smith and Jim Bridger, among others.

1847: Gen. Kearny is ordered to establish a new government in California, following the Mexican War takeover. It will be located in Monterey.

1861: America's first medal of honor action occurs when Col. Bernard Irwin, an assistant surgeon, takes charge of the troops and defeats a party of hostile Chiricahua at Apache Pass in New Mexico Territory, present-day Arizona. This event, ending the "Bascom Affair," precipitated Cochise's war with the U.S. which lasted until 1872.

1866: The distinction of being the first financial institution to be robbed by the James brothers goes to the Clay County Savings & Loan of Liberty, Missouri. (Historians quibble; Jesse may have been recuperating from a bullet wound, but Frank was definitely present.) Total withdrawal: $15,000 in gold and $45,000 in securities. In the process, bystander George Wymore is slain.

1913: Johanna Troutman named to create a Texas Lone Star flag.

1945: Navy transport plane crashes into San Francisco Bay 13 minutes after takeoff, killing 24.

FEBRUARY 14

1682: Father Zenobe Membre, chaplain of a minor French expedition, reaches the mouth of the Missouri after descending the Mississippi. He writes: "The Indians assure us that this river is formed by many others, and that they ascend it for ten or twelve days to a mountain where it rises; that beyond this mountain is the sea where they see great ships...."

1776: Father Garces is the first recorded Spaniard to visit a Mohave settlement near present Needles, California.

1844: Fremont's Rocky Mountain expedition reaches the Sierra Madre.

1859: Oregon, with a population of 50,000 enters the Union as the 33rd state. First governor is John Whiteaker.

1886: The first trainload of oranges leaves for the east from Los Angeles.

1892: A report from the Interior Department confirms that forest reserves have been violated for years by American, Canadian, and Indian lumbermen.

1912: Arizona enters the Union as the 48th state. President Taft signs the measure before movie cameras.

1931: *Fighting Caravans* with Gary Cooper released by Paramount.

1935: Ladies Golf Hall of Famer Mickey Wright born in San Diego.

1983: General Motors and Toyota of Japan agree to produce subcompact automobiles in a joint venture at a California GM plant.

FEBRUARY 15

1870: Work on the second transcontinental railroad begins on Lake Superior in Duluth, Minnesota. The Northern Pacific will not be finished for 13 years due to the Panic of 1873.

1876: Last constitution of Texas is formally adopted.

1905: Lew Wallace, former governor of New Mexico and author of *Ben Hur*, dies at age 78 in Indiana.

1922: Lawman/legislator/cattleman "Texas" John Slaughter dies at age 80 in Douglas, Arizona.

GERONIMO
Born: June, 1829
Died: February 17, 1909
War leader (Chiricahua Apache)

1839: Raised near the headwaters of the Gila River.
1858: Mexican soldiers slay wife and children.
1860s: Fights under Cochise.
1874: Assumes Chiricahua leadership after the death of Cochise.
1876: Escapes reservation after it is moved to San Carlos, goes to Mexico.
1877: Arrested; returns to the reservation.
1881: Leaves reservation again to go on the warpath.
1883: Surrenders to Gen. George Crook.
1885: Leads a hundred Apaches in an escape from the San Carlos Reservation in Arizona Territory; terrorizes countryside.
1886: Surrenders to Gen. Nelson A. Miles, the last American Indian to formally surrender to the United States. Imprisoned in Florida.
1903: Joins Dutch Reformed Church; appears at St. Louis World's Fair.
1905: Attends Theodore Roosevelt's inaugural.
1906: Dictates his memoirs, *Geronimo's Story of His Life*.
1909: Dies of pneumonia at age 80.

1922: Dashiell Hammett quits his job with Pinkerton's National Detective Agency in San Francisco to write detective fiction.

1936: North Dakota record low reached as Parshall hits -60 degrees.

1940: Football quarterback John Hadl born in Lawrence, Kansas. In 1965 he will be the leading passer in the AFL with 2,798 yards.

1955: R.W. Bliss of Tucson builds this country's first solar heated and radiation cooled house.

FEBRUARY 16

1877: The first train arrives in Texas.

1878: The silver dollar is legalized.

1900: Carry Nation marks this date by busting her first barrel of booze in Kansas.

1914: First flight from San Francisco to Los Angeles is made by Silas Christofferson.

FEBRUARY 17

1820: The Missouri Compromise is passed by the Senate. It will bring in slave state Missouri, free state Maine, and forbid slavery above latitude 36 degrees 30 minutes. Slave and free states are now tied at 12 each.

1851: Alice Ivers, who will gamble her way across the Wild West as Poker Alice, is born in Sudbury, England.

POKER ALICE TUBBS

1889: Texas oil billionaire Haroldson Lafayette Hunt born in Vandalia, Illinois. He will hit the big strike in the eastern part of the state during the 1930s.

1904: Lawman turned train robber Burt Alvord is wounded, then arrested by Arizona Rangers just across the border at Nigger Head Gap, Mexico.

1909: Prisoner of war Geronimo dies of pneumonia at approximately age 80 at Fort Sill in Lawton, Oklahoma.

1927: The first run of a talking motion picture begins at Denver's Aladdin Theatre.

FEBRUARY 18

1823: Mexican authorities acknowledge that the land grant made to the late Moses Austin by Mexico may be transferred to his son, Stephen F. Austin.

1849: California's first regular steamboat service begins with the arrival of Pacific Mail's *California*.

1861: Cheyenne and Arapaho leaders give up their claim on much of present Colorado, although they are entitled to it by terms of an 1851 treaty. They will relocate to a reservation situated between the Arkansas River and Sand Creek in the eastern portion of the state.

1875: Two of five cattle rustlers are lynched in Mason County, Texas.

1878: New Mexico's bloody "Lincoln County War" begins with the murder of John Tunstall by a group that includes Jesse Evans, William Morton, and Tom Hill.

1896: Vulcan mine explosion at New Castle, Colorado kills 49.

1900: Complying with a new law that dictates all gambling be conducted on the second floor, Cripple Creek, Colorado bar owners build six-foot platforms above their main floors.

1902: Artist Albert Bierstadt dies, broke and forgotten.

1915: Frank James dies at the Samuel Farm in Missouri. His last job saw him charging admission to tour the Samuels home where he and his brother Jesse had hidden during their glory years.

1920: Actor Jack Palance, villain of *Shane*, born in Lattimer Mines, Pennsylvania.

1927: At the White House, President Coolidge presses a button that triggers an explosion under Colorado's James Peak, completing the Moffat Tunnel.

1930: Clyde Tombaugh becomes the only person in the 20th century thus far to discover a planet when he finds Pluto from Lowell Observatory in Flagstaff, Arizona. He does it by comparing exposed photographic plates. The elusive planet is 3.5 billion miles from the sun, which it orbits every 248 years.

1939: The Golden Gate International Exposition opens on an island in San Francisco Bay.

1960: The eighth Winter Olympics open at Squaw Valley, California.

1977: Actor Andy Devine, "Jingles" on TV's "Wild Bill Hickok," dies at age 71.

1987: An avalanche at Colorado's Breckenridge Ski Area claims four skiers.

FEBRUARY 19

1806: President Jefferson's report on the Lewis and Clark expedition is issued today. It is called *Message from the President of the United States Communicating Discoveries*

BIERSTADT LANDSCAPE

Made in *Exploring the Missouri, Red River and Washita by Captains Lewis and Clark, Doctor Sibley and Mr. Dunbar.*

1846: Texas state government is installed at Austin.

1847: A small rescue party reaches the ill-fated Donner party at Donner Lake. Of the 86 who followed George Donner, 36 perished. Survivors are found eating human flesh.

1881: Kansas becomes the first state to prohibit the use of alcohol except for scientific or medical reasons.

1914: Thomas Jonathan Jeffers dies at his home near Tucson. The scout, rancher, miner, and Indian agent negotiated his own personal peace with Cochise in 1867 and was later instrumental in effecting an armistice between Cochise and Gen. O.O. Howard. His friendship with the chief was later the basis for the novel *Blood Brother* by Elliot Arnold.

1924: Actor Lee Marvin, who will win the best actor Oscar for his performance in *Cat Ballou* (1965), born in New York City.

1959: North American record snowfall is set over a five-day period at California's Mount Shasta: 189 inches.

1983: Two men kill 13 people during a robbery at a Seattle gambling club in the city's Chinatown.

FEBRUARY 20

1725: First known scalping of Indians by white men occurs when a group of New Hampshire volunteers encounters ten sleeping Indians and kills them to collect the reward. The Boston treasury offers 100 pounds per scalp.

1902: Western wilderness photographer Ansel Adams is born in San Francisco, California.

1915: San Francisco Panama-Pacific International Exposition closes after a successful run, attracting 13 million visitors in two weeks.

1931: Actress Amanda Blake, Miss Kitty on TV's "Gunsmoke," born in Buffalo, New York.

1936: Last of 41 one straight days of below zero temperatures in North Dakota.

1946: Actress Sandy Duncan born in

The Cherokee Alphabet — Sequoyah

Henderson, Texas.

1954: Newspaper heiress Patricia Hearst born in San Francisco, California.

1963: *How the West Was Won* released by MGM.

FEBRUARY 21

1794: Antonio Lopez de Santa Anna born in Jalapa, Vera Cruz, Mexico.

1828: In Echota, Georgia a printing press is received by the Cherokee Council. This year, Sequoyah and Elias Boudinot will found the first American newspaper published in the Indian language, the *Cherokee Phoenix*.

1836: Santa Anna passes through Medina en route to the Alamo.

1896: Judge Roy Bean hosts the Maher-Fitzsimmons heavyweight championship fight on an island in the Rio Grande. Fitzsimmons knocks out his opponent in 1:30 of the first round.

1913: Production of the "buffalo" nickel begins.

1916: Outlaw Cole Younger, survivor of the Northfield bank raid with the James boys and a resultant 25-year prison sentence, dies at age 72, 15 years after his release, at the place of his birth, Lee's Summit, Missouri.

1936: Barbara Jordan, future Congresswoman from Texas, born in Houston.

1959: *The Hanging Tree* with Gary Cooper released by Warner Brothers.

1971: Elk City, Oklahoma receives a record 36 inches of snow in 24 hours.

FEBRUARY 22

1847: 15,000 troops under Santa Anna attack Zachary Taylor's 5,000 men, beginning the Battle of Buena Vista in the Mexican War.

1880: Utah editor Charles King, of

the *Ogden Morning Rustler*, is tarred and feathered by a crowd of masked hoodlums.

1889: The Omnibus Bill, signed today by President Cleveland, will admit Washington, Montana, North Dakota and South Dakota into the Union.

1894: Texas Gov. James Hogg arrested for poaching on federal land.

1897: President Grover Cleveland establishes the Bitterroot Forest Reserve that includes much of northern Idaho.

1911: Quanah Parker, last chief of the Comanches, dies of pneumonia in Oklahoma.

1920: The first racing dogs to chase a mechanical rabbit do so at Emeryville, California.

1921: Outlaw/actor Henry Starr is shot dead by William J. Meyers while trying to rob a bank in Harrison, Arkansas. He is the last Old West bank robber to be slain during a holdup.

1923: First American chinchilla farm established in Los Angeles.

1984: Houston's "boy in the bubble," known only as David, dies after two weeks of freedom from the plastic shell he was housed in for 12 years. Cause of death is fluid developing around his heart and lungs.

FEBRUARY 23

1540: Francisco Vasquez de Coronado begins his search for the Seven Cities of Cibola, fabled cities of gold, in the American southwest. With him are 300 Spaniards and a party of Indians.

1836: The siege at the Alamo begins as Santa Anna surrounds the mission and demands the rebels' surrender. A red flag in the San Fernando church tower signals "no quarter." Col. William Barret Travis answers with a shot from a cannon. Mexican soldiers begin shelling the mission that afternoon.

1861: Texas residents vote to secede from the Union, a measure passed by their legislature on February 1.

1935: The serial *The Phantom Empire* starring Gene Autry is released by Mascot. It is the story of a cowboy who discovers a subterranean civilization under his ranch.

1940: Folk singer Woody Guthrie writes "This Land is Your Land."

1945: Ira Hayes, a Pima Indian from Arizona, helps to raise the flag on Iwo Jima during some of the heaviest fighting in the Pacific. Photographer Joe Rosenthal snaps the most famous photograph of World War II, and things will never be the same for Hayes.

1955: Walt Disney airs part three of his frontier adventure, "Davy Crockett at the Alamo."

FEBRUARY 24

1821: Mexico declares independence from Spain.

1835: First Kansas newspaper, the *Shawnee Sun*, is printed by Jotham Meeker.

1836: William B. Travis writes his famous plea for help from the Alamo. He signs it "Victory or Death."

1847: Gen. Zachary Taylor defeats Santa Anna at the Battle of Buena Vista.

1855: U.S. troops destroy a Mescalero Apache village in New Mexico.

1863: Arizona becomes a United States territory, formed from half of

February

New Mexico territory west of the 109th meridian.

1878: The Sam Bass gang robs the Houston and Texas Central at Allen station.

1884: A coal mine explosion at Crested Butte, Colorado kills 59.

1885: World War II U.S. Navy Admiral of the Fleet Chester W. Nimitz born in Fredericksburg, Texas.

1949: First rocket to reach space is launched from White Sands proving ground in New Mexico.

FEBRUARY 25

1510: Explorer Francisco Vasquez de Coronado is born in Salamanca, Spain. He will lead an expedition into present-day Kansas, Oklahoma, and Texas, and a detachment from his party will ascend the Colorado River and discover the Grand Canyon.

1836: First message for help from the Alamo reaches James W. Fannin at Goliad, Texas.

1836: Samuel Colt receives patent number 138 from the United States for "an improvement on revolving firearms."

1848: Edward H. Harriman, future head of the Union Pacific railroad and Boys Club founder, born in Hempstead, New York.

1858: Self-appointed Mormon ambassador, Thomas Kane, arrives in Brigham Young country to convince the leader to recognize Alfred Cummings as governor of the territory. Young agrees, as long as troops are not brought in.

CORONADO
Born: February 25, 1510
Died: September 22, 1554
Explorer

1535: Arrives in Mexico with first Spanish government officials.
1538: Becomes governor of Nueva Galicia.
1540: Sets off on the expedition through American southwest to find the Seven Cities of Cibola, reported lost cities of gold.
1542: Dejected, he reports to officials that his mission was unsuccessful.
1554: Dies in Mexico City.

1885: Fencing of public lands in the West prohibited by Congress.

1906: Playwright Mary Chase (*Harvey*) born in Denver.

1921: Record February high in Los Angeles set at 92 degrees.

1950: Largest crowd in Denver's history, 350,000, turns out to watch a smelter destroyed by dynamite.

1956: *The Lone Ranger* with Clayton Moore released by Wrather / Warner.

FEBRUARY 26

1807: One hundred Spanish dragoons and militia arrest Zebulon Pike near Alamosa, Colorado on suspicion of spying.

1846: William F. Cody, Buffalo Bill,

born in Le Claire, Iowa. In one of the more stellar careers in the west he will be a Pony express rider, cavalry scout, and creator of the Wild West show.

> **WILLIAM F. CODY**
> **Born:** February 26, 1846
> **Died:** January 10, 1917
> **Scout, buffalo hunter, showman**
>
> **1850:** Moves with family to Kansas.
> **1857:** Following the death of his father, he supports the family working for various wagon trains.
> **1860:** Goes to work as a rider for the Pony Express.
> **1864:** Scouts for Kansas Regiments of the Union Army during Civil War.
> **1865:** Works as a stagecoach driver.
> **1868:** Gets his nickname providing buffalo for the railroads expanding west.
> **1869:** Becomes a scout/Indian fighter for the 5th Cavalry.
> **1869:** Meets Ned Buntline, who writes and publishes "Buffalo Bill, King of the Border Men" before the year is out.
> **1872:** Appears on stage for the first time in Buntline's *Scouts of the Plains*.
> **1883:** Starts the first Wild West show, an outdoor extravaganza that will play for 30 years all over the world.
> **1913:** At 68, his show is attached and put up for auction to pay debts.
> **1917:** Dies in Denver.

WILLIAM F. CODY

1875: Hostages Catherine and Sophie Germain are released with the surrender of Stone Calf's Cheyennes. The incident had received national attention and raised feelings of bitterness against Native Americans.

1882: First illustration by Frederic Remington is published in *Harper's Weekly*.

1887: Baseball pitcher Grover Cleveland Alexander born in Elba, Nebraska. His 374 wins will put him in the Baseball Hall of Fame in 1938.

1892: Another rush to Colorado begins as N.C. Creede discovers silver in the southern part of the state. The town of Creede will soon be born.

1898: Lincoln County War survivor James J. Dolan dies.

1919: Grand Canyon National Park established in Arizona. The massive gorge carved by the Colorado River is 217 miles long; the park covers 657,575 acres.

1906: Idaho and Colorado authorities kidnap union leader Big Bill Heywood and two others in Denver, whisk them to the Boise penitentiary, and charge them with the murder of former governor Frank Steunenberg.

1920: Actor Tony Randall born in Tulsa, Oklahoma.

1928: The Moffat Tunnel, Colorado's train link through the Rocky Mountains, is formally dedicated.

1929: Grand Teton National Park established in Wyoming. A spectacular landmark in the Grand Teton range, the area encompasses 310,442 acres.

1932: Singer Johnny Cash born in Kingsland, Arkansas. His many hits will include "Folsom Prison Blues" and "Don't Take Your Guns to Town."

1957: Gangster Bugs Moran dies of cancer in Leavenworth Penitentiary.

FEBRUARY 27

1845: Senate agrees on the annexation of the Republic of Texas by passing a joint resolution.

1865: Gunfighter/lawyer Elfego Baca born on a softball diamond in Socorro, New Mexico, shortly after his mother had finished playing a game. In an exciting life that will link the Old West with the Atomic Age, Baca will be known as one of the region's tougher hombres, always on the side of justice.

1895: Nebraska requests a $1.5 million government loan to aid its farmers through a terrible dry spell. Hay is selling for $2 a ton.

1902: Author John Steinbeck born in Salinas, California. His novels will include *Of Mice and Men* (1937), and *The Grapes of Wrath* (1939).

1906: Avalanche buries 75 residents of Wallace, Idaho.

1907: Author Zane Grey moves to Arizona to see if the change of scenery will have any effect on his writing. Soon, he will begin his first Western.

1917: Future Texas Gov. John Connally born in Floresville, Texas.

1934: Author N. Scott Momaday born in Oklahoma. A member of the Kiowa tribe, his first novel, *House Made of Dawn* (1968), will win the Pulitzer Prize.

1937: Floods in San Bernardino, California cause $79 million in damages killing 87.

1963: Denver records the 202nd tremor in eight months. The repeated earthquakes are a mystery until it is learned that hazardous materials have been dumped in massive loads into the earth's core by the Rocky Mountain Arsenal.

1973: Siege begins at Wounded Knee, South Dakota as 200 members of the American Indian Movement barricade themselves inside a Roman Catholic church in the small town. They call on Sen. William Fulbright to investigate 371 United States treaties, and for Sen. Edward Kennedy to look into the Bureau of Indian Affairs.

FEBRUARY 28

1803: Congress approves the Lewis and Clark expedition.

1836: After receiving a plea for help from the Alamo, Fannin leaves Goliad. Less than a mile out of town, two of his wagons break down; he orders his soldiers home. This will be their only attempt to reach San Antonio.

1847: Col. Doniphan and the Missouri Mounted Volunteers begin their victorious Battle of Sacramento during the Mexican War.

1849: The first gold seekers to reach California by ship arrive in San Francisco Bay aboard the *California*. There are 365 passengers on board.

1861: Congress establishes Colorado Territory, created from parts of Nebraska, Utah, and New Mexico territories, and the state of Kansas. William Gilpin is appointed governor of the population of 35,000.

1864: George Armstrong Custer leaves his bride of less than three weeks to return to the fighting in the Civil War.

1897: Most precipitation for one month in Colorado is recorded at Ruby: 23.28 inches.

1898: In *Holden vs. Hardy*, the Supreme Court upholds a Utah law that limits work days in the mines to eight hours.

1900: A posse of Pinkertons kills Lonny Logan in a gunfight in Dodson, Missouri.

1901: Linus Pauling born in Portland, Oregon. He will win the 1954 Nobel Prize in chemistry for his work on molecular structures. During his life he will actively oppose nuclear weapons and become a strong advocate of Vitamin C in treating the common cold.

1902: Three separate avalanches kill a total of 19 people near Telluride, Colorado. Many of the fatalities are rescue workers, trying to free previous victims.

1906: Avalanche destroys Mace, Colorado killing 60.

1918: Texas state legislature adopts prohibition.

1927: The Supreme Court rules that Interior Secretary Albert B. Fall's lease of the Elk Hills oil reserve to Edward Doheny was illegal and fraudulent. The Teapot Dome scandal is nearly over.

1930: Poker Alice, 79, dies during a gall bladder operation in Rapid City, South Dakota. Reports the Associated Press, "Poker Alice Tubbs coppered her last and biggest bet today ~ and lost."

1945: Rodeo champ Fritz Truan, who hollered "Let 'er buck!" when his craft landed on Iwo Jima in World War II, is killed in action.

1960: The eighth Winter Olympics close at Squaw Valley, California.

FEBRUARY 29

1836: William Oury leaves the Alamo with a communique to Sam Houston during the seventh day of the siege.

1908: Pat Garrett shot and killed by Wayne Brazel en route from his ranch in the Organ Mountains to Las Cruces. Brazel will be acquitted in the slaying, which was the result of an argument over Garrett's negotiating to sell land on which the assailant was living. Although Wayne Brazel was the only one brought to trial for Garrett's murder, there is evidence that Jim Miller or Carl Adamson actually killed him.

1932: Oklahoma Gov. "Alfalfa" Bill Murray appears on the cover of *Time* after announcing his "Bread, Butter, Bacon, and Beans" Presidential candidacy.

March

MARCH 1

1784: Thomas Jefferson's Congressional committee proposes a temporary government in the western territories of Ohio, Indiana, Illinois, Michigan, Wisconsin, and part of Minnesota, which calls for dividing the region into states.

1831: Sitting Bull born during this month, near Bullhead, South Dakota.

1836: In the dead of night, 32 men from Gonzales, about 80 miles distant, arrive to help defend the Alamo, fully aware that the situation is hopeless. Inside the old mission, 187 prepare to defend themselves against a force of 2,400.

1845: President Tyler signs a joint resolution annexing the Republic of Texas.

1867: Nebraska enters the Union as the 37th state. Its name comes from *Nibthaska*, an Omaha Indian word meaning "flat water."

1872: President Grant signs the bill designating Yellowstone as the nation's first national park. Over 3,000 geysers cover 2,221,772 acres in northwestern Wyoming Territory; bear, moose, and elk are plentiful.

1873: Billy the Kid's mother, Catherine McCarty, marries her second husband, William Antrim, in Santa Fe when Billy is 13.

1877: Jack McCall, convicted murderer of Wild Bill Hickok, is hanged high in Yankton, Dakota Territory.

1903: The worst avalanche in history claims 99 lives as a snowslide buries two trains east of Seattle in Washington's Cascade Mountains.

1904: Bandleader Glenn Miller born in Clarinda, Iowa. His family will move to Fort Morgan, Colorado in 1918; he will attend the University of Colorado.

1910: Two trains are tossed down a canyon during a storm near Wellington, Washington, killing 96.

CATHERINE McCARTY

1933: Saguaro National Monument is established in Arizona.

1933: Zane Grey's *The Thundering Herd* is released by Paramount.

1935: Zane Grey's *Rocky Mountain Mystery* is released by Paramount.

1952: *Viva Zapata!* with Marlon Brando is released by 20th Century Fox.

1954: Actor/director Ron Howard born in Duncan, Oklahoma.

MARCH 2

1793: Sam Houston born in Rockbridge County, Virginia. He will play an instrumental part in Texas' break from Mexico and become that state's first president.

1819: Congress establishes Arkansas as a U.S. territory, creating it from Mississippi Territory.

> **1836: Texas declares independence** from Mexico. The declaration is made from the village of Washington-on-the-Brazos, on Sam Houston's 43rd birthday.

1853: Washington becomes a U.S. territory.

1861: Nevada becomes a U.S. territory.

1861: Territories of North Dakota and South Dakota are created.

1861: The United States signs a contract with Russell, Majors, and Waddell to provide a daily overland mail and a semiweekly Pony Express for $1 million annually.

1864: Nevada is proclaimed the 36th state by President Lincoln.

1876: The House of Representatives impeaches Secretary of War William Belknap for taking bribes in exchange for the sale of Indian Territory trading posts.

1889: Congress transfers the Unassigned Lands in Indian Territory, (Oklahoma) into the public domain, after working out the last of the Indian claims.

1899: Mount Rainier National Park established in Washington. An ancient volcano, it is this country's greatest single-peak glacial system.

1923: Hovenweep National Monument established in Utah and Colorado.

SAM HOUSTON
Born: March 2, 1793
Died: July 26, 1863
Texas founding father

1812: Serves under Andrew Jackson in War of 1812. Wounded at Battle of Horseshoe Bend.
1823: Elected to Congress from Tennessee.
1827: Elected governor of Tennessee.
1829: Resigns as governor. Lives among the Cherokee Indians.
1832: Commissioned by President Jackson to meet with Indians in Texas.
1835: Becomes commander of the Texas Army.
1836: Texas declares independence from Mexico. After the fall of the Alamo, defeats Santa Anna at the Battle of San Jacinto. Sworn in as the first president of Texas.
1840: Weds Margaret Lea.
1844: Succeeded as president by Anson Jones.
1845: Texas statehood. Elected to Senate.
1854: Baptized.
1859: Elected governor of Texas.
1861: Submits the Texas resolution of secession.
1863: Dies in Huntsville, sure that Texas is lost.

1933: Black Canyon National Monument established in Colorado.

1958: Artist John Held, Jr., famous for his sheik and Sheba illustrations of the Roaring 20s, dies at age 69.

MARCH 3

1805: Congress changes District of Louisiana to Territory of Louisiana.

1807: Meriwether Lewis succeeds Gen. Wilkinson as governor of Louisiana Territory. Wilkinson is removed by President Jefferson's order for his alleged part in the Aaron Burr conspiracy to establish a new country in the western territories.

1807: Zebulon Pike and his party, prisoners of Mexico, are moved from Santa Fe to Chihuahua.

1817: A commercial steamboat route between Louisville and New Orleans is begun. One can book passage on the *Washington* and tour the Mississippi River for around $100.

1831: George Pullman, who will spend time prospecting in Colorado before inventing the railroad sleeping car that will bear his name, is born in Brockton, New York.

1837: On his last day in office, President Jackson recognizes the Republic of Texas.

1849: Minnesota becomes a United States territory.

1849: The Home Department is established to regulate settlement, land policies, and Indians. It will later be known as the Department of the Interior.

1853: Congress gives the go ahead for a railroad survey that will extend from the Mississippi River to the Pacific.

1855: Congress earmarks $30,000 to introduce camels into the American southwest, at the suggestion of Secretary of War Jefferson Davis; 33 are ordered from Egypt.

1857: Butterfield stage service begins by connecting Memphis, Tennessee and Tipton, Missouri. The Overland Mail Service offered by the line will begin a direct mail connection to the Old West. In a related incident, Congress authorizes the Postmaster General to seek bids for an overland stagecoach service that will carry mail as well as passengers from the Missouri River to San Francisco.

1859: First white child born in Denver.

1871: The Indian Appropriation Act passed today in Congress says that no tribe will be considered a sovereign power that the United States must deal with by treaty. All treaties will remain in force, but now Indians will be governed by the laws of the U.S.

1879: Congress establishes the U.S. Geological Survey. The first director will be Clarence King.

1890: Buffalo Bill meets with Pope Leo while his Wild West show makes a stop in Rome.

1905: Congress opens 1.5 million acres of Wyoming's Wind River Indian Reservation for settlement.

1911: Actress Jean Harlow born in Kansas City, Missouri.

1930: Film version of Zane Grey's *The Light of Western Stars* is released by Paramount.

MARCH 4

1801: Thomas Jefferson is inaugurated as the third U.S. President.

1805: Thomas Jefferson is inaugurated for his second term.

1829: In his inaugural speech,

Andrew Jackson asks for just treatment of and a liberal policy toward Indians.

1833: Andrew Jackson is inaugurated for his second term.

1837: Cannon fired at Fort Leavenworth, Kansas in honor of the inauguration of President Martin Van Buren.

1856: Anti-slavery factions in Kansas petition the United States for statehood.

1861: The Pony Express makes its best time, delivering President Lincoln's inaugural address to California (1,966 miles) in seven days, 17 hours.

1863: Idaho becomes a United States territory.

1868: Jesse Chisholm, whose name is immortalized on the most famous of the cattle trails, dies in Oklahoma of food poisoning.

1878: The Central City Opera House opens in this Colorado mountain and mining community.

1881: Almy, Wyoming mine explodes killing 38.

1886: University of Wyoming chartered at Laramie.

1899: Snow ceases in Leadville, Colorado after 38 days nonstop.

1917: First woman in Congress, Jeanette Rankin of Montana, begins her first term.

1921: Hot Springs, Arkansas becomes a national park. Over a million gallons of 143-degree water flow from the 47 mineral springs each day.

1923: With scandal clouds on the horizon regarding the Teapot Dome oil reserves, Interior Secretary Albert Bacon Fall resigns.

1928: First cross-country foot race begins in Los Angeles, as 274 men start for New York.

1929: Charles Curtis, America's first Vice-President of Indian heritage is sworn in.

1930: President Coolidge dedicates Coolidge Dam near Globe, Arizona. To appease the Apaches, who fought the dam for 55 years because it would interfere with ancient burial grounds, an $11,000 slab of concrete was laid over the grounds.

1936: British playwright George Bernard Shaw visits San Francisco.

1940: King Canyon in California becomes a national park.

MARCH 5

1766: First Spanish governor of Louisiana, Antonio de Ulloa, arrives in New Orleans.

1836: The shelling of the Alamo ceases at 5:00 P.M., to be replaced by a more disturbing quiet. Col. Travis draws his famous line in the dirt (the authenticity of which has been questioned in later years), giving any who wish to leave the opportunity to do so; 187 men cross the line and elect to fight. In his tent, Gen. Santa Anna prepares for his final assault at dawn.

1836: Samuel Colt incorporates the Patent Arms Manufacturing Co. in Patterson, New Jersey to produce his revolvers.

1836: Cattle industry innovator Charles Goodnight, creator of the chuck wagon and the hybrid "cattalo," is born in Madison County, Illinois.

1879: President Hayes approves the Reno Court of Inquiry findings clearing Maj. Marcus Reno of any wrongdoing in the events surrounding the Battle of the Little Bighorn.

1918: Louis John Jordan becomes the first officer from Texas killed in World War I.

1925: The country's first old-age pension laws are enacted by Nevada and Montana.

1959: Fire at Little Rock's Negro Boys Industrial Reformatory claims 21.

1963: Singer Patsy Cline, 30, killed in a plane crash in Camden, Tennessee. Also killed in the crash, are singers Cowboy Copas, 49, and Hawkshaw Hawkins, 41.

1980: California's Channel Islands designated a national park.

MARCH 6

1820: The Missouri statehood bill is passed, authorizing residents to decide on the issue of slavery within their boundaries.

> **1836: The Battle of the Alamo** ~ The mission falls as Santa Anna's band plays the throat-slitting anthem "Deguello," signifying no quarter, only death. Col. Travis is one of the first to die, shot from the top of the wall after emptying his shotgun on some attackers. Jim Bowie fights to the finish from his sickbed in the chapel. Historians now believe that Davy Crockett was captured, then put to death after the actual battle. By 6:30 A.M., it is all over, and the bodies of the 187 men are tossed into a massive funeral pyre. The fight for Texas independence now has a stirring rallying call: "Remember the Alamo!"

1844: Second Fremont expedition reaches Sutter's Fort on the Sacramento River.

1846: Fremont raises the American flag near Monterey on Gavilan Peak.

1853: John Henry Turnstall, a major participant in the Lincoln County War, is born in England.

1861: "The Birdman," Samuel Franklin Cody, is born at Birdville, Texas. He will quit the Wild West show business to pursue his aviation dreams in Europe, and will become the first pilot to fly over British soil.

1866: William F. Cody marries Louisa Frederici, his sweetheart from St. Louis.

1878: During the Lincoln County War, the Regulators, including Billy the Kid, arrest William Morton and Frank Baker.

1893: Idaho's office of state mine inspector established.

1900: Temperatures in Havre, Montana take only three minutes to rise 31 degrees.

1927: Astronaut Leroy Gordon Cooper born in Shawnee, Oklahoma. He will fly missions in both Mercury and Gemini programs.

1941: Gutzon Borglum, who spent the better part of the past 20 years carving the heads of four Presidents on Mount Rushmore, dies of a heart attack.

1986: Artist Georgia O'Keeffe dies at age 98 in Santa Fe.

MARCH 7

1782: In Gnadenhutten, Ohio 96 Christian Delaware Indians are massacred by soldiers in retaliation for raids conducted by other tribes.

JIM BOWIE
Born: ?, 1796
Died: March 6, 1836
Land owner, inventor, Texas rebel

1796: Born in Logan County, Kentucky.
1815: Arrives in New Orleans, works in slave trade, rides alligators.
1826: Moves to Texas from New Orleans.
1830: Marries Maria Ursula de Veramendi in San Antonio. Granted Mexican citizenship.
1830: Becomes a colonel in the Texas Rangers.
1831: Develops the Bowie knife. It measures 15 inches and weighs two pounds.
1832: Begins participation in Texas fight for independence.
1833: Wife and two children die of cholera.
1835: Helps to take the Alamo from Mexican forces.
1836: Dies at the Battle of the Alamo.

1849: Botanist/horticulturist Luther Burbank, who will do his major work in California, is born in Lancaster, Massachusetts.

1876: A Pueblo, Colorado newspaper announces "the biggest drunk of the present century" to be held in celebration of the arrival of the Atchison, Topeka and Santa Fe railroad.

1885: The Kansas state legislature makes it illegal to drive Texas cattle through Kansas between March 1 and December 1, in an effort to protect citizens from an epidemic of hoof-and-mouth disease.

1897: Lucy Factor, an Indian woman living in Oklahoma, is accused of being a witch and is shot.

1935: The body of Baby Doe Tabor is found frozen at Leadville's Matchless Mine. Colorado's Silver Queen of the Gay 90s, her husband's fortunes came crashing down with the Silver Panic of 1893. Baby Doe went from enjoying performances in her private box in the family-owned opera house to a gaunt figure, haunting the streets of Leadville and Denver, "hanging on to the Matchless" as her husband, H.A.W. Tabor had advised before he died.

MARCH 8

1862: The Battle of Pea Ridge in Arkansas is the most important Civil War battle to be fought west of the Mississippi. Confederate Generals McCulloch and McIntosh are both killed in this Union victory. Young Wild Bill Hickok serves as a Union scout.

1881: The completion of the Southern Pacific railroad gives the United States a second continental railroad as it joins the Atchison, Topeka and Santa Fe at Deming, New Mexico Territory.

1890: Writer Gene Fowler, whose works will include *Timber Line*, is born in Denver.

1893: Emmett Dalton, only Dalton survivor of the ill-advised raid on Coffeyville, begins a life sentence at the Kansas State Penitentiary. He will be pardoned in 1907.

1948: J. Frank Dalton, who will claim to be Jesse James in 1949, celebrates his 100th birthday at Lisbon Veterans Hospital in Dallas.

MARCH 9

1804: Upper Louisiana is officially transferred from France to the

United States at a ceremony in St. Louis.

1804: Capt. Meriwether Lewis arrives in St. Louis to begin the great westward exploration.

1842: Placer gold is discovered in California's San Fernando Valley, in Santa Feliciana Canyon.

1855: Lawman/stage driver Warren Earp, younger brother of Wyatt, born in Pella, Iowa.

1878: In the Lincoln County War, Frank Baker, William Morton, and William McCloskey are gunned down by a member of the Regulators, possibly Billy the Kid.

1895: Idaho Irrigation District Act is approved.

1914: Fire at the Missouri Athletic Club in St. Louis kills 37.

1916: Gen. Pancho Villa leads 1,500 troops in a raid on Columbus, New Mexico, killing 17 U.S. soldiers and residents. It is the largest attack of its kind in a series of depredations by Mexican rebels. American troops led by John J. Pershing chase them, kill 50, then follow them to Mexico to slay another 70.

MARCH 10

1849: Mormons vote to form the State of Deseret in present Utah, and to uphold the United States Constitution.

1864: Jack Slade is hanged in Virginia City, Montana.

1884: Colorado's most deadly single avalanche claims 13 as a slide demolishes a telegraph office near St. Elmo.

1910: Shwayder Trunk Manufacturing, the forerunner of the Samsonite Corporation, opens in Denver.

1922: KLZ is Denver's first radio station on the air.

1925: Amnesty is granted to impeached former Texas Gov. James Ferguson, while his wife is governor.

1933: Long Beach, California earthquake kills 120 and does $50 million damage.

1933: First state narcotic regulations go into effect in Nevada.

MARI SANDOZ
The
BEAVER MEN
SPEARHEADS OF EMPIRE

1966: Historian/novelist Mari Sandoz dies at age 64 in New York City.

MARCH 11

1755: Scottish explorer and fur trader Sir Alexander MacKenzie is born. He will make the first overland journey from Fort Chipewyan, in northeastern Alberta, to the Pacific coast.

1805: Gen. James Wilkinson is appointed governor of Louisiana Territory by President Jefferson. His regime will be a black mark in American history, as he plots with Aaron Burr to establish a new country in the western territories.

1836: In Gonzales, Texas, Sam Houston first hears of the fall of the Alamo.

1884: Gunslinger Ben Thompson dies in San Antonio, Texas.

1918: The Save the Redwoods League is established.

1950: Charles Windolph, the last Army survivor of the Battle of the Little Bighorn (he was with Reno) dies in Lead, South Dakota.

1971: Inventor Philo Taylor Farnsworth, known for his television pioneering, dies of cardiac arrest at age 64 in Salt Lake City.

MARCH 12

1802: First non-Indian child, a black, born in what is now North Dakota.

1850: California formally asks for statehood.

1888: Chinese laborers are excluded from entering the United States for 20 years under the terms of a treaty signed today by Secretary of State Charles Bayard and the Chinese minister.

1922: Jack Kerouac, whose beat generation will take him all over the west and produce classic portraits of postwar Denver and Wyoming, born in Lowell, Massachusetts.

1934: Earthquakes rock Utah and Idaho.

1935: *Rainbow Valley* with John Wayne released by Lone Star/Monogram.

1969: Levi Strauss begins production of bell-bottom jeans.

MARCH 13

1836: Sam Houston's troops move out of Gonzales on the trail of Santa Anna, less than a week after the fall of the Alamo.

1868: Captain Jack Harvey, good friend of Wild Bill Hickok, dies in Ellsworth, Kansas of tuberculosis.

1878: In the Lincoln County War, Tom Hill is killed and Jesse Evans wounded during an attack on the John Wagner camp.

1895: Six Italians are lynched by a mob during riots in the Colorado coal region.

1928: The St. Francis Dam breaks 50 miles from Los Angeles, emptying over 12 billion gallons of water into L.A. and Ventura County. The disaster kills 451, doing $12 million in damage.

1930: The announcement of the first planetary discovery in this century is made from the Lowell Observatory in Arizona. Young Clyde Tombaugh is the proud father of the new world, having worked on calculations and theories by the late Percival Lowell. After several suggestions, the name Pluto is chosen, for the Lord of the Underworld.

MARCH 14

1887: Louis Thoen finds a piece of sandstone, with a message carved in 1834 by a band of hapless goldminers under attack by Indians near Spearfish, South Dakota.

1894: Denver's "City Hall War" ends. The standoff saw members of the city's fire and excise commission, along with 200 armed sympathizers, holed up in the massive City Hall building. Gov. Davis "Bloody Bridles" Waits ("I should rather see our men riding through the streets through blood to the bridles than to surrender our liberties to the corporations") calls out the national guard, but the confrontation ends without a shot. A series of legal maneuvers keeps the defenders in the building until April 18.

1919: The first Max Brand book, *The Untamed*, is published by Putnam's.

1924: Charles Lindbergh begins pilot training at San Antonio, Texas.

1944: Salt Lake City sets a city record with 21.6 inches of snow in one storm.

1961: A B-52 loaded with nuclear weapons, on a training mission, crashes in California.

MARCH 15

1767: Called the first President from the West, Andrew Jackson is born in Waxhaw, South Carolina.

1845: Thomas Ward Custer, George Armstrong Custer's brother, is born.

1848: First published account of the California gold discovery is printed in the San Francisco *Californian*.

1881: The Benson stage is robbed by the Clanton gang near Bisbee, Arizona, setting in motion a number of events. Gambler Doc Holliday will be accused of murder for killing the stage driver. A feud between the Clantons and Holliday's friends, the Earps, will climax with the Gunfight at the OK Corral on October 26, 1881.

1912: Bluesman Lightnin' Hopkins is born in Centerville, Texas.

1916: Gen. Pershing leads 6,000 men into Mexico in search of Pancho Villa.

1941: Blizzard claims 71 in Minnesota and North Dakota.

MARCH 16

1775: Daniel Boone and a party of 30 begin chopping down trees, clearing the Wilderness Road to pass through the Cumberland Gap to Kentucky.

1874: The Youngers have a shoot out with Pinkerton agents in Osceola, Missouri. John Younger is killed along with agents E.B. Daniels and Louis Lull.

1894: John Wesley Hardin receives full pardon from Texas Gov. Jim Hogg after serving 16 years of a 25-year sentence.

1903: Judge Roy Bean, "Law West of the Pecos," dies at Langtry, Texas.

1905: The state of Colorado has three governors in one day.

1906: A head-on collision of Denver and Rio Grande trains at Florence, Colorado kills 34.

1942: Singer Jerry Jeff Walker ("Mr. Bojangles") born in Oneonta, New York.

1974: Roy Acuff gives President Nixon yo-yo lessons at the all-new Nashville Opry House.

1975: Oregon record reached with 119 inches of snow falling on Crater Lake in one season.

MARCH 17

1775: Cherokees sell parts of present Kentucky to the Transylvania Company.

1804: Mountain man James Bridger born in Richmond, Virginia. He will join Ashley's famed expedition to the Rockies in 1822 and become one of the charter members of the Rocky Mountain Fur Company. One of the most popular figures at rendezvous, Bridger will be known for his bravery and his tall tales. He will establish Fort Bridger (in today's Wyoming) in 1843, but run into trouble with Brigham Young's "Avenging Angels."

> **JIM BRIDGER**
> **Born:** March 17, 1804
> **Died:** July 17, 1881
> **Mountain man**
>
> **1804:** Born in Richmond, Virginia.
> **1822:** Joins William Ashley's party to fur trap Missouri River.
> **1825:** Sees the Great Salt Lake; mistakes it for the Pacific Ocean.
> **1830:** Begins a four year partnership in the Rocky Mountain Fur Company.
> **1832:** Wounded in battle with Gros Ventre Indians.
> **1843:** Builds Fort Bridger in Wyoming.
> **1850:** Discovers Bridger's Pass while leading Stansbury expedition.
> **1865:** Guides Powder River expedition.
> **1881:** Dies in Missouri.

1848: Peace negotiator Nicholas P. Trist is arrested after representing the U.S. in the Treaty of Guadalupe Hidalgo. He has negotiated the treaty after being ordered home.

1859: Gun sight inventor John Hill Redfield born in Oregon.

1876: Reynolds attacks Two Moon's Cheyenne and He Dog's Sioux Indians as campaigns on the plains heat up.

1879: New Mexico Gov. Lew Wallace holds a secret meeting with Billy the Kid. The governor is in the middle of writing *Ben Hur*, the Kid is trying to arrange a pardon. Arrangements are made, but the Kid does not choose to abide, remaining a wanted man.

1896: Cherokee Bill Goldsby hanged for murder in Fort Smith, Arkansas.

1897: Bob Fitzsimmons whips James J. Corbett in the 14th round of their heavyweight championship bout in Carson City, Nevada.

1906: An avalanche wipes out a boarding house near Silverton, Colorado killing a dozen miners.

1914: Pro football Hall of Famer Sammy Baugh born in Temple, Texas.

1932: Colorado's Great Sand Dunes designated a national monument.

1949: Shamrock Hotel has a $1.5 million grand opening in Texas.

MARCH 18

1852: Wells Fargo & Co., a subsidiary of American Express, begins operation in the California gold fields. Founders Henry Wells and William Fargo meet with seven financial backers at New York's Astor House and organize with $300,000 in capital.

1878: Sam Bass gang robs the Houston and Texas train at Hutchins, Texas.

1882: As revenge for the Gunfight at the OK Corral, Morgan Earp is murdered while playing pool in Tombstone, shot in the back at Bob Hatch's Billiard Parlor. Among his last words, "This is the last game of pool I'll ever play." His brothers prepare their revenge.

1911: Theodore Roosevelt dedicates Roosevelt Dam on Arizona's Salt River. This government project will allow widespread irrigation in the southwest.

1911: David Moffat dies at age 71 of a heart attack in New York City, after being refused a loan for his railroad and proposed tunnel under the Continental Divide.

1912: Boiler explodes on a train in San Antonio, killing 26.

1919: Pershing County, Nevada established in honor of Gen. John J. Pershing.

1926: Actor Peter Graves born in Minneapolis, Minnesota.

1937: Natural gas explosion in a schoolhouse kills 294 in New London, Texas.

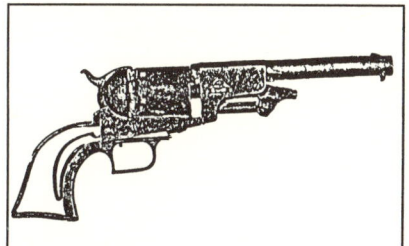

MARCH 19

1687: French explorer Robert Cavalier, Sieur de La Salle, attempting to reach help for his ill-fated Matagorda Bay Colony, is murdered by mutinous followers in eastern Texas.

1743: Pierre de la Verendrye, returning from his western explorations, reaches the Missouri River.

1836: James Fannin's men (the command that didn't make it to the Alamo) are surrounded by Mexicans when their ammo cart breaks down en route from Goliad to Victoria in Texas.

1840: Texans invite Comanches to bring in white prisoners and talk peace at the San Antonio Council House. When the Comanches show with only one prisoner, the settlers lock the doors. A fight breaks out and 35 Indians are killed.

1848: Lawman Wyatt Berry Stapp Earp is born in Monmouth, Illinois.

WYATT EARP
Born: March 19, 1848
Died: January 13, 1929
Lawman, con man

1868: Becomes proficient at gambling while working on the Union Pacific.

1872: After being arrested for stealing a horse in Indian Territory, makes a living as a buffalo hunter in Kansas.

1875: Hired as a policeman in Wichita, Kansas.

1876: Dismissed in Wichita; serves as a deputy and faro dealer in Dodge City; joins police force.

1877: Departs for Black Hills to seek gold.

1878: Returns to Dodge, becomes assistant marshal. Shoots gunman George Hoyt during a disturbance.

1879: Arrives in Tombstone with his brothers, goes to work as a Wells Fargo shotgun messenger.

1880: Becomes partner in the Oriental Saloon, hires Bat Masterson.

1881: Feud with Clanton/McLaury "cowboy element" of Tombstone results in the Gunfight at the OK Corral.

1882: Following shootings of brothers Virgil and Morgan, goes on a revenge rampage against alleged assassins. Hides in Colorado.

1883: Returns to Dodge City to help Luke Short.

1884: Lives in Idaho; legal problems with a mining claim.

1889: Runs a San Diego gambling hall.

1897: Follows gold hunt to Alaska.

1906: Moves to Los Angeles. Serves as unpaid consultant for several Westerns as his finances dwindle.

1928: Meets author Stuart Lake, whose biography will make Earp famous two years after his death.

1929: Dies at age 80.

1860: Politician/orator William Jennings Bryan born in Salem, Illinois. He will become a major figure in the Silver Panic of 1893.

1864: Western artist Charles Marion Russell, related through his paternal ancestors to William and Charles Bent of Bent's Fort, born in Oak Hill, Missouri. A self-taught artist, he will move from the cattle trail to the studio, leaving a legacy of the white and red experience during the twilight of the Old West.

1868: Crazy Horse attacks the Horsecreek Station.

1873: Gunfire erupts at the Matador Saloon in Lampasas, Texas, when authorities try to arrest Clint Barkley, alias Bill Bowen. Three officers die.

1920: *Trailin'* by Max Brand published by Putnam's.

1931: Gambling, outlawed since 1910, is legalized in Nevada. Gov. Fred Balzar signs into law a statute that requires only six weeks of residency for a divorce.

1950: Greatest snow depth in Oregon is reached at Timberline Lodge, a total of 246 inches.

1954: First rocket-driven sled on rails is tested by Air Force Lt. Col. John Paul Stapp in Alamogordo, New Mexico. Six rockets propel him to speeds reaching 421 MPH.

MARCH 20

1822: Ashley's ad appears in the *Missouri Republican*. Looking for a few good men to trap for his fur enterprise, he will attract Jim Bridger and Jedediah Smith, among others.

1823: Ned Buntline, the "dime millionaire," king of pulp fiction born Edward Zane Carroll Judson in Stamford, New York. He will switch from writing nautical adventure hogwash to western adventure hogwash, and make a fortune. In his prime, he will be this country's top literary money-earner, pulling in a better living than Whitman, Longfellow, or Twain. His most important contribution, though, will be his discovery and promotion of Buffalo Bill.

1842: Charles A. Reynolds who, as Custer's chief guide, will be called "Lonesome Charlie" by his cohorts and the "White-Hunter-Who-Never-Goes-Out-for-Nothing" by the Indians, is born in Warren County, Illinois.

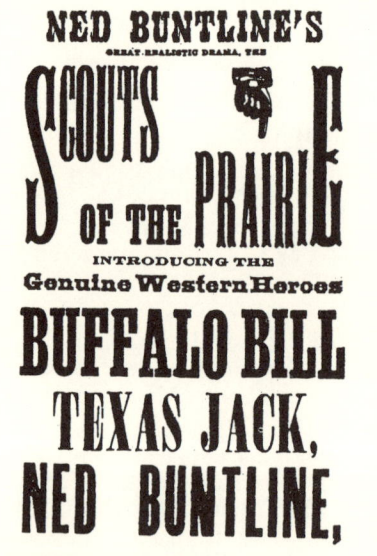

1882: Two days after the murder of Morgan Earp, his brother Virgil, who had been wounded several months earlier, is put on a train from Tucson to California by brothers Wyatt and Warren, Doc Holliday, Sherman McMasters, and Turkey Creek Jack Johnson. The boys have another reason to be in town ~ to seek out Frank Stillwell,

March

rumored killer of Morgan. They find him, and blast him out of existence.

1895: Explosion at Coal Mine No. 5 in Red Canyon, Wyoming, kills 62.

1909: Navajo National Monument is created in Arizona.

1930: *Montana Moon* with Johnny Mack Brown, released by MGM.

1932: Movie cowboy Tom Mix marries Mabel Ward in Yuma, Arizona.

MARCH 21

1852: No birth record exists, but John Henry Holliday, who will be known in the Old West as the deadly consumptive dentist Doc Holliday, is baptized in Griffin, Georgia.

1868: Jesse and Frank James, Jim and Cole Younger, and four others rob the Southern Bank of Kentucky at Russellville; Jesse wounds bank president Nimrod Long. The gang rides away with $14,000.

> **1882:** First western film star, G.M. "Broncho Billy" Anderson born. He will star in the first film of the genre, 1903's *The Great Train Robbery*, and will receive a special Oscar in 1957 for his "contribution to the development of motion pictures."

1890: Gen. George Crook dies of heart failure while lifting weights in his Chicago headquarters.

1910: Rock Island train derails at Green Mountain, Iowa killing 55.

1916: Outlaw Cole Younger dies at age 72 in Lee's Summit, Missouri. He is buried with 17 bullets in his body.

1916: Fire sweeps through Paris, Texas engulfing 1,500 buildings and doing $14 million in damage.

1947: *Jesse James Rides Again* serial with Clayton Moore released by Republic.

MARCH 22

1622: First massacre of white people by Indians takes place at Jamestown, Virginia, as 347 of 1,240 are slain.

1774: Juan Bautista de Anza reaches Mission San Gabriel from Sonora after traveling overland.

1858: Wild Bill Hickok, 20, elected village constable of Monticello Township, Johnson County, Kansas.

1881: Flat-nosed George Manuse is taken from jail by a mob in Rawlins, Montana and lynched from a telegraph pole. A suspect in the killing of Deputy Sheriff Bob Widdowfield, his hide was tanned and made into a pair of moccasins and a tobacco pouch.

1882: Still seeking revenge for the murder of Morgan Earp, brothers Wyatt and Warren, accompanied by Doc Holliday and two others, return to Tombstone to find Pete Spence. Instead they locate another suspect, Florentino Cruz, and kill him.

1882: The Edmunds Act, passed today in Congress, is aimed squarely at the Mormon Church. Polygamy is declared a felony with up to five years and a $500 fine awaiting those who adhere to it. Unlawful cohabitation is a misdemeanor. Also, a board appointed by the President will assume the duties of all registered and elected officers in the territory of Utah. Over 1,300 will be jailed for polygamy or, more correctly, polygyny, the taking of plural wives.

1896: Ira Terrell, author of Oklahoma's statute on the death penalty, is the first to die under it when it is learned he is a convicted felon.

1908: Author Louis L'Amour born in Jamestown, North Dakota. The best-selling Western author's works will include *Hondo, Sackett, Bendigo Shafter,* and many, many others.

1941: Construction of the Grand Coulee Dam on Washington's Columbia River begins.

MARCH 23

1806: Lewis and Clark expedition breaks camp at Fort Clatsop on the Columbia River and begins the journey back east.

1823: Politician Schuyler Colfax is born in New York City. On a visit to Denver as Speaker of the House, a major thoroughfare will be named in his honor.

1889: Following President Harrison's announcement today that a part of Indian Territory will be opened for settlement, a mass migration from all over the globe converges on present Oklahoma. "Harrison's Hoss Race," where land will be offered on a first come, first served basis, is coming soon.

1895: Denver's St. James Hotel burns.

1908: Actress Joan Crawford born in San Antonio, Texas.

1913: Omaha tornado levels the town, kills 94, and does $3.5 million in damage.

MARCH 24

1825: Mexican state of Texas-Coahuila declares itself open for American settlers.

1834: Explorer John Wesley Powell born in New York City.

1860: Clipper ship *Andrew Jackson* arrives in San Francisco from New York after 89 days at sea.

1883: Two dozen Canadian River cowboys strike for a 50 cents a day pay raise.

1909: Outlaw Clyde Barrow born in Teleco, Texas.

1930: Actor Steve McQueen born in Indianapolis, Indiana. He will make his name in such Western films as *Magnificent Seven, Nevada Smith, Tom Horn,* and the TV series, "Wanted, Dead or Alive."

MARCH 25

1842: Myles Keogh, a soldier of fortune who will serve with the Papal Guards and with the Union forces during the Civil War, is born in Ireland.

1867: Gutzon Borglum, who will carve the heads of four American Presidents on South Dakota's Mount Rushmore, born in Bear Lake, Idaho.

1867: Pat Garrett's mother Elizabeth dies.

1879: Little Wolf, called "the greatest of the fighting Cheyennes," is overtaken and pursuaded to surrender by his friend, Lt. W.P. Clark. Little Wolf and Dull Knife had been leading their people toward their old homeland, away from the reservation in Indian Territory. The flight of the 300 was the basis of Mari Sandoz' *Cheyenne Autumn.*

MARCH 26

1804: Louisiana becomes the Territory of Orleans.

1804: Public lands in the West are put on sale under the Land Act, establishing a minimum of 160 acres at $1.64 per acre.

1825: California becomes a territory of the Mexican Republic.

1832: American Fur Company's steamship *Yellowstone* departs from

St. Louis on her second expedition up the Missouri. Among the passengers is artist George Catlin.

1872: California earthquake kills 30, destroying many small towns.

1882: Samsonite Corp. founder Jesse Shwayder born in Black Hawk, Colorado.

1930: Sandra Day O'Connor, first woman on the U.S. Supreme Court, born in El Paso, Texas.

1937: Statue of Popeye is unveiled at the Spinach Festival in Crystal City, Texas. It is the world's first statue of a cartoon character.

1951: Attorney Jesse Edward James, son of the Missouri outlaw, dies at age 75 in California.

1984: The Medal of Freedom, the highest American civilian honor, is awarded to western author Louis L'Amour.

MARCH 27

1836: The Goliad Massacre – Troops under Gen. Urrea put 417 Texas revolutionaries to the sword.

1886: Apache leader Geronimo, having escaped from his reservation in May 1885, agrees to return and surrender in Arizona, then changes his mind at the last minute. En route to Fort Bowie, Arizona, he encounters a whiskey merchant, gets drunk, and disappears.

1877: Mattie Silks makes Denver's *Rocky Mountain News*: "Madame Silks was fined $12 for drunkenness yesterday, and paid it like a woman. She ought to play it finer when she gets on a spree."

1901: Passing through Paint Rock, Texas, Harvey Logan, *aka* Kid Curry, gets into a heated discussion with local Oliver Thornton and shoots him dead.

1907: Zane Grey, on his first trip to the West, arrives at the Grand Canyon.

1915: Henry Starr, attempting to rob two banks at once in Stroud, Oklahoma, is wounded and taken prisoner.

1930: Actor David Janssen born in Naponee, Nebraska.

1951: Dumont, South Dakota gets 34 inches of snow in 24 hours.

1964: Alaskan earthquake kills 117.

1973: Marlon Brando turns down the Oscar for his role in *The Godfather*. Brando expresses regret at his country's and the media's treatment of Native Americans, in a statement read at the ceremonies by Sacheen Little Feather.

1980: First steam is seen rising from Washington's Mount St. Helens.

MARCH 28

1776: Juan Bautista de Anza reaches the site of San Francisco with 247 colonists, where he will found the presidio of San Francisco.

MATTIE SILKS

1845: As a preamble to the Mexican War, Mexico cuts off diplomatic relations with the United States.

1846: Gen. Worth directs 4,000 U.S. soldiers to erect Fort Texas. Meanwhile, at Matamoros, Gen. de Ampudia begins fortification.

1868: Wild Bill Hickok and Buffalo Bill oversee a prisoner move from Fort Hays to Topeka, Kansas.

1882: British literary figure Oscar Wilde visits San Francisco.

1883: During one of their many raids, Chiricahua Apaches under Chief Chato murder Judge and Mrs. H.C. McComas. Chato's rebel band will be forced to surrender in 1884.

1890: Bandleader Paul Whiteman, the "King of Jazz," born in Denver.

1904: Kansas Sen. Joseph Burton is convicted of accepting bribes and illegally hindering the post office from issuing a fraud order.

1908: A cave-in at the Union Pacific Coal Company's Mine No. 1 Hanna, Wyoming kills 59.

1953: Athlete of the half-century Jim Thorpe dies of a heart attack.

1984: Brownsville, Texas reports a high of 106 degrees.

MARCH 29

1836: San Felipe, Texas is put to the torch, keeping it from falling into Mexican hands.

1840: Antonio Zapata, found guilty of treason by Mexican authorities, is beheaded. His head is placed on a pole in front of his house as an example for future traitors.

1857: Capt. Alexander Fancher's wagon train of nearly 150 men, women, and children, departs Arkansas en route to California. They will never make it. In September, in Utah, they will be the victims of the Mountain Meadows Massacre.

1879: Wyoming Stock Growers Association formed in Laramie.

1888: Rich Hill, Missouri mine explosion kills 24.

1909: Singer Moon Mullican ("Mona Lisa," "Cherokee Boogie") born in Polk County, Texas.

1955: Football great Earl Campbell born in Tyler, Texas.

MARCH 30

1870: Military rule in Texas ceases following the Civil War. The state is readmitted to the Union.

1889: Maj. Marcus Reno, who commanded three companies under Custer at the Battle of the Little Bighorn, dies during an operation for cancer of the mouth in Washington, D.C.

1899: A record 141-inch snowfall ends in Ruby, Colorado.

1913: Singer Frankie Laine ("Mule Train") born in Chicago. He will also gain fame with his theme songs for the TV show "Rawhide" and the movie *Gunfight at the OK Corral*.

MARCH 31

1861: In the days before the Civil War, Fort Bliss in Texas surrenders to state troops.

1878: Heavyweight champion Jack Johnson, who will send racist America seeking a "great white hope," born in Galveston, Texas.

1895: Author Vardis Fisher, whose works will include *Toilers of the Hills* and *Children of God* born in Annis, Idaho.

1899: Ruby, Colorado records the most snow ever in a calendar month: 249 inches.

1925: Cattle baroness Henrietta

King of the famous King Ranch dies at age 92.

1928: Singer Lefty Frizzell ("If You've Got the Money, I've Got the Time") born in Corsicana, Texas.

1935: Actor Richard Chamberlain born in Beverly Hills, California.

1943: *Oklahoma!* opens on Broadway. The Rodgers and Hammerstein musical is a milestone, depicting real, everyday people in song and dance. In addition to the title tune, other hits include "Oh, What A Beautiful Mornin'," and "The Surrey With the Fringe On Top." It will run for 2,248 performances in New York.

April

APRIL 1

1807: Captive Zebulon Pike and company arrive in Chihuahua, where they are interviewed by Gen. Nemesio Salcedo.

1818: Davy Crockett becomes town commissioner of Lawrenceburg, Tennessee.

1875: Wild Bill Longley murders his old friend Wilson Anderson when he learns Anderson is responsible for the death of his cousin, Cale Longley. This shotgun murder on a farm in Bastrop County, Texas, will earn Longley the death sentence.

```
Welcome to Tombstone
   AND BOOTHILL GRAVEYARD.
      BURIED HERE, ARE THE REMAINS OF
TOM McLOWERY - FRANK McLOWERY  | KILLED IN EARP CLANTON BATTLE
AND BILLIE CLANTON             |    SEPT. 26 TH. 1881
DAN DOWD, RED SAMPLE, TEX HOWARD, | HANGED LEGALLY BY J.T. WARD SHERIFF,
BILL DeLANEY AND DAN KELLY        | FOR THE BISBEE MASSACRE MAR. 8TH 1884
      JOHN HEATH           :        M. R. PEEL
SALTY GODENS, DUTCH ANNIE, INDIAN BILL, PAT LYNCH, RED GERMAN, BLACK JACK, FISHER BROTHERS
JIM HOOKAH
```

1877: Ed Schieffelin, 29, begins prospecting in Apache country in present Arizona. Fellow miners scoff, telling him all he will discover will be his tombstone. After striking one of the richest silver veins in the Old West, seven inches wide and 50 feet long, Schieffelin names his bonanza Tombstone. A major social center of the Wild West develops on the location.

1878: Sheriff Bill Brady, Deputy George Hindman, and three others are ambushed by Billy the Kid and five Regulators in Lincoln, New Mexico. Billy is later indicted for the murder of Brady.

1883: Actor Lon Chaney, who will become film's "Man of a Thousand Faces" in classics such as *The Phantom of the Opera* and *The Hunchback of Notre Dame*, is born to deaf mute parents in Colorado Springs, Colorado.

1892: Trouble begins at the Coeur D'Alene mines in Idaho as miners walk out on strike. They will return to the mines only after federal intervention in July, 1892.

1912: Tornado leaves a 300-foot chasm in downtown Houston. The water table is broken and a waterspout develops.

1930: *Under a Texas Moon* released by Warner Brothers

1932: Actress Debbie Reynolds, who will star in movies like *The Unsinkable Molly Brown* born in El Paso, Texas.

APRIL 2

1880: Outlaw Dave Rudabaugh participates in the murder of jailer Antonio Lino Valdez in Las Vegas, New Mexico.

1901: Wild Bunch member William Carver is shot dead by authorities in Sonora, Texas.

1902: Suffragist Esther Morris dies at age 88 in Cheyenne, Wyoming.

1932: The recognized inventor of bulldogging, black rodeo star Bill Pickett, dies after being kicked in the head by a horse. At age 60, he is laid to rest in Oklahoma.

1949: Singer Emmy Lou Harris born in Birmingham, Alabama.

1959: *Alias Jesse James* with Bob

Hope released by United Artists.

APRIL 3

1817: Texas Ranger William "Big Foot" Wallace born in Lexington, Virginia.

1848: First American public school in San Francisco opens.

1860: Pony Express begins as Billy Richardson departs St. Joseph, Missouri at 7:15 P.M.. James Randal starts the first leg from San Francisco.

1861: William Clarke Quantrill barely escapes a lynching in Paola, Kansas.

1882: Robert Ford shoots Jesse James in the back of the head while the famed outlaw is adjusting a picture on the wall of his Missouri home. Historians argue as to whether it was really a painting or an embroidery of "Home Sweet Home." A heated debate over whether the victim was the real Jesse or not turns into a true Wild West controversy, especially when 101-year-old J. Frank Dalton emerges in the 1940s to announce to the world that he is the once and future Jesse. James scholars debunk the old man's story and stick with the accepted version, that Jesse is viciously murdered by "that dirty little coward," who will drift to the boom town of Creede, Colorado, where he too will be murdered by a glory seeker.

1898: Fourteen-year-old Douglas Fairbanks is kicked out of Denver's East High School for "a lavish and unauthorized use of green paint" on St. Patrick's Day.

1900: The greening of California's Imperial Valley begins through irrigation.

1929: Singer Johnny Horton ("The Battle of New Orleans," "North to Alaska") born in Tyler, Texas.

1924: Actor Marlon Brando born in Omaha, Nebraska. His Westerns will include *One-Eyed Jacks* and *The Missouri Breaks*.

APRIL 4

1843: Photographer William Henry Jackson born in Keesville, New York. He will pack hundreds of pounds of photographic equipment on the backs of mules to record many of the the West's wonders on film. His photos of Yellowstone will lead directly to the creation of this country's first national park.

1878: Lincoln County War participant Dick Brewer has his head blown off by Andrew "Buckshot" Roberts at Blazer's Mill. Roberts is then killed by Charles Bowdre. Billy the Kid is grazed.

1878: The Sam Bass gang robs the Texas and Pacific train at Eagle Ford, Texas.

1882: Headline of the *Kansas City Daily Journal* reads "Goodbye, Jesse!"

1887: America's first woman mayor is elected, Susanna Medora Salter of Argonia, Kansas.

1887: Mine disaster at Savannah, Oklahoma kills 18.

1888: Baseballer Tris Speaker born in Hubbard, Texas.

1894: Third Cavalry called in to put down a disturbance of Cheyenne Indians stealing cattle near El Reno, Oklahoma. Trouble is, the cows are illegally feasting on Indian lands.

1934: Heavy rains in western Oklahoma claim 22 lives.

1959: *Rio Bravo* with John Wayne, Dean Martin, and Ricky Nelson released by Armada/Warner Brothers.

"GOOD-BYE JESSE!"

APRIL 5

1915: Jesse Willard, "the Potawatomie Giant" from Kansas, decks Galveston's Jack Johnson, first black heavyweight champ, in the 26th round of their battle in the Havana sun. Willard's moment of victory, with Johnson sprawled on the canvas shading his eyes from the sun, will be enshrined on barroom walls for years to come.

1922: Actress Gale Storm born in Bloomington, Texas.

1946: *The Virginian* with Joel McCrea released by Paramount.

1976: Billionaire recluse Howard Hughes dies in his airplane en route from Acapulco to Houston.

APRIL 6

1830: Mexico decides to prohibit Americans from settling in Texas, as they have been for the past seven years. The stage is set for revolution.

1830: Joseph Smith and six others form the Church of Jesus Christ of Latter-day Saints in Palmyra, New York. Within 16 years the church, under the direction of Brigham Young, will begin a westward migration to escape religious persecution.

1832: Black Hawk War begins as Sauk and Fox Indians try to regain lands ceded to the United States.

1862: Explorer John Wesley Powell loses his right arm during the Civil War Battle of Shiloh in Tennessee.

1892: Journalist/traveler Lowell Thomas born in Ohio. His family will move to Cripple Creek, Colorado in 1907.

1924: First round-the-world flight takes off from Seattle. It will be completed September 28.

1926: The first domestic air mail contractor is Varney Air Lines, which will fly mail between Elko, Nevada and Pasco, Washington.

1933: Elizabeth Bacon Custer, widow of George Armstrong Custer for 57 years, dies in New York City and is buried beside her husband at West Point.

1937: Singer Merle Haggard born in Bakersfield, California.

1944: Rose O'Neill, who invented the Kewpie Doll while watching the snow fall in Durango, Colorado, dies in Springfield, Missouri.

1983: Record Denver low is set at seven degrees.

APRIL 7

1805: After camping north of Bismarck, North Dakota for the winter, the Lewis and Clark Expedition resumes its trek up the Missouri River. A party of 16 will go back to St. Louis to report on the exploration.

1891: Nebraska enforces one of the country's first eight-hour work day laws.

1891: P.T. Barnum, showman and Western enthusiast, dies.

1898: Little Dick West is slain by Bill Tilghman and Heck Thomas near Guthrie, Oklahoma.

1900: Jack London marries Bessie Maddern in Oakland, California.

1922: Wyoming's Teapot Dome is secretly leased by Interior Secretary Albert B. Fall to Mammoth Oil's Harry Sinclair. The events surrounding these shady deals will make for Washington's biggest scandal until Watergate.

1928: Actor James Garner, whose TV show "Maverick" will be one of the top shows of the Western television era, born in Norman, Oklahoma.

1933: Prohibition ends after 13 years.

1935: Singer Bobby Bare born in Ironton, Ohio. His big hits will include "Detroit City," and "500 Miles".

1958: Frank Eaton, better known as Pistol Pete, dies at age 97 in Anadarko, Oklahoma.

1959: First atomic-generated electricity produced at Los Alamos, New Mexico.

1959: Oklahoma repeals prohibition.

APRIL 8

1842: Elizabeth Clift Bacon, future bride of George Armstrong Custer, born in Monroe, Michigan.

1853: Exploration for a rail route between the 47th and 49th parallels is begun.

1920: A Ponca City, Oklahoma rooming house explodes, killing 32.

APRIL 9

1682: French explorer Robert Cavelier, Sieur deLa Salle lands at the mouth of the Mississippi. He names all land drained by it and its tributaries Louisiana in honor of Louis XIV, and claims it for France.

1856: Lt. Col. Robert E. Lee is assigned to fight frontier hostilities from Camp Cooper, Texas.

1878: Marshal Ed Masterson, Bat's oldest brother, is shot dead by a drunk cowhand, Jack Wagner, in the Lady Gay Dance Hall, Dodge City, Kansas.

1881: After a heated trial, Billy the Kid is convicted of murder in New Mexico, and sentenced to hang. Soon after, the sheriff will leave the jail to go shopping for wood to build a gallows, and the Kid will escape.

1892: Suspected rustler Nate Champion surrounded in his Johnson County, Wyoming cabin. When he makes a run for it, he is felled by 28 bullets. Nick Raya, another suspected rustler, was killed earlier in the day.

1892: The Solid Muldoon, a fake petrified man, is "rediscovered" near Creede. It will be managed this time around by shyster *extraordinaire* Soapy Smith, and tour under the name "Colonel Stone."

1905: Actor Ward Bond, star of TV's "Wagon Train" is born in Nebraska.

1932: Pretty Boy Floyd evades an ambush at his stepfather's house near Bixby, Oklahoma, killing state special agent Erv Kelley with a blast from his submachine gun.

1965: The Houston Astros take on the New York Yankees in the first game ever played in the Houston Astrodome.

APRIL 10

1830: William L. Sublette leads 81 men in ten wagons out of St. Louis to the annual mountain man rendezvous. These will be the first wagons to go as far as the Rocky Mountains.

1865: Following the signing of the surrender at Appomattox Court House on April 9, Gen. Phil Sheridan purchases the table used by Grant and Lee for the historic occasion. He presents it to Gen. George Armstrong Custer to give to his wife, Elizabeth. Custer rides home with the table strapped across his horse.

1869: Congress creates the Board of Indian Commissioners.

1878: The Sam Bass gang robs the Texas and Pacific near Mesquite, Texas. They are foiled when the passengers pull back their curtains and open fire. Worst wounded is gang member Seaborn Barnes.

1891: Rodeo champ Lee Robinson born in Haskell County, Texas.

1899: Former Silver King H.A.W. Tabor dies of appendicitis in Denver. A man of overwhelming riches and power, he was wiped out with the Panic of 1893 when the United States went to a gold standard. He was made Postmaster of Denver, a position he served with honor until his death.

1905: A three-day meeting begins that will result in the formation of the Wyoming Wool Growers Association.

1921: Actor Chuck Connors of TV's "The Rifleman" born in New York, New York.

1933: Civilian Conservation Corps created.

1962: Texas gets major league baseball. In the first official game, the Houston Colt .45's beat the Chicago Cubs 11-2.

APRIL 11

1803: Negotiations begin on the Louisiana Purchase as France's Talleyrand asks America's Livingston what the U.S. might pay for the land.

1819: Margaret M. Lea, future wife of Sam Houston born in Marion, Alabama.

1822: Fur trade entrepreneur William H. Ashley receives his license to operate on the upper Missouri River and forms a partnership with Andrew Henry. In 1830, five of Ashley's successors, including Tom Fitzpatrick and Jim Bridger will initiate the Rocky Mountain Fur Company.

1873: Fighting breaks out during peace talks with California's Modoc Indians. Modocs kill Gen. E.R.S. Canby and Rev. Eleazer Thomas. A thousand soldiers take up the chase against the Indians, which ends in the surrender of their leader,

PONY EXPRESS ARRIVES

Captain Jack. Canby receives the dubious distinction of being the only regular army general to be killed during the Indian wars.

1900: The *Denver Daily News* reports the death of Cort Thomson, lover of Mattie Silks, citing "the combined effects of whisky and opium."

1935: Massive dust storms destroy several crops throughout the region.

1962: *The Man Who Shot Liberty Valance* with John Wayne, James Stewart, and Lee Marvin, released by Paramount.

1971: Patience Latting is sworn in as Oklahoma City's mayor, the first woman mayor of an American city with a population over 200,000.

APRIL 12

1844: Texas agrees to cede public lands to the United States in return for $10 million to pay its public debt.

1858: Gov. Alfred Cummings is welcomed in Salt Lake City. When he informs the populace that troops are coming, 30,000 Mormons hurry out of town. They will hide in Provo until the confusion is over.

1875: Jesse James kills farmer Daniel H. Askew of Kearney, Missouri, for harboring a Pinkerton agent.

1879: Brewer Adolph Coors marries Louisa M. Weber in Golden, Colorado.

1882: Oscar Wilde delivers a lecture on aesthetics at Denver's Tabor Opera House. Admission is $1.50. The week before, newspaperman Eugene Field pretended to be the great wit, leading folks to believe the event had already happened when the real Wilde arrived.

1886: Command of the Department of Arizona is taken over by Gen. Nelson A. Miles. He succeeds Gen. George Crook, removed from office for promising Geronimo that, should he surrender, he would be able to live on his Arizona reservation.

1923: Actress/dancer Ann Miller is born Lucille Ann Collier in Chirino, Texas.

1981: Former heavyweight champion Joe Louis, 66, dies in Las Vegas.

APRIL 13

1860: First Pony Express rider arrives in San Francisco with dispatches only ten days after his departure from St. Joseph, Missouri.

1866: Robert Leroy Parker, who will gain fame as the dashing Butch Cassidy, last of the great train robbers, born in Utah.

> **BUTCH CASSIDY**
> **Born:** April 13, 1866
> **Died:** 1909 or 1937
> **Outlaw**
>
> **1866:** Robert Leroy Parker born in Utah.
> **1883:** Idolizes Utah bandit Mike Cassidy.
> **1889:** Pulls his first holdup in Telluride, Colorado.
> **1892:** Works at a butcher shop in Rock Springs, Wyoming, where he gets the nickname "Butch".
> **1894:** Begins an 18-month jail sentence in Laramie for horse stealing.
> **1896:** Heads for Hole in the Wall region; meets Sundance Kid and forms the Wild Bunch. More than five years of train robbing begins.
> **1897:** First Utah holdup.
> **1899:** The Wild Bunch rob a train near Wilcox, Wyoming.
> **1901:** Last American robbery by the Wild Bunch occurs near Wagner, Montana.
> **1902:** Goes to New York City, then on to South America and more bank robbing.
> **1909:** Possibly slain by Bolivian cavalry.
> **1937:** According to some, the death date of Butch Cassidy in Spokane.

1892: Wyoming's "Johnson County War" between homesteaders and cattlemen ends when federal troops rescue cattle forces from the "Ark of Vengeance," a wagon loaded with dynamite.

1893: As the Mississippi floods, 250 die in St. Louis.

1918: Fire at the Oklahoma State Hospital for the Insane in Norman claims 38 lives.

1954: Harry Orchard, convicted of the assassination of Idaho Gov. Frank Steunenberg, dies in prison.

1984: Space shuttle *Challenger* lands at Edwards AFB in California after a successful week in space.

APRIL 14

1823: Stephen Austin's settlement of Texas is confirmed by new leadership in Mexico. The revoking of settlers' rights will bring on the Texas battle for Independence during the 1830s.

1860: Franklin, the oldest town in Idaho, is founded just north of the Utah border.

1902: J.C. Penney opens his first dry goods store as a partner in "The Golden Rule Store" in Kemmerer, Wyoming.

1921: Record United States 24-hour snowfall occurs at Silver Lake, Colorado: 75.8 inches.

1924: Chiricahua National Monument created in Arizona.

1932: Singer Loretta Lynn, whose hits will include "You Ain't Woman Enough to Take My Man," and "Coal Miner's Daughter" born in Butcher's Hollow, Kentucky.

1935: Woody Guthrie writes "So Long, It's Been Good to Know You" during a dust storm in Pampa, Texas.

1958: Texan Van Cliburn wins the Tschaikovsky Piano Competition in Moscow, USSR.

1981: Space shuttle *Columbia* lands in the California desert after a 54.5-hour flight.

APRIL 15

1850: City of San Francisco is incorporated.

1871: Wild Bill Hickok appointed marshal of Abilene, Kansas for a salary of $150 a month.

1889: Artist Thomas Hart Benton (*Cotton Pickers, Lonesome Road*) born in Neosho, Missouri.

1892: The Sisseton Indian reservation in South Dakota is opened for settlement by run; 3,000 claim land before nightfall.

1912: The "unsinkable" Molly Brown is physically tossed into a *Titanic* lifeboat on the night to remember. Her heroics at sea include rescuing a drowning sailor, keeping her boat calm with stories of the Old West, and threatening to throw a particularly snide crewman overboard. Rich and more than a little overblown, she will bask in fame for the rest of her life, and be immortalized on stage and in the movies.

1949: On tax day, Robert Niles becomes the first person to make a stunt jump off the Golden Gate Bridge for reasons other than suicide.

APRIL 16

1847: After making camp for the winter, Brigham Young's exodus continues from Council Bluffs, Iowa.

1866: An explosion at the Wells Fargo office in San Francisco is set off by nitroglycerine, the first time freight has exploded on the line.

1881: Bat Masterson arrives in Dodge City, Kansas to help brother Jim in some business affairs. A few hours later he shoots Alabama Updegraff dead and leaves for Colorado.

1884: Annie Oakley billed as a markswoman for the first time, touring with the Sells Brothers Circus at Columbus, Ohio.

1903: Baseballer Paul Waner, 1927's MVP, born in Harrah, Oklahoma.

1908: Natural Bridges National Monument established in Utah.

1947: The French liner *Grandcamp*, a fertilizer ship, explodes in the harbor at Texas City, Texas; 552 are killed, 3,000 are injured, and $100 million in damage is done.

APRIL 17

1824: Russia agrees to a treaty that limits its territory in the Pacific Northwest to the lands above the 54' 40" mark.

1882: The Library of Congress receives its copyright-deposit copies of *The Authentic Life of Billy the Kid, the Noted Desperado of the Southwest* by Sheriff Pat Garrett, the man who killed said noted desperado.

1894: Percival Lowell founds his Lowell Observatory near Flagstaff,

Arizona. Here, 36 years later, young astronomer Clyde Tombaugh will discover the planet Pluto.

1900: Flat Nose George Curry is killed while rustling the wrong steers in Thompson, Utah.

1923: Newsman Harry Reasoner born in Dakota City, Iowa.

1930: Charles Sanford Skilton's opera *The Sun Bride*, based on Native American folklore, premieres on New York radio.

APRIL 18

1846: Gen. Stephen W. Kearny takes Santa Fe without firing a shot during the Mexican War.

1859: Trial run of the Leavenworth and Pikes Peak Express Company is held between Fort. Leavenworth and gold fields in Kansas Territory, present-day Colorado.

1880: Baseball Hall of Famer Samuel Earl Crawford, who will record 2,964 hits in his life, born in Wahoo, Nebraska.

> **1906: The San Francisco earthquake begins** with the first of two tremors at 5:13 A.M. this Wednesday morning. The jolt is recorded in Cape Town, South Africa. The city's water mains are destroyed, leaving the 585-man fire department to stop the inferno with no water. The quake/fire combination kills 700 and does over $500 million in damage, destroying 28,000 buildings. The rains come Saturday night, as citizens contemplate 3,000 burned acres which once were 520 city blocks. Writes Jack London, "Surrender was complete."

1934: Fort Worth, Texas claims the world's first laundromat.

1936: Gene Autry records his best known song, "Back in the Saddle Again."

1969: Former Army Sgt. Patrick Stout dies of leukemia, contracted after he stepped into the atomic bomb crater in Alamogordo, New York, shortly after the world's first nuclear blast in 1945, to prove there was no danger.

APRIL 19

GENE AUTRY

1852: Incorporation of the California Historical Society.

1859: Fort Mojave built on the Colorado River near present-day Mojave, Arizona, to protect settlers.

1863: A massive fire nearly destroys the young city of Denver.

1864: Cherry Creek flood wipes out most of Denver.

1867: Troops under Gen. Winfield S. Hancock attack an abandoned Sioux-Cheyenne village on the Arkansas River in present Kansas, destroying 241 lodges.

1874: Barracks at Alcatraz Island in San Francisco Bay destroyed by fire.

1876: A Wichita commission votes against rehiring policeman Wyatt Earp.

1906: In the wake of the earthquake,

176 prisoners are moved from the San Francisco city jail to Alcatraz.

1909: Jim "Killer" Miller and three others are lynched in an Ada, Oklahoma livery stable for the murder of rancher Gus Bobbitt.

1930: Actor Hugh O'Brian, TV's "Wyatt Earp" born in Rochester, New York.

1937: Amelia Earhart flies 1,700 miles from Burbank, California to Mexico City.

APRIL 20

1893: Comic actor Harold Lloyd, who will become the highest-paid film star of the 1920s, born in Burchard, Nebraska.

1905: American retailer Harold S. Marcus born in Dallas, Texas.

1910: Author Samuel L. Clemens, Mark Twain, who predicted his own demise with the return of Halley's Comet, dies on schedule three days after the comet circles around the sun.

> **1914: The Ludlow Massacre** ~ Striking miners and their families, camped in small tents in Ludlow, Colorado, are fired upon by militia. Approximately 20 are killed in a sickening slaughter that will alert the country to the gravity of American labor problems.

APRIL 21

1811: Wilson P. Hunt, a partner with John Jacob Astor in his fur and trading enterprise, departs St. Louis, bound for Oregon and colonization.

1833: On her third voyage up the Missouri, the *Yellowstone* passes the mouth of the Kansas River. On board are Prince Maximilian and Swiss artist Charles Bodmer.

> **1836: The Battle of San Jacinto** ~ Gen. Sam Houston and his Texans surprise Santa Anna's 1,400 troops. Seven Texans are killed vs. 630 Mexican dead, 208 wounded. Houston takes 730 prisoners, including Santa Anna, who is forced to sign surrender papers and recognize Texas independence following this, the decisive battle for Texas freedom.

1838: Naturalist John Muir born in Dunbar, Scotland. Raised in Wisconsin in the 1850s, he will explore the Sierras, and will become the moving force behind the first United States land and conservation laws. In 1892 he will form the Sierra Club for the purpose of "exploring, enjoying and rendering accessible the mountain regions of the Pacific Coast." He will also be involved in the establishment of the Sequoia and Yosemite National Parks.

1844: Artist George Catlin and Iowa Indians are received by King Louis Phillip in France.

1856: First train crosses the Mississippi River on that river's first bridge, between Davenport, Iowa and Rock Island, Illinois.

1875: Wyatt Earp is hired as a policeman in Wichita, Kansas, a position he will hold for nearly a year.

1875: Cave of the Winds discovered, near Colorado Springs, Colorado.

1897: A new era of Wild West crime begins as Butch Cassidy pulls his first holdup in Utah.

1898: Pro Football Hall of Famer Steve Owen born in Cleo Springs, Oklahoma.

APRIL 22

1831: Future Alamo hero Jim Bowie

marries Maria Ursula de Veramendi, daughter of the vice-governor of Texas, in San Antonio de Bexar, later San Antonio, Texas.

1887: Author James Norman Hall, who with Charles Nordhoff will write *Mutiny on the Bounty*, born in Colfax, Iowa.

1889: The Oklahoma Land Run ~ A portion of Indian Territory is opened for white settlement with the first of many runs. The United States purchased the former Seminole and Creek lands for $4 million. In today's great race, over 1,920,000 acres of land will be claimed on a first come first served basis, beginning with a gun shot at noon. By day's end the cities of Guthrie, Norman, Oklahoma City, and others have been born. Many find that choice spots were picked out ahead of the official gun by people called the "Sooners."

1904: "Father of the Atomic Bomb" Julius Robert Oppenheimer, who, with a top secret crew, will test his accomplishment in the New Mexico desert, born in New York City.

1935: *The Desert Trail* with John Wayne released by Lone Star/Monograph.

1936: Singer Glen Campbell ("By the Time I Get to Phoenix," "Rhinestone Cowboy") born in Delight, Arkansas.

1952: The first live atom bomb telecast occurs in Nevada.

1966: Military plane crashes during a thunderstorm at Ardmore, Oklahoma, killing 82.

APRIL 23

1859: William Byers publishes the first issue of the *Rocky Mountain News* in Denver, beating his competition, the *Cherry Creek Pioneer*, by 20 minutes. The *Pioneer* ceases publication with the first issue. The *News* is still in business today.

1868: Josefa Jaramillo Carson dies ten days after giving birth to the last child of her husband, Kit Carson.

1907: Accused cannibal Alfred Packer dies after a peaceful retirement and is buried in Littleton, Colorado.

1936: Singer Roy Orbison ("Pretty Woman") born in Vernon, Texas.

1940: Actor Lee Majors born in Wyandotte, Michigan.

APRIL 24

1851: Lawman Morgan Earp born in Pella, Iowa.

1874: Jesse James marries his double first cousin, Zerelda Mims, in Kearny, Missouri.

1947: Willa Cather, author of *My Antonia*, *Death Comes For the Archbishop*, and *O Pioneers* dies.

1984: An earthquake centered near San Jose, California registers 6.2 on the Richter Scale.

APRIL 25

1831: *The Lion of the West*, a play based loosely on the legend of Davy Crockett, opens at New York City's Park Theatre with James Hackett as Nimrod Wildfire.

1834: Davy Crockett begins a three-week speaking engagement through eastern states.

1846: Mexican troops fire on Zachary Taylor's troops, in a preamble to the Mexican War.

1898: United States declares war on Spain when that nation refuses to remove troops from Cuba and recognize her independence. In its declaration, the U.S. maintains that a state of war has existed between the two since April 21, 1898.

1898: Highest April temperature in the United States recorded at Volcano Springs, California, a torrid 118 degrees.

1935: Glenn Miller records under his own name for the first time.

1967: Abortion is first legalized by Colorado Gov. John Love in cases where a three-doctor licensed board agrees unanimously.

APRIL 26

1791: Most Cherokee lands are ceded to the United States with the Treaty of Holston River, in return for a promise that the Indians will be able to stay on the remaining lands for all time.

1798: The date mountain man James Beckwourth gave as his birth, though historians believe it probably occurred in 1800 in Frederick County, Virginia. The son of Sir Jennings Beckwith and a mulatto slave, Beckwourth will become the first black man to be named chief of an Indian tribe, the Crows.

1805: Lewis and Clark reach the mouth of the Yellowstone River.

1818: Lawman/Indian fighter John Coffee Hays born in Wilson County, Kansas.

1837: John James Audubon spends his 52nd birthday sketching the birds of Texas.

1854: Concerned Bostonians form the Massachusetts Emigrant Aid Society for the purpose of settling Kansas with anti-slavery sympathizers.

1858: California passes a bill prohibiting Chinese from landing at any port in state, the first of many attempts to quash Chinese immigration.

1869: First official run of the Atchison, Topeka, and Santa Fe railroad, the "Picnic Special" travels on seven miles of completed track, between Atchison and Topeka, Kansas, towns 50 miles apart.

1882: President Arthur asks for authority to act against "cowboy" terrorists in Arizona.

1901: Train robber Tom "Black Jack" Ketchum hanged in Texas. His last words are, "I'll be in Hell before you start breakfast. Let her rip!"

1934: Actress / comedienne Carol Burnett born in San Antonio, Texas.

1957: First Air Force Academy woman officer is Capt. Naomi M. McCracken.

APRIL 27

1813: Explorer Zebulon Pike, 34, is killed while leading his troops in the

Battle of York during the War of 1812.

1896: Baseball Hall of Famer Rogers Hornsby born in Winters, Texas. He will be the National League batting champion in 1920, 21, 22, 23, 24, 25, and 28, and will record a lifetime batting average of .358 over 23 years.

1896: Wallace Carothers, inventor of neoprene and nylon synthetic materials, born in Burlington, Iowa.

1930: *Roaring Ranch* with Hoot Gibson released by Universal.

1930: *The Texan* with Gary Cooper released by Paramount.

1930: *The Arizona Kid* with Warner Baxter released by Fox.

1937: Actress Sandy Dennis born in Hastings, Nebraska.

APRIL 28

1869: The beginning of the final track in the first great transcontinental railroad is laid in a dramatic demonstration by the Central Pacific railroad. Beginning 14 miles outside Promontory Point, Utah, at 7:00 A.M., a crew of Chinese backed by eight husky rail carriers attempts to lay ten miles of track in a day. Before the sun sets, they have laid ten miles, 56 feet, a total of 3,520 rails. Each rail handler has carried 25,800 ties weighing a quarter of a million pounds.

1878: During the Lincoln County War, the Seven Rivers gang forms under Marion Turner and John Jones to fight John Chisum. On a ride to Lincoln, they kill Frank Macnab, shoot Ab Sanders, and capture Frank Coe.

1880: Apache Chief Victorio lays waste to Cooney, New Mexico.

JIM BECKWOURTH

1881: While Pat Garrett is out of town shopping for gallows wood, Billy the Kid escapes from the Lincoln County Jail, killing Deputy Sheriff J.W. Bell and Bob Olinger in the process.

1896: The sun comes out in Leadville, Colorado a little too early for town planners who built the Ice Palace. The great structure melts during an unseasonably warm spring, and is closed to visitors.

1896: Fire in Cripple Creek, Colorado, the second major one in a week, wipes out much of the boom town.

1897: The Dawes Commission reaches an accord with Chickasaw and Choctaw Nations that will abolish tribal government, and divide lands into 40-acre homesteads. Also in the pact is a provision for no future liquor sales.

1897: Outlaw Will "Black Jack" Christian slain by a posse in Black Jack Canyon, Arizona.

1933: Actress Carolyn Jones born in Amarillo, Texas.

APRIL 29

1863: Publishing tycoon William Randolph Hearst born in San Francisco. On his 50th year in journalism he will own 25 daily newspapers, 17 Sundays, 13 magazines, ten radio stations, and two wire services.

1868: At Fort Laramie, Wyoming, the United States agrees to abandon three forts in the Powder River region and to cease Bozeman Road improvements if Sioux and Cheyenne Indians will live on their Dakota Territory reservation, where they will have full access to their hunting grounds in Montana Territory.

1872: Frank and Jesse James, Cole Younger, and Clell Miller rob the Columbia Kentucky Deposit Bank of $600, killing teller R.A.C. Martin.

1899: Labor war erupts at Coeur d'Alene Mine, as the Bunker Hill & Sullivan concentrator is dynamited by the Western Federation of Miners at Wardner, Idaho. President McKinley is outraged; sends troops to arrest miners and have them jailed in makeshift bull pens.

1907: Lawman David J. Cook dies in his Denver home after an illustrious career described in *Hands Up! or Twenty Years of Detective Life in the Mountains and on the Plains*.

1925: Colorado's Dr. Florence Sabin becomes the first woman elected to the National Academy of Science in New York.

1931: The lark bunting is chosen as Colorado's state bird, despite the school children's vote for the mountain bluebird. Because the lark bunting is black and white, lawmakers maintain it will be less expensive to print on government stationery.

1947: Jim Ryun born in Wichita, Kansas. In 1966 he will set a world record running the mile at 3:51.3, then will break it the following year with 3:51.1. This record will stand until 1975.

1978: Anti-nuclear demonstrations begin at Rocky Flats, a manufacturer of plutonium triggers for H-bombs, located between Denver and Boulder.

APRIL 30

1598: Juan de Onate proclaims Spain's sovereignty over all the "lands, pueblos, cities, villas, of whatsoever nature now founded in the kingdom and province of New Mexico," a stretch of country that reaches from present Texas to California.

1803: Official date of the Louisiana Purchase. France cedes Louisiana to the United States for 80,000,000 francs, or $15,000,000.

1806: Zebulon Pike's northern expedition arrives back in St. Louis. The team erroneously names Leech Lake and Cass Lake the sources of the Mississippi, a fact geographers accept until 1832.

1812: Louisiana enters the Union as the 18th state.

1867: Lawman Burton C. Mossman, future captain of the Arizona Rangers, born near Aurora, Illinois.

1871: Over 100 federally protected Apaches are massacred by a mob at Camp Grant in Arizona Territory. A 15-year on-again off-again war ensues, ending with the surrender of Geronimo.

1885: Philadelphia *Press* reviews Elizabeth Custer's book on the 7th

Cavalry, *Boots and Saddles*.

1904: In St. Louis, the $31.5 million "Louisiana Purchase Exposition" opens. More than 20,000 will attend.

1933: Singer Willie Nelson ("Whiskey River," "Mama Don't Let Your Babies Grow Up to be Cowboys") born in Abbot, Texas.

1935: Film version of Jack London's *Call of the Wild* with Clark Gable and Loretta Young released by United Artists.

1947: Boulder Dam is renamed Hoover Dam.

May

MAY 1

CALAMITY JANE

1718: The mission San Antonio de Valero, the Alamo, founded during the term of Spanish Gov. Martin de Alarcon by Father Antonio Olivares.

1769: Daniel Boone and five companies leave North Carolina to go exploring in Kentucky.

1830: Mary Harris Jones, future labor activist "Mother Jones," born in Cork, Ireland.

1832: A wagon train under the leadership of Capt. Benjamin Louis Eulalie de Bonneville departs Fort Osage on the Missouri for Oregon.

1843: Thomas Larkin appointed first and only U.S. consul to California.

1846: Gen. Taylor calls for 5,000 reinforcements as Mexican troops attack Fort Texas.

1852: Martha Jane Canary, Calamity Jane, born near Princeton, Missouri. During her life she will be a scout, bullwhacker, Wild West show performer, and prostitute. She will also spend most of her life hopelessly in love with Wild Bill Hickok, and possibly bear one of his children.

CALAMITY JANE
Born: May 1, 1852
Died: August 1, 1903
Guide, bullwhacker, prostitute, gambler
1865: Relocates with family to Montana.
1869: Moves to Wyoming, does railroad labor.
1870: Befriends, possibly marries Wild Bill Hickok.
1875: Dressed as a man, she joins a geological expedition into the Black Hills.
1876: Scouts for Gen. George Crook.
1885: Marries Charles Burke
1893: Tours with Buffalo Bull's Wild West Show.
1903: Dies in Terry, near Deadwood, South Dakota.

1860: San Francisco's first school for the deaf founded on Tehama Street.

1878: No one is hurt in the streets of Lincoln, New Mexico as Billy the Kid and a group of Regulators shoot it out with members of the opposition.

1880: First issue of the *Tombstone Epitaph* published.

1880: Adolph Coors buys out his partner, Jacob Scheuler, to go it alone in the brewing industry from his base in Golden, Colorado.

1890: Grand opening of Denver's Elitch Gardens, the largest zoological exposition in the West.

1891: Alaskan Exploratory Expedition under E. Hazard Wells discovers the source of the Yukon River.

1893: President Cleveland presides over opening ceremonies of the World Columbian Exposition at Chicago.

1900: Mine disaster at Scofield, Utah kills 200.

1913: Texas Ranger John Barclay Armstrong dies at age 63 in Armstrong, Texas.

1925: Astronaut Malcolm Scott Carpenter born in Boulder, Colorado. One of the original Project Mercury astronauts, he will orbit the earth three times in his *Aurora 7* capsule in 1962.

1934: Film version of Zane Grey's *The Last Roundup* released by Paramount.

MAY 2

1803: Treaty that solidifies the Louisiana Purchase signed between the United States and France. Final price: $15 million for 828,000 square miles.

1890: Oklahoma Territory created by Congress.

1924: Craters of the Moon National Monument established in Idaho.

1972: Silver mine fire in Kellogg, Idaho kills 91 miners.

MAY 3

1833: Mormons adopt the name "Latter-day Saints."

1851: Fire wipes out 70 percent of San Francisco, killing 30, while doing $3.5 million in damage.

1859: Andy Adams, cowboy and author of 1903's *The Log of a Cowboy* born in Columbia City, Indiana.

1882: Outraged by Wild West lawlessness in Arizona, President Arthur threatens Tombstone with martial law.

1933: Nellie Tayloe Ross named the first woman Director of the U.S. Mint.

1968: A Braniff International Electra crashes during a snowstorm at Dawson, Texas, killing 88.

MAY 4

1850: Fire destroys much of San Francisco.

1851: Future fire fighter Lilly Coit arrives in San Francisco via the Golden Gate.

1922: Austin, Texas struck by two separate tornados in 30 minutes.

1952: *The Outcasts of Poker Flat* with Anne Baxter and Dale Robertson released by 20th Century Fox.

MAY 5

1832: Historian Hubert Howe Bancroft born in Granville, Ohio. He will painstakingly engineer a 39-volume history of the West.

1852: Alonzo Hickok, father of Wild Bill, dies.

1871: With a band of Chiricahua Apaches, Cochise (or possibly his associate, Juh,) surprises the U.S. 3rd Calvary at Bear Springs in Arizona's Whetstone Mountains, killing Lt. Cushing and ten of his 22 men who had been chasing them.

1877: Sitting Bull leads his people into Canada, which he calls Grandmother's Land after Queen Victoria.

1902: Author Bret Harte dies in New York City at age 65 after an illustrious career.

1917: One-day record May snowfall for Denver is recorded -- 12 inches.

MAY 6

1812: A big day at Astoria in Oregon as the ship *Beaver* arrives with supplies.

1859: John Gregory finds gold at what will be called Gregory's Gulch on Clear Creek near the new city of Denver. Horace Greeley, on his western venture, is a witness to the discovery.

1877: Crazy Horse surrenders, leading a procession of warriors, women and children into the White River Valley in Nebraska. Soldiers confiscate 1,700 ponies and 117 rifles from the 800-1,200 people. It is the beginning of the end for the great chief, whom the whites fear will cause a rebellion.

1882: His veto overridden, President Arthur signs the Chinese Exclusion Act into law. It will halt labor immigration from China for ten years.

1911: George Maledon, chief executioner for "Hanging Judge" Isaac Parker, dies in Johnson City, Tennessee. George once said, "I never hanged a man who come back to have the job done again."

1912: First rain in San Bernardino County, California since August 16, 1909.

1921: Mary Partridge, an Indian woman who took her ownership case of a Tulsa residential area to court, wins her settlement. She names over 100 property owners as defendants, and is granted the property in question.

1930: Texas tornadoes kill 82 and cause $2.5 million in damage.

1951: An Air Force B-36 crashes while attempting to land in a sandstorm at Kirkland AFB, New Mexico, killing 23.

1975: Nguyen Cao Ky, former South Vietnamese premier, arrives at a refugee camp at Camp Pendleton, California.

1978: Cheyenne, Wyoming gets 18 inches of snow.

1979: Gas rationing on an odd-even license plate basis begins in California.

MAY 7

1824: The Mexican Federal Republic organizes Texas and Coahuila as one of its states.

1838: Mormon houses burned by a mob in Jackson County, Missouri.

1877: Gen. Nelson Miles and his soldiers attack Lame Deer's Miniconjous near the Tongue River. The chief himself is murdered after he presents a white flag of truce.

1880: Madame Mattie Silks petitions the Denver city council to build a carriage house in the rear of block 12 on Holladay Street, the city's main avenue of prostitution.

1885: Actor George "Gabby" Hayes born in Wellesville, New York. In over 80 films, he will play the perennial comic old-timer.

1901: Actor Gary Cooper born in Montana. He will win his second acting Oscar as the sheriff under pressure in 1952's *High Noon*.

MAY 8

1785: Land Ordinance of 1785 is passed by Congress, providing for six-mile square townships in the Northwest Territories, comprised of present-day Ohio, Indiana, Illinois, Wisconsin, Michigan, and part of Minnesota.

1827: Site chosen for Cantonment Leavenworth in Kansas. Its purpose will be to aid pioneers along the Santa Fe Trail.

1843: Secretary of State Daniel Webster resigns in the wake of the battle over Texas annexation.

1846: Gen. Zachary Taylor defeats the Mexican army at Palo Alto, Texas.

1861: Arkansas legislature votes to secede from the Union.

1871: Wyatt Earp indicted for stealing a horse in Van Buren, Arkansas. He will jump bail and head for Kansas.

1895: Utah attempts statehood for the sixth time with a new constitution that prohibits polygamy.

1911: First long-distance telephone call placed from Denver. Three minutes to New York City costs $11.25.

1937: Amelia Earhart is the first person to fly solo from Mexico City to Newark, New Jersey.

1973: Siege at Wounded Knee, South Dakota ends when Oglala Sioux leaders agree to meet with United States representatives to discuss treaty violations.

1981: Softball-sized hail pounds Dallas causing $200 million in damage.

1987: Colorado presidential hopeful Gary Hart withdraws his candidacy, less than a week after the *Miami Herald* alleges that he spent the night with a woman other than his wife.

MAY 9

1813: Fort Meigs in present Ohio defended by Gen. Harrison against Tecumseh and British troops.

1840: Sam Houston weds Margaret Lea.

1846: Gen. Zachary Taylor with 200 troops meets 6,000 Mexicans at the Battle of Resaca de la Palma; 500 Mexican casualties to nine American.

> **1846: Francis Parkman's party** leaves Westport, Missouri. During a summer of travels, Parkman will record scenes of Indian life and existence among the settlers. He will publish his memoir as *The Oregon Trail*, the most important book on the West for its time. For many, this will be a first glimpse at a wild and wonderful region.

1859: First Leavenworth and Pikes Peak stagecoach arrives in Denver.

1887: Buffalo Bill's Wild West opens at the Earls Court show ground in London, giving the British their first look at cowboys and Indians.

1891: The Dalton Gang holds up the Santa Fe Limited in the Cherokee Strip near Wharton, Oklahoma.

1902: Actor Will Geer ("The Waltons") born in Frankfort, Indiana.

May

1907: Jury selection gets under way for the trial of union leader Big Bill Heywood, charged with the murder of former Idaho Gov. Frank Steunenberg.

1916: Texas, New Mexico, and Arizona militia are ordered to the Mexican border by President Wilson to protect Americans from Mexican rebels.

1945: Sunnyside, Utah mine explodes, killing 23.

1969: Problems arise when students, intent on having a Mother's Day "Zap-Out" in Zap, North Dakota, begin fighting and looting, resulting in $2,000 damage.

1987: William Garlow Cody, 74-year-old grandson of Buffalo Bill, unveils a plaque in London commemorating the 100th anniversary of his famous ancestor's appearance there. Says Cody, "Grandad was really the first ambassador of good will not only to England but to all of Europe."

MAY 10

1800: Harrison Land Act of 1800 is passed, providing liberal credit terms for western land purchases.

1859: The *New York Tribune* announces that its editor's western excursion has begun: "Mr. Greeley left this city by the Erie Railroad last evening, on his way to the Pacific States. We shall probably receive from Kansas the first letters of the series he proposes to write during his journey."

1865: William Clarke Quantrill receives his death wound in a barn in Bloomfield, Kentucky, after being hunted down by soldiers.

1869: The Driving of the Golden Spike ~ At Promontory Point, Utah, the rails of the Union Pacific and the Central Pacific are joined, completing the first transcontinental line. The Central Pacific's Jupiter 90 and the Union Pacific's 119 face each other, as the spike is laid in place by California Gov. Leland Stanford. Stanford misses when he tries to strike the spike. It is eventually driven by Grenville Dodge of the U.P.

1883: Sioux chief Sitting Bull released from prison.

1899: The first automobile in Denver is delivered to David Brunton.

1908: Politician Carl Albert, U.S. Speaker of the House from 1971-76, born in McAlester, Oklahoma.

1909: Singer Maybelle Addington who, as "Mother Maybelle Carter" will be a cornerstone of modern country music, born in Nickelsville, Virginia.

1929: President Hoover designates Colorado's Mount of the Holy Cross as a national monument. It will lose this status on May 5, 1950, after erosion makes the cross nearly unrecognizable.

MAY 11

1846: President Polk charges, "Mexico has invaded our territory and shed American blood upon American soil" in his war message to Congress.

1858: Minnesota enters the Union as the 21st state.

1896: Western historian/writer Mari Sandoz born in the Niobrara River country of Nebraska. Her first, and one of her best books, is a biography of her father, *Old Jules* (1935). Her 1942 biography, *Crazy Horse*, is remarkable in that it is told from an Indian perspective. Her masterpiece will come in 1953, though *Cheyenne Autumn* will initially be rejected by eight publishers.

1905: Snyder, Oklahoma tornado kills 100.

1907: Southern Pacific derailment at Surf, California kills 33.

1933: Dirt from a Montana and Wyoming dust storm blows across the United States, falling in New York City and Boston.

1938: Actor Doug McClure, star of TV's "The Virginian," born in Glendale, California.

1941: Jane Hickok McCormick, 68, announces on a Mother's Day radio broadcast that she is the daughter of Wild Bill Hickok and Calamity Jane. With a stack of letters from her mother, Jane says, "My heart burned to think that my mother lived out her life in loneliness so that her daughter would have a better fate."

1953: Waco, Texas tornado injures 1,097, kills 114, and does $50 million in damage.

1954: Candy tycoon Russell Stover, who introduced the Eskimo Pie in Iowa and his own brand of quality candy in Denver, dies at age 66 in Miami, Florida.

1970: Lubbock, Texas tornado kills 26 and does $135 million in damage.

MAY 12

1794: The Missouri Company forms in St. Louis to explore and trade on the upper Missouri River.

1825: First sighting of the Great Salt Lake in Utah by a white man, mountain man Jim Bridger. Bridger returns to his mountain man buddies, telling them he has been all the way to the Pacific Ocean.

1832: William Sublette leads a pack train out of Independence, Missouri, headed for the rendezvous at Pierre's Hole, Idaho.

1846: Francis Parkman, gathering information for his book, *The Oregon Trail*, visits a Kickapoo village in present Kansas.

1870: Trains collide head-on at Eureka, Missouri, killing 19.

1875: The James and Younger brothers rob a stagecoach of $3,000 near Austin, Texas.

1897: Paiute Indian Ahvote goes berserk and kills six residents of Eldorado, Nevada. Ahvote had tracked his brother in 1890, and killed him for the murder of a U.S. mail carrier. This was a result of an agreement with the United States military forces that kept Paiutes from reprisals as long as they punished Indians that committed crimes against whites. After Ahvote's murderous outburst, he is killed by a member of his tribe, possibly his father, uncle, or brother.

1921: Farley Mowat, author of *Never Cry Wolf*, born.

1947: Trunk murderess Winnie Ruth Judd escapes Arizona State Insane Hospital for the third time, and is captured 12 hours later.

MAY 13

1846: War declared between the United States and Mexico.

1861: Lewiston, Idaho established as a service community for mines.

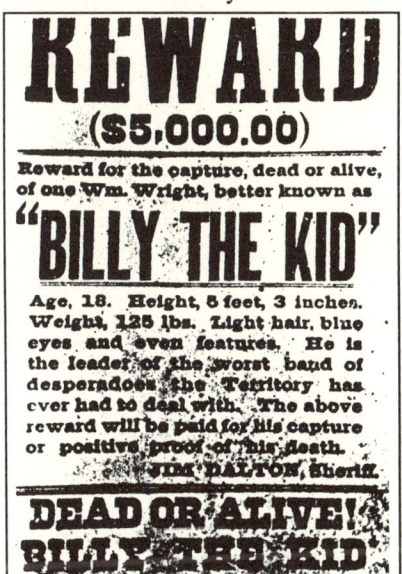

1881: The day Billy the Kid was to have been hanged for the murder of Lincoln County Sheriff William Brady. Judge Warren Bristol's sentence was ignored by the Kid, who had already escaped from jail.

1902: The first pornographic movies in the West are shown in Denver by the Colorado Mutoscope Company, on Mr. Edison's remarkable invention.

1913: Heavyweight champ Jack Johnson is sentenced to a year in prison for violating the Mann Act, legislation prohibiting the transportation of women across state lines for immoral purposes. He will skip bail posing as a Canadian baseball player and sail for Europe.

1916: The first observance of Indian Day, sponsored by the Society of American Indians, is held.

1930: First U.S. death caused by hail occurs in Lubbock, Texas, as a farmer is killed in his field.

1961: Actor Gary Cooper dies of cancer at age 60.

1975: The inventor of western swing, Bob Wills, dies in Texas.

1978: Asa Maxson, 102, of Longmont, Colorado, a veteran of the Spanish American War, becomes the oldest veteran to join the VFW.

MAY 14

1797: Trader Francisco Derouin reports in St. Louis about raging battles between Kansa and Otoe Indians.

> **1804:** The Lewis and Clark Expedition starts up the Missouri River from St. Louis. The exploration of the newly acquired western territories will take two years, four months, and ten days. Early on, Lewis writes: "This scenery, already rich pleasing and beautiful, was still farther hightened by missles herds of Buffaloe, deer Elk and Antelopes which we saw in every direction feeding on the hills and plains."

1836: Texas and Mexican presidents meet at Velasco to sign a peace treaty officially ending the Texas fight for independence.

1852: James King, editor of San Francisco's *Evening Bulletin*, is murdered. A mob seizes his assassin and executes him.

1870: Indians attack Kansas Pacific construction crews near Kit Carson, Colorado, killing 11, wounding 19, and driving off 500 head of livestock.

1878: A group of Regulators, possibly led by Billy the Kid, steals 27 horses from a ranch on the Pecos River outside Lincoln, New Mexico Territory.

1896: Record May low for the continental United States is recorded at Climax, Colorado: -10 degrees.

1901: First water from the Colorado River is brought via a new canal to California's Imperial Valley.

1903: John Muir accompanies Theodore Roosevelt on a trip to the Yosemite. The President returns more determined than ever to protect wilderness lands.

1930: New Mexico's Carlsbad Caverns, the most breathtaking subterranean caverns on the planet, become a national park.

MAY 15

1882: Arizona authorities attempt to extradite Doc Holliday from Denver to question him about his involvement in the Gunfight at the OK Corral. Friend Bat Masterson speaks to Colorado Gov. Pitkin. The request is denied.

1890: Katherine Anne Porter, author of *Ship of Fools*, born at Indian Creek, Texas.

1905: Las Vegas, Nevada founded.

1926: Hopi Indians from Arizona perform religious dances before 5,000 onlookers in Washington D.C., including Vice-President Dawes. The purpose is to show the rites are not cruel, as some have charged.

1918: Crooner Eddy Arnold ("Cattle Call," "Turn the World Around") born in Henderson, Texas.

1925: Famed Indian fighter Gen. Nelson A. Miles dies of a heart attack at a circus in Washington, D.C.

1948: Father Edward J. Flanagan, founder of Nebraska's Boys Town, dies while on a mission for Uncle Sam, offering advice on what to do with war orphans in Berlin.

Stanley Zamonski
MOUNT OF THE HOLY CROSS

1950: Congress abolishes national monument status of Colorado's Mount of the Holy Cross.

1954: *Billboard* magazine reports 30 million country and western records sold in 1953, accounting for 13 percent of all record sales.

1963: Youngest of the original astronauts, Leroy Gordon Cooper of Oklahoma, orbits the earth 22 times in 34 hours in his *Faith* 7 capsule.

MAY 16

1846: Francis Parkman links up with the Oregon Trail and heads west.

1905: Actor Henry Fonda born in Grand Island, Nebraska.

1910: The Bureau of Mines is established within the framework of the

Department of the Interior.

1914: The Horseshoe Pitchers' Association is formed in Kansas City, Missouri.

ANNIE OAKLEY

1946: Rodgers and Hammerstein's *Annie Get Your Gun* opens at the Imperial on Broadway. The musical comedy based on the life of Annie Oakley will feature such hits as "You Can't Get a Man With a Gun" and "There's No Business Like Show Business." Ethel Merman is Annie; it will play 1,147 performances.

MAY 17

1673: Father Jacques Marquette and Louis Joliet set out to explore the North American interior. They journey from Lake Michigan down the Mississippi River to the Arkansas River.

1849: Fire in St. Louis destroys 15 city blocks, 25 steamboats, and does $4 million in damage.

1876: Lt. Col. George Armstrong Custer and 12 companies of 7th Cavalry move out of Fort Abraham Lincoln under Gen. Alfred H. Terry, meeting Indian resistance in the Yellowstone country.

1877: Mr. and Mrs. Tom Thumb perform at Denver's Guard Hall. The most famous midgets in the world are on a successful western tour. In Central City, Colorado schools will empty when General Thumb drives a miniature coach down the main street of town.

1879: Denver customs agents auction tins of opium at $2 a can.

1885: One hundred Apaches led by Geronimo, Mangas, and Nana, escape the San Carlos Reservation in Arizona Territory.

1891: A prospector, poking around Truckee, California, finds cash and other buried items left behind by the ill-fated Donner Party during the winter of 1846-47.

1932: *The Last of the Mohicans* with Harry Carey released by Mascot.

1936: Actor Dennis Hopper is born in Dodge City, Kansas.

1958: *The Left Handed Gun* starring Paul Newman as Billy the Kid released by Warner Brothers.

MAY 18

1846: Zachary Taylor's troops cross the Rio Grande during the Mexican War, occupying Matamoros, Mexico.

1871: Massacre at Salt Creek, Texas. Kiowa Satanta leads a charge, killing seven members of a wagon train.

1904: Western Union ceases all service to pool halls.

1926: Evangelist Aimee Semple McPherson disappears in Los Angeles. Though she will claim that she was kidnapped, she has really escaped

the public eye to be with a lover.

1973: First woman elected to the U.S. House of Representatives, Jeannette Rankin, dies at age 92 in Carmel, California.

1980: Washington's Mount St. Helens erupts, killing 22 and devastating 122 square miles of surrounding lands.

MAY 19

1836: Cynthia Ann Parker kidnapped ~ Comanche, Kiowa, and Caddo Indians attack the residents of Parker's Fort, a civilian stockade 40 miles east of present Waco, Texas. Amidst the rape and slaughter, nine-year-old Cynthia Ann Parker is ripped from her mother's arms. She grows up to be the bride of Peta Nocona and the mother of Quanah Parker, last chief of the Comanches.

1853: The United States begins talks with Mexico to acquire land below New Mexico's southern border for a Texas to California railroad.

1864: Cherry Creek floods Denver, wiping out much of the infant city.

1887: Halley's electric light plant begins operation in Idaho.

1890: Supreme Court sustains Edmunds-Tucker law, another Mormon defeat. The law dictates the church is to be dissolved.

1898: Spanish-American war volunteers from Idaho leave for the Philippines.

1913: The California Land Act goes into effect, preventing Japanese ownership of agricultural land.

1955: Record 24-hour rainfall showers 11.28 inches on Lake Maloya, New Mexico.

MAY 20

1770: Pedro Piernas, first Spanish lieutenant governor of upper Louisiana, arrives at St. Louis to begin his duties.

1818: William G. Fargo, co-founder of the Wells Fargo Co., born in Pompey, New York.

1868: The James-Younger gang robs a bank in Russellville, Kentucky.

1891: Earl R. Browder, U.S. Communist Party head from 1921-1946, born in Wichita, Kansas.

1908: Actor James Stewart, whose Westerns will include *Two Rode Together*, *Bend of the River*, and *Winchester '73*, born in Indiana, Pennsylvania.

1916: Tornado hits Codell, Kansas.

1917: Tornado hits Codell, Kansas.

1918: Tornado hits Codell, Kansas, marking the third consecutive year a tornado has struck the small town on the same date.

1932: On the fifth anniversary of Lindbergh's flight, Amelia Earhart takes off from Newfoundland. When she lands in Ireland, she will have become the first woman to solo the Atlantic.

1954: Thirty thousand people greet Hopalong Cassidy at Denver's Elitch Gardens.

1972: Twenty-one thousand acres of Washington tribal lands returned to the Yakima Indians.

MAY 21

1856: Pro-slavery forces kill one man in Lawrence, Kansas. Abolitionist John Brown retaliates by killing five pro-slavers at the massacre at Potawatomie Creek.

1904: Actor Robert Montgomery born in Beacon, New York.

1906: The United States and Mexico agree to divide equally the waters of the Rio Grande.

1908: Floods evacuate 6,000 from Dallas/Fort Worth; 26 are killed.

1919: Explosion at the Douglas Starch Works in Cedar Rapids, Iowa kills 25, injures 100.

MAY 22

1807: Former Vice-President Aaron Burr goes on trial for treason for his plan to "seize New Orleans...and to separate the Western from the Atlantic states."

1816: Davy Crockett remarries, following the death of his first wife, this time to widow Elizabeth Patton.

1822: Trader William Becknell and a party of 20 depart Franklin, Missouri, for his second trip to Santa Fe.

1843: Western migration begins in force as 1,000 leave St. Louis for Oregon.

1848: Lincoln County War participant James J. Dolan born at Loughrea, County Galway, Ireland. After accompanying the 1878 posse that murders J.H. Tunstall he will be arrested for the murder of Huston Chapman. An acquittal will follow.

1856: James P. Casey and Charles Cora are executed in San Francisco by a vigilance committee in the wake of events surrounding the murder of newspaper editor James King.

1867: The James Gang robs the Hughes and Mason Bank of Richmond, Missouri, killing three including Mayor Shaw. They net $4,000 in gold.

1871: Maj. John Wesley Powell begins the second expedition of the Green and Colorado Rivers.

1876: Denver's Cherry Creek floods.

1878: Denver's Cherry Creek floods.

1902: Crater Lake National Park established in Oregon.

1909: President Taft authorizes 700,000 acres for settlement in Idaho, Montana, and Washington.

1957: A 42,000 pound hydrogen bomb, 600 times more powerful than the atomic bombs used against Japan, accidentally falls 1,700 feet from an Air Force B-36 bomber, just south of Albuquerque, New Mexico. The bomb does not explode. The story is suppressed for 29 years until 1986.

1962: A Boeing 707 explodes over Centerville, Iowa, killing 45.

MAY 23

1838: Early traveller Samuel Parker returns home to Ithaca, New York after two years of exploring in the

West and Hawaii.

1868: Kit Carson dies at age 58 in Fort Lyon, Colorado.

1872: Cole and Bob Younger, Jesse James, and Bill Stiles rob the Savings Association Bank of Ste. Genevieve, Missouri of $4,000.

1873: First post cards sold in San Francisco.

1883: Actor Douglas Fairbanks, Sr. born in Denver.

1908: A 450-foot dirigible explodes over San Francisco Bay. Sixteen fall into the water, but are not killed.

KIT CARSON

1923: Crow scout Curley, who worked for Custer's 7th Cavalry and survived the Little Bighorn battle by allegedly disguising himself as a Sioux, dies and is buried at the National Cemetery of the Custer Battlefield in Montana.

1934: Bonnie Parker and Clyde Barrow are killed in a Louisiana ambush.

1950: *Annie Get Your Gun* with Betty Hutton is released by MGM.

1958: Mass murderer Charlie Stark-weather convicted in Nebraska.

MAY 24

1856: John Brown leads the Potawatomie Massacre, the murder-mutilation of five pro-slavery Kansans in return for the March 21 slaying of a Lawrence abolitionist.

1869: Maj. John Wesley Powell and a crew of nine embark on an historic expedition down the Green and Colorado Rivers. They depart from Green River Station, Wyoming on the 100-day, 1000-mile voyage, the first white men to travel down the Colorado.

1883: Apache warrior Chato returns to the San Carlos Reservation after nearly two years of raiding white settlements.

1911: Colorado National Monument established near Grand Junction, Colorado.

1913: The pier collapses at Long Beach, California, killing 35.

1968: Last U.S. Army Cavalry horse, Chief, dies.

MAY 25

1850: New Mexico adopts a new constitution prohibiting slavery.

1892: The Mississippi River floods, killing 250 in St. Louis.

1917: Fastest tornado on record, 65 MPH, hits southeastern Kansas.

1934: The *Pioneer Zephyr*, a stainless-steel train built for comfort and speed, races the sun beginning at 5:30 A.M. in Denver. It will zoom to the Chicago World's Fair in just over 13 hours.

1948: San Francisco's first television broadcast.

1975: The grizzly bear is classified as "threatened."

MAY 26

1804: Congress divides Louisiana at the 33rd parallel. Territory of Orleans lies south and District of Louisiana north of that line. The parallel today marks the northern border of the state of Louisiana.

1805: With the Lewis and Clark Expedition, Meriwether Lewis spots the Rocky Mountains for the first time, from a hill near present-day Cow Creek, Montana.

1853: Outlaw John Wesley Hardin born in Bonham, Texas. Perhaps the greatest killer of the Old West, Hardin will slay 20 men between his 15th and 25th birthdays.

1863: Gold is discovered in Idaho Territory (present-day Montana) near what will become Alder Gulch. The lucky party is led by Bill Fairweather. Within the first year, some 10,000 prospectors will take $10 million in gold dust. Virginia City will be incorporated here in January, 1864.

1864: Montana becomes a United States territory. The first capital is Bannack, the governor, Sidney Edgerton.

1892: The Idaho Populist Party is organized in Boise by members of the Farmers Alliance and the Knights of Labor.

1900: Wild Bunch triggerman Harvey Logan kills two members of a posse when they come after him near Thompson, Utah. His victims are Moab County Sheriff Jesse Tyler and Sam Jenkins.

1907: Actor John Wayne born Marion Morrison in Winterset, Iowa. The king of the modern Westerns, his long line of hits will include *Red River*, *The Alamo*, and *True Grit* for which he will win a Best Actor Oscar.

JOHN WESLEY HARDIN
Born: May 26, 1853
Died: August 19, 1895
Outlaw

1868: Kills his first man, a black, for "shaking a stick" at him. Becomes a fugitive.
1869: Kills James Bradley after a poker game in Towash, Texas.
1871: Leaves Abilene after murdering a Mexican; travels to Gonzales County, Texas where he kills a posse of five black police.
1872: Is shot after a bowling argument. Shoots a police officer dead who comes to his room while he is recuperating.
1874: Kills a deputy sheriff of Comanche, Texas while celebrating 21st birthday.
1875: Runs a saloon in Gainesville, Florida. Works in southern cattle trade.
1877: Arrested in Florida by Ranger John Armstrong. Sentenced to 25 years in Huntsville state prison.
1894: Released from prison.
1894: Studies law, sets up practice in Gonzales.
1895: Shot to death in the Acme Saloon in El Paso, Texas by John Selman.

1919: Actor Jay Silverheels, best known for his role as "Tonto" on "The Lone Ranger" TV series, born in Canada.

1923: Actor James Arness, TV's Marshal Matt Dillon on "Gunsmoke", born in Minneapolis, Minnesota.

1928: Andrew Payne, a Cherokee from Oklahoma, wins the first cross-country foot race from Los Angeles to New York, crossing the finish line at Madison Square Garden. His time for the 3,422 miles is 573 hours, begun on March 4.

WILD BILL HICKOK
Born: May 27, 1837
Died: August, 1876
Gunfighter, lawman, gambler

1855: Moves to Kansas; employed as constable and stagecoach driver.
1861: Shoot out with the McCanles Gang at Rock Creek Station, Nebraska.
1862: Scouts at The Battle of Pea Ridge in Arkansas during the Civil War.
1865: Participates in the first Western duel, killing Dave Tutt.
1866: Appointed deputy U.S. Marshal.
1867: First dime novel appearance: "Wild Bill the Indian Slayer".
1867: Loses Ellsworth County, Kansas sheriff election.
1868: Oversees a prisoner move with Buffalo Bill in Kansas.
1869: Elected sheriff of Ellis County, Kansas.
1869: Kills Samuel Strawhun in a saloon brawl in Hays City.
1869: Kills John Mulrey in Hays City for resisting arrest.
1870: Becomes marshal of Abilene, Kansas.
1870: During a barroom brawl with 7th Cavalry members in Hays City, Kansas, kills Pvt. John Kile. Leaves town.
1870: Romantically involved with Calamity Jane.
1871: Appointed marshal of Abilene, Kansas.
1871: Accidentally kills friend Mike Williams during a disturbance.
1871: Dismissed as sheriff of Abilene.
1872: Rides in the Grand Buffalo Hunt at Niagara Falls.
1873: Appears with Buffalo Bill Cody on stage in *The Scouts of the Plains*; relocates to Deadwood.
1876: Murdered in Deadwood.

1930: Sunset Crater National Monument is established in Arizona.

1933: Singer Jimmie Rodgers dies of tuberculosis at age 35, two days after recording twelve songs in eight days at New York's Victor Studios, including "Fifteen Years Ago Today."

1949: Singer Hank Williams, Jr. born in Shreveport, Louisiana. The son of the country music legend will carve his own niche in the 1970s.

1956: John Ford's *The Searchers* with John Wayne and Jeffrey Hunter released by Warner Brothers It is considered by some to be Ford's masterpiece and John Wayne's finest role.

MAY 27

1831: Mountain man Jedediah Strong Smith, first man to lead a party overland to California, is slain by Comanches while journeying on the Santa Fe Trail.

1837: James Butler Hickok, later known as Wild Bill, born in Homer, Illinois. He is the fourth son of William Alonzo and Polly Butler Hickok.

1856: While attending Hopedale Normal School in Ohio, George Armstrong Custer writes to Rep. John A. Bingham, inquiring about the qualifications required to enter West Point.

1862: The Homestead Act becomes law today. For a ten-dollar filing fee and a promise to live on the site for five years, a settler may claim up to 160 acres of free public land.

1887: Jim Thorpe, Olympic and professional athlete, born near Shawnee, Oklahoma. A Sauk and Fox, his Indian name is Wa-Tho-Huck, which means Bright Path.

1896: St. Louis tornado kills 306,

leaving 5,000 homeless, and doing $13 million in damage.

1957: "That'll Be the Day," recorded in Clovis, New Mexico, released by the Crickets with Buddy Holly.

1975: Alaska Supreme Court legalizes the use of marijuana in the home.

MAY 28

1830: President Jackson signs the Indian Removal Act, authorizing the great movement of the eastern Indian tribes to the West.

1845: American troops ordered to the Mexican border by President Polk to protect settlers in Texas from a Mexican invasion.

1848: Francis X. Aubry rides into Independence, Missouri, breaking his own January 5 record for the 780-mile Santa Fe Trail ride by five and a half days. He completes the distance in eight days, ten hours.

1892: The Sierra Club founded by John Muir. Its purpose will be to preserve forests from lumber concerns, but it will eventually deal with many other environmental projects.

1902: The first serious Western, *The Virginian: A Horseman of the Plains* by Owen Wister, is published by Macmillan. Set on the Wyoming frontier between the years of 1874 and 1890, it is a collection of previously published as well as new stories on the exploits of the Virginian and his courtship of schoolmarm Molly Stark Wood. The book is dedicated to President Theodore Roosevelt.

1948: The Columbia River floods, killing 26 in Vanport City, Oregon.

1955: *Billboard* magazine reports that "The Ballad of Davy Crockett" is the most popular tune in the country. All the available versions have sold 18 million copies in the past six months.

1971: War hero/actor Audie Murphy dies in a plane crash in Virginia.

MAY 29

1843: John C. Fremont's second expedition into the West begins. Guide Kit Carson will take the party through the Snake River Valley in today's Idaho, and on to California's San Joaquin Valley.

1892: Western writer Frederick Faust, who will become famous as Max Brand, born in Seattle, Washington.

1962: Astronaut M. Scott Carpenter is greeted by his hometown of Boulder, Colorado.

1973: Thomas Bradley is elected the first black mayor of Los Angeles.

MAY 30

1854: Kansas and Nebraska become United States territories.

1893: Bill Doolin's gang escapes a posse led by Chris Madsen as they try to cross the Cimarron River into Oklahoma. Madsen is on their tail for a train robbery committed three days earlier. The boys get away, but Doolin's foot is torn up by a steel-jacketed rifle bullet.

1899: Amateur robbers Pearl Hart and her boyfriend Joe Boot hold up the Benson-Globe stage in Arizona. Pearl dresses like a man; they get away with $400. Ultimately nabbed by authorities, Joe gets 35 years in the Yuma slammer, but Pearl wins parole after two years. This launches a career in show business, and for a while she is on the lecture circuit billing herself as "The Arizona Bandit."

1908: Lakeside Amusement Park, also known as "White City" opens in Denver.

1910: Rainbow Bridge National Monument is established in Utah.

1914: Lassen Peak, a California volcano believed dormant, begins to erupt.

1927: Actor Clint Walker, TV's "Cheyenne", born in Hartford, Illinois.

1935: Republican River Valley floods; 21,000 cattle drown in Nebraska and Colorado; 110 people lose their lives.

1943: Football star Gale Sayers born in Wichita, Kansas.

MAY 31

1847: Col. Richard B. Mason becomes the new governor of California as Kearny, Fremont, and Stockton return to Washington.

1921: President Harding approves transfer of the Teapot Dome oil reserves in Wyoming and the ones at Elk Hills, California from the Navy Department to the Interior, then guided by Albert Bacon Fall.

1923: Pipe Spring National Monument created in Arizona.

1926: A Ku Klux Klan parade through the streets of downtown Denver marks its point of strongest influence in the West.

1930: Actor Clint Eastwood, who will star in such Westerns as *The Good, the Bad, and the Ugly* and *Hang 'Em High*, and direct some of his own films, before becoming the mayor of Carmel, California, born in San Francisco.

June

JUNE 1

1801: Brigham Young born in Whitingham, Vermont. As the inheritor of the Church of the Latter-day Saints from founder Joseph Smith, Young will manage a remarkable exodus, moving his Mormon followers from persecution in Illinois to religious freedom in the Wild West.

BRIGHAM YOUNG
Born: June 1, 1801
Died: August 23, 1877
Mormon leader

1824: Marries his first wife, Miriam Works, moves to New York.
1832: Baptized in Mormon church.
1833: Leads group of Mormons to Ohio.
1835: Designated an apostle. Travels in U.S. and England as a missionary.
1838: Helps move his people to Missouri, then to Nauvoo, Illinois.
1841: Becomes president of the Quorum of the Twelve Apostles.
1844: Takes over as head of church following murder of Joseph Smith.
1846: Mormon exodus begins from Nauvoo.
1847: Exodus continues from Council Bluffs, Iowa. Mormons reach Utah that July.
1850: Named governor as territorial government established in Utah, formerly Deseret.
1855: Has idea for followers to come to Utah using handcarts instead of covered wagons.
1857: Obtains a contract from the United States to haul mail and freight.
1857: Troops occupy Mormon empire. Salt Lake City evacuated.
1857: Replaced by Alfred Cummings as Utah territorial governor, per order of President Buchanan.
1861: Participates in construction of transcontinental telegraph line.
1865: Sealed to his 50th bride.
1868: Aids construction of transcontinental railroad.
1871: Tried for bigamy; not convicted.
1877: Dies of peritonitis at age 76. At time of death, his Mormon stronghold numbered 140,000.

1829: Geronimo born near the headwaters of the Gila River in Arizona. The exact date cannot be verified, only the month.
1850: The *San Francisco Daily Herald* publishes its first issue.
1867: Cullen Baker kills a Cass County, Texas shop owner when the latter complains of Baker's bills.
1871: Texas outlaw John Wesley

Hardin and his trail crew arrive in Abilene, Kansas. Lawman Ben Thompson tries to convince him to gun down town marshal Wild Bill Hickok, a task which Hardin declines.

1876: Custer's 7th Cavalry is stalled in its march from Fort Abraham Lincoln against the Sioux by a freak June snow that will leave 2 inches and force a two-day halt.

1881: Denver's Union Station opens. Built at a cost of $525,000, the city's first union station is connected by tunnel with both the Windsor Hotel and the Denver Omnibus and Cab Company.

1905: Lewis and Clark Centennial Exposition opens in Portland, Oregon.

1915: Singer Johnny Bond ("Smoke Smoke Smoke," "Hot Rod Lincoln") born in Enville, Oklahoma.

1921: Tulsa, Oklahoma race riots claim the lives of nine whites and 21 blacks. Problems started the evening before, when a black man was arrested for attacking a white girl.

1924: The Border Patrol is established as a branch of the Immigration and Naturalization Service.

1939: Actor Cleavon Little, star of *Blazing Saddles*, Hollywood's top-grossing Western, born in Chickasha, Oklahoma.

1954: Security clearance of J. Robert Oppenheimer is withdrawn by the Atomic Energy Commission, when it is rumored the atomic bomb creator may have pro-Communist ties.

1958: *From Hell to Texas* released by 20th Century Fox.

JUNE 2

1739: Brothers Paul and Pierre Mallet come to the Platte River and name it the Plate River.

1823: Two keelboats of trappers led by William H. Ashley are attacked before dawn by Arikara Indians. Many are killed. The trapping enterprise suffers a serious setback.

1873: Ground is broken on Clay Street in San Francisco for the world's first cable street railroad.

1875: Quanah Parker and his band of Comanches surrender, the last of this tribe to do so.

1892: The Dalton Gang steals $2,000 from the Santa Fe Express at Red Rock, Arizona.

1895: Kid Curry and Flat Nose George Curry lead a gang in robbing the Union Pacific's Overland Flyer at Wilcox, Wyoming.

1899: The Wild Bunch robs a train near Wilcox, Wyoming, dynamiting the forward section. When employee C.E. Woodcock refuses to open the baggage door, Butch Cassidy orders it blown off with one stick. Alas, that is a little too much, and $30,000 in cash and a shipment of raspberry jam are blown sky high. The Bunch picks up as much money as they can before making their escape.

1924: The Snyder Act grants citizenship to all Native Americans born within the territorial limits of the United States.

1931: Amelia Earhart pilots an autogiro from Cheyenne to Denver.

JUNE 3

1846: Col. Stephen W. Kearny ordered to occupy California with naval backup from Commodore John D. Sloat.

1865: Speaker of the House Schuyler Colfax, on a mission to carry out

Lincoln's last wish, to deliver a message to the miners in Nevada, departs Denver. A major thoroughfare is named in his honor.

JESSE JAMES

1871: Frank and Jesse James, Jim, John, and Cole Younger, and three others rob the Ocobock Brothers Bank in Corydon, Iowa of $45,000. Before he rides out of town, Jesse addresses a political rally.

1873: Prostitute Emma Stanley is wounded in the thigh during an argument with cavalrymen in Delano, Kansas. Dance hall owner Red Beard opens fire, wounding two.

1907: Following Clarence Darrow's dismissal of every businessman or banker, a jury is finally impaneled for the trial of Big Bill Heywood.

1913: Last horse-drawn streetcar runs in San Francisco.

1921: Three days of flooding begin in Pueblo, Colorado as the Arkansas River crests. More than 120 are killed and a thousand homes destroyed. Loss estimates reach $25 million.

1936: Larry McMurtry, author of *Lonesome Dove* and *The Last Picture Show* born in Wichita Falls, Texas.

1959: Hail falls for nearly an hour and a half in Seldon, Kansas, reaching a depth of 18 inches.

JUNE 4

1782: Indians and Loyalists work together to kill Col. William Crawford, who gave the order for the massacre at Gnadenhutten, Ohio on March 7 of that year.

1812: The Territory of Louisiana becomes the Territory of Missouri.

1860: The "Comanche Tornado" (weather, not Indians) devastates parts of Iowa.

1863: One is killed and five are wounded during a fight between a group of Italians and workers at the Farallone Egg Company in San Francisco.

1870: Wild Bill Hickok takes the oath of office as marshal of Abilene, Kansas.

1876: The Transcontinental Express arrives in San Francisco after speeding from New York in just over 83 hours.

1923: The Supreme Court tosses out laws in Iowa, Nebraska, and 19 other states that make the teaching of foreign languages in school illegal.

1924: Actor Dennis Weaver, Chester on "Gunsmoke," born in Joplin, Missouri.

1968: Sen. Robert F. Kennedy, winner of the Presidential primary in California and South Dakota, is fatally wounded after addressing a throng at the Ambassador Hotel in Los Angeles.

JUNE 5

1813: St. Louis *Missouri Gazette* reports on mountain man Manuel Lisa's successful trading mission with the Mandans.

1849: Eleazar Adams, father of Grizzly Adams, commits suicide.

1850: Pat Garrett born in Chambers County, Alabama. He will grow up to become one of the more notable sheriffs of the Old West, and become internationally famous as the killer of Billy the Kid.

1859: Herman Lehman, son of German settlers, born in Loyal Valley, Texas. During his life, he will be captured by Apaches, then live with Comanches.

1862: George Armstrong Custer becomes a Union captain during the Civil War.

1873: Upset soldiers in Delano, Kansas burn Red Beard's dance hall to the ground in revenge for his shooting two of their men. Prostitute Emma Stanley is shot for the second time in as many nights.

1875: The Pacific Stock Exchange opens in San Francisco.

1878: Doroteo Arango, the future Francisco "Pancho" Villa, born in San Juan del Rio, Mexico. As a military guerilla leader, he will kill 16 Americans during a raid on Columbus, New Mexico in 1916.

1898: William Boyd, movie and TV's "Hopalong Cassidy," born in Cambridge, Ohio. Riding a horse named Topper, he will star in 118 films.

1899: Following a Wilcox Siding train robbery, the Sundance Kid, Kid Curry, and Flat Nose George Curry shoot it out with a posse. Kid Curry kills Sheriff Joe Hazen.

1922: George W. Carmack, first to discover gold in Alaska, dies in Vancouver.

1929: Colorado brewer Adolph Coors, 82, is killed in a fall from a hotel window in Virginia Beach, Virginia.

1943: Zoot Suit riots rock Los Angeles.

1976: Idaho's Teton River Dam breaks; 40,000 are evacuated, 4,000 homes are lost, and nine are killed.

JUNE 6

1819: Secretary of War John Calhoun sends Maj. Stephen Long from Pittsburgh to find the source of the Red River. This is the first government-funded western expedition since Zebulon Pike's in 1806.

1842: German topographer Charles Preuss, traveling with the Fremont expedition, writes in his journal, "Annoyed by that childish Fremont."

1859: Horace Greeley arrives in one-year-old Denver and observes that the inhabitants are "prone to deep drinking, soured in temper, always armed, bristling at a word, ready with the rifle, revolver, or bowie knife."

1865: Civil War guerila leader William Clarke Quantrill, 27, dies after being shot by Union forces in Louisville, Kentucky.

1894: Cherokee Bill kills Deputy Sequoyah Houston near Tahlequah, Oklahoma.

1924: Cowgirl yodeler Rosalie Allen, "The Prairie Star," born in Old Forge, Pennsylvania.

1938: First degree in dude ranching awarded to Donald Ellsworth Smith at the University of Wyoming. Offered by the School of Agriculture, it was an optional program officially titled "Recreational Ranching."

1976: Texas oil billionaire J. Paul Getty, 83, dies at Surrey, England.

JUNE 7

1769: Daniel Boone first spots Kentucky from the Cumberland Gap.

1866: Seattle, the Indian chief for whom the city in Washington was named when white settlers arrived in 1852, dies on this date.

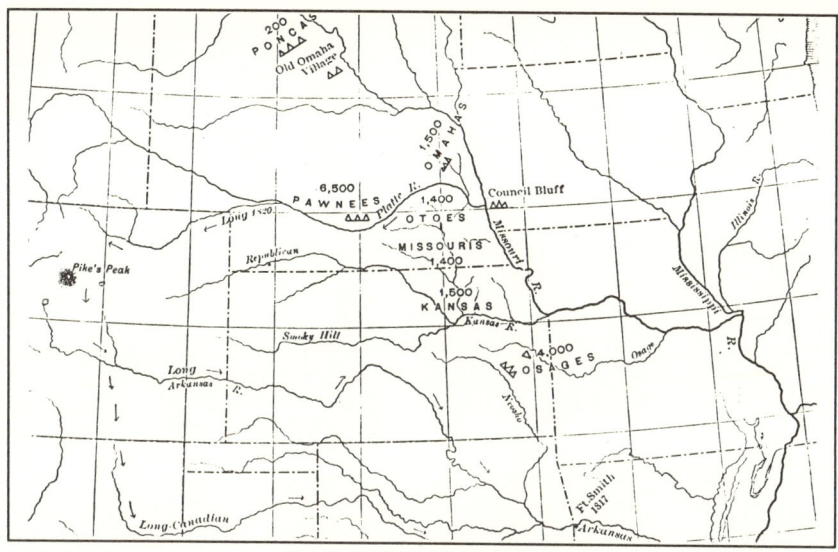
MAP OF LONG'S ROUTE

1888: Sheriff John Slaughter and deputy Burt Alvord are involved in a shootout with bandits in Cochise County, Arizona. Slaughter kills Guadalupe Robles and wounds another.

JUNE 8

1874: Chiricahua Apache leader Cochise dies in his Dragoon mountain stronghold in southeastern Arizona. He had carried out a ten-year war with the U.S. until he made peace, assisted by his trusted friend Thomas J. Jeffers, with Gen. O.O. Howard in 1872.

1892: Bob Ford, murderer of Jesse James, is slain by glory seeker Edward O'Kelly in Creede, Colorado. He is done in by a double-barreled shotgun blast to the throat. O'Kelly basks in his fame as the man who shot the man who shot Jesse James, until he himself is later slain by police in Oklahoma City.

1904: Six striking union members are slain by Colorado Militia at Dunnville.

1908: The National Conservation Commission is created to monitor land use and natural resources.

1917: Future football great and Justice of the Supreme Court Byron Raymond "Whizzer" White born in Fort Collins, Colorado.

COCHISE
Born: 1815?
Died: June 8, 1874
Chief (Chiricahua Apache)

1860: Wrongly accused of kidnapping Micke Free. Begins eleven year war with the whites. During the conflict, makes friends with Tom Jeffords.
1871: Makes peace.
1874: Dies of natural causes at 63 on Chiricahua Reservation in New Mexico.

1917: A fire at Butte, Montana's Speculator Mine kills 162 miners. They die because metal bulkheads that could be opened had not been installed, although required by law. A labor strike ensues; 15,000 walk off the job.

1923: Bryce Canyon National Park is established in Utah. It encompasses 36,010 acres of unusual erosional effects.

JUNE 9

1856: Four hundred ninety-seven Mormons pushing a hundred handcarts depart Iowa City for Salt Lake City.

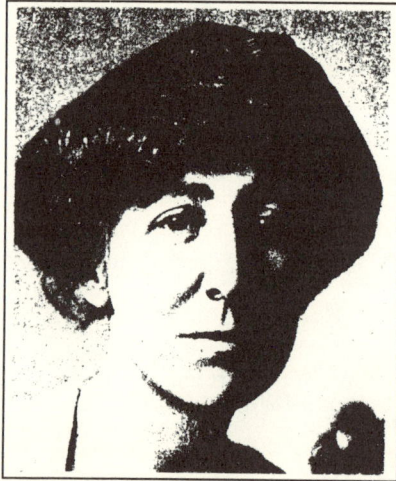
JEANETTE RANKIN

1860: The first dime novel is *Malaeska, the Indian Wife of the White Hunter*, by Ann Sophia Stevens, published today by Irwin P. Beadle.

1911: Bar smasher Carry Nation, 64, dies in Leavenworth, Kansas just before her dream of national prohibition comes true.

1972: Heavy rains and floods kill 242 in Rapid City, South Dakota and do $163 million in damage.

JUNE 10

1821: Texas colonizer Moses Austin dies.

1833: Beauty Pauline Cushman is born in New Orleans. During her life she will appear on stage, become a Union spy during the Civil War, and horsewhip those who question her virtue out West. In Arizona, she will referee gunfights.

1857: Brigham Young obtains a contract from the United States for his XY Company to haul mail and freight.

1859: The Comstock Lode becomes the biggest mining discovery in American history. In Six Mile Canyon in Nevada's Washoe Mountains, Patrick McLaughlin and Peter O'Riley make a discovery that will produce $300 million in silver and gold over the next two decades. Henry Comstock insists that he get some of the credit, since they are using his water. Ironically, Comstock, McLaughlin, and O'Riley will all die broke.

1946: Former heavyweight champ Jack Johnson killed when he loses control of a Lincoln Zephyr in North Carolina.

1958: An El Dorado, Kansas woman is sucked out a window of her home by a tornado.

1962: Rodeo champ Oral Zumwalt killed while flanking a bucking horse at Montana's Big Timber Rodeo.

JUNE 11

1845: Gen. Zachary Taylor moves his troops to the disputed border of Mexico and Texas.

1865: On orders from Maj. Gen. G.M. Dodge, 2,000 Sioux Indians living under United States protection near Fort Laramie are forcibly moved to Fort Kearney, Nebraska. Atrocities along the way include the whipping of youngsters and the raping of maidens.

1880: First woman U.S. Representative, Jeanette Rankin, born near Missoula, Montana. She will serve in the House from 1917-19, and again from 1941-43, and go down in history as the only member to vote against the declaration of war against Japan.

1971: Federal marshals recapture Alcatraz Island from Indians after 19 months of occupation.

1972: 1.64 inches of rain fall on Phoenix, Arizona, more than had ever fallen in June on that city.

1978: Two days after the Church of the Latter-day Saints throws out its 148-year-old edict excluding blacks from the priesthood, Joseph Freeman, Jr. becomes the first black Mormon priest.

1979: Actor John Wayne, 72, dies in Los Angeles.

JUNE 12

1838: Iowa created as a U.S. territory, from the western part of Wisconsin Territory.

1858: Gold seekers from Georgia, accompanied by Cherokee Indians, arrive at Bent's Fort on the Santa Fe Trail in present-day Colorado. They will soon move on to the Cherry Creek diggings, near present Denver.

1867: Old Man Afraid, representing 200 Oglala Sioux lodges, meets with whites at Fort Laramie to discuss peace. When accused of wanting ammunition to wage war, he storms out, breaking off the negotiations.

1983: Heavy flooding in Utah. Downtown Salt Lake City is sandbagged. A mud slide causes a natural dam, completely wiping out the town of Thistle on the Denver and Rio Grande railroad route.

JUNE 13

1805: The Lewis and Clark expedition reaches Great Falls on the Missouri River.

1865: Crazy Horse sneaks into the Sioux camp that is being relocated to Fort Kearney, Nebraska. With other leaders, he plots an escape.

1875: Miriam Amanda Wallace, first female governor of Texas, born in Bell County.

1878: Texas Rangers shoot it out with the Sam Bass Gang at their Salt Creek camp in Wise County, Texas. Outlaw Arkansas Johnson is killed before the others escape.

1893: A horse race begins at Chicago's World Columbian Exposition. Nine men will ride for two weeks to see who can be first to reach Buffalo Bill's Wild West show at Chadron, Nebraska. John Berry will be the winner.

1911: Physicist Luis Alvarez born in San Francisco, California. His contributions will include the discovery of resonance particles, as well as a method for X-raying the great pyramids of Egypt. Nobel Prize winner, 1968.

1918: Actor Ben Johnson born in Oklahoma. He will be in a number of Westerns, and win an Oscar for *The Last Picture Show*.

1966: Supreme Court defines police interrogation practices in *Miranda vs. Arizona*.

1979: Sioux Indians awarded $105 million for South Dakota's Black Hills, confiscated by the United States in 1877.

JUNE 14

1740: The Mallet brothers, exploring in New Mexico, abandon their horses and build a canoe to travel on a river that will be named Canadian in honor of their heritage.

> **1846: California's Bear Flag Revolt** ~ William B. Ide and homesteaders take over Sonoma and declare California independent. With aid from Capt. John C. Fremont, they raise a bear flag.

1850: Fire destroys part of San Francisco.

1865: Crazy Horse leads an escape of Sioux, Loafers, and Brules from U.S. cavalry.

1877: Shootout in the streets of Lampasas, Texas. Friends and brothers of Clint Barkley run into rival ranchers. One dies.

1913: Rodeo champ Clyde Burk born in Comanche, Oklahoma.

1917: Actor Lash La Rue born. He will be the man in black with the bullwhip in a series of 1940s cliffhangers.

1918: Former Billy the Kid gang member D.L. Anderson, *aka* Billy Wilson, now sheriff of Terrell County, Texas, is shot dead by a drunk named Ed Valentine. Valentine is lynched an hour after Anderson dies.

1919: Actor Gene Barry, TV's "Bat Masterson," born in New York City.

1961: Singer Patsy Cline seriously injured in a Madison, Tennessee car crash.

1984: Grapefruit-sized hail leaves six-foot ice mountains in some parts of Denver. Snow plows are used for removal.

JUNE 15

1806: Lewis and Clark begin their ascent of the western slope of the Rocky Mountains on their return trip from the Pacific.

1836: Arkansas, a slave state, enters the Union as the 25th state.

1843: Texas and Mexico declare a truce. Hostilities between the two had been going on since September 1842, when Mexican recaptured San Antonio.

1845: Texas is guaranteed federal protection from Mexico if it will agree to the annexation treaty.

1846: Francis Parkman's party reaches Fort Laramie in present Wyoming. Soon the young Harvard man will be among the Sioux Indians, gathering material for *The Oregon Trail*.

1934: *Randy Rides Alone* with John Wayne released by Lone Star/Monograph.

1937: Singer Waylon Jennings born in Littlefield, Texas.

1941: Red Rocks, a natural outdoor theatre in the foothills west of Denver, opens with Metropolitan Opera soprano Helen Jepson.

1952: Dwight D. Eisenhower opens his Presidential campaign headquarters at Denver's Brown Palace.

1958: *The Lone Ranger and the Lost City of Gold* released by United Artists.

JUNE 16

1873: President Ulysses S. Grant signs an order to remove all whites from Washington's Wallowa Valley, home of the Nez Perce. Two years later, that order will be rescinded.

1906: The Enabling Act, signed today by President Theodore Roosevelt, will combine Indian Territory and Oklahoma Territory into a single state.

1933: FBI agents capture Frank Nash at Hot Springs, Arkansas, an event that will lead directly to the Kansas City Massacre.

1965: Colorado's Platte River floods, causing $500 million in damage throughout the state.

1975: Oregon is the first state to prohibit aerosols with chlorofluorocarbon propellants.

JUNE 17

1579: Francis Drake sails into a northern California bay on his ship *Golden Hind* and names it "Nova Albion" for Queen Elizabeth.

> **1876:** In the Battle on the Rosebud, the dress rehearsal for the Little Bighorn, Gen. Crook and 1,000 troopers are attacked by columns of mounted Sioux and Cheyenne forces. Estimated at 1,500, the Indians are directed by field marshal Crazy Horse. They manage to divide the command, leaving Crook with 57 dead and wounded.

1882: A tornado devastates 200 miles of Iowa, killing 130.

1931: First contracts are awarded for the construction of the Golden Gate Bridge.

1933: The Kansas City or Union Station Massacre ~ Gangsters open fire on law officers in an attempt to spring Frank Nash from custody. Officers Raymond J. Caffrey, Frank Hermanson, Otto Reed, and W.J. Grooms are all killed, as is Nash. The FBI believes the crime to be the work of Pretty Boy Floyd, though it is never proven. Floyd will deny the crime with his dying breath.

RED ROCKS AMPHITHEATER

RED ROCKS PARK — Fred Thumhart III

JUNE 18

1859: A group of settlers from Boston organizes the Colorado settlement of Golden City, claiming 1,280 acres.

1880: John Sutter, on whose property the first California gold was discovered, dies penniless in Pennsylvania.

1970: A $5 million hailstorm pounds Oberlin, Kansas.

1973: Last official veteran of the Indian wars, Fredrak Fraske, dies at age 101. A member of the 17th Infantry designed to quell an Idaho uprising in 1894, he saw no action. Recalled Fraske, "The chief explained to his Indians that they couldn't do much against 400 soldiers, so they drifted quietly back to the reservation at Pocatello."

JUNE 19

1845: Brigham Heber Young, often referred to as "the first child of Mormon polygamy," is born to Brigham Young and Lucy Decker.

1865: Juneteenth ~ Today is Emancipation Day in Texas. Gen. Robert S. Granger, commander of the Texas militia, issues a proclamation that notifies blacks that they are free under the Emancipation Proclamation, which officially took effect six months before, on January 1.

1902: Annie Rogers is acquitted of being Kid Curry's accomplice.

1921: Heaviest one-day rainfall in Montana at Circle -- 11.5 inches.

1939: Public administrator, former director of the United States Children's Bureau, Grace Abbot dies at age 60.

Boy Meets Teacher

1947: Denver educator Emily Griffith, who founded a unique Opportunity School, and her sister are found shot to death in their retirement cabin near Pinecliffe, Colorado.

1970: U.S. Air Force announces MIRV's (missiles capable of delivering independently targetable reentry vehicles) are deployed in Minot, North Dakota.

JUNE 20

1882: The date on the marriage certificate of Annie Oakley and Frank Butler, though the two were really married in 1876. Historians believe that Frank's divorce might not have been final for the '76 vows, and that they were reaffirmed in '82.

1899: Texas Brazos River runs over its banks after four days of rain. Flooding eventually will kill 284.

1910: Arizona Territory and New Mexico Territory are authorized by Congress to form state governments and to apply for admission to the U.S.

1921: Alice Robertson of Oklahoma is the first woman to preside over a session of the United States House of Representatives.

1924: War hero/actor Audie Murphy born in Kingston, Texas.

1924: Guitarist Chet Atkins born on a farm in Knoxville, Tennessee.

1935: Big Bend National Park established in Texas. Deserts, mountains, and geological formations cover 708,221 acres.

1979: The Corn Palace in Mitchell, South Dakota catches fire. The structure, adorned on the outside by corny designs, will reopen August 8.

JUNE 21

1851: First town in Colorado, San Luis, founded by New Mexican colonists.

1876: Lt. Col. George Armstrong Custer meets with Gen. Terry and Lt. Col. Gibbon aboard the steamship *Far West* to discuss their strategy against the Indians. Gibbon and Terry will follow the Yellowstone River to the Bighorn River and go on to the Little Bighorn to meet Custer. They are unaware of the June 17th Battle on the Rosebud.

1877: John Sallee, Jr. dies. One of his pallbearers will be Jesse James, in disguise.

1894: In his famous "Cross of Gold" speech, Nebraska Representative William Jennings Bryan advocates free silver as a solution to American economic woes resulting from a depletion of the gold supply to back American currency.

1921: Actress Jane Russell, who will play in Howard Hughes' *The Outlaw* (about Billy the Kid) and with Clark Gable in *The Tall Men*, born in Bemidji, Minnesota.

1924: Charles Banta, Arizona lawyer/newspaperman, dies in Prescott at age 81.

1978: A major forest fire burns 12,000 acres in New Mexico and comes dangerously close to an explosives storage area at Los Alamos.

JUNE 22

1835: Badman Cullen Baker is born in Weakly County, Tennessee.

1850: Lewis Ralston, prospecting with a group of Cherokee Indians near present Arvada, Colorado, discovers gold.

1870: The first railroad passenger train arrives in Denver. The future of the young city had been in doubt when the Union Pacific railroad announced in 1866 that it would build the transcontinental railroad through Cheyenne, by-passing the mile-high city. Denverites formed their own corporation and began laying track.

1876: Lt. Col. George A. Custer takes 675 men, 12 companies of the 7th Cavalry, and splits off from Col. Gibbon and Gen. Terry as the search continues for a reported Indian gathering near the Little Bighorn. On this date, he also pens his last letter to his wife Libbie: "Do not be anxious about me, I hope to have a good report to send you by the next mail."

1876: Antonio Lopez de Santa Anna dies an embittered old man in Mexico City.

1880: Buckskin Frank Leslie takes May Killeen to a dance in Tombstone, despite the fact that she is married to the very jealous Mike Killeen. Killeen attacks Leslie while he is escorting May home, clubbing him in the head. Leslie goes for his guns. Killeen is laid out in the streets of Tombstone. He will die in five days.

1890: Frederick Benteen, the captain who took three companies on a scouting mission when Custer divided his troops at the Little Bighorn, dies of a stroke in Atlanta.

1900: In Idaho, the New York Canal opens to expand irrigation in the Boise valley.

1936: Singer/actor Kris Kristofferson who will write hits like "Help Me Make It Through the Night" and play the Kid in *Pat Garrett and Billy the Kid*, is born in Brownsville, Texas.

1981: Lubbock, Texas woman lives after she is struck by lightning that blows off her tennis shoes.

JUNE 23

1810: The Pacific Fur Company is organized by John Jacob Astor.

1845: The Republic of Texas legislature votes to accept annexation by the United States.

1865: Cherokee Chief Stand Watie becomes the last Confederate general to surrender. He gives his sword to Union commissioners at Doaksville in the Choctaw Nation of southeastern Oklahoma. Lee had surrendered to Grant on April 9, 1865.

1931: Texas aviator Wiley Post takes off in his *Winnie Mae* on a trip around the world which he will complete in just eight days.

1946: Film great William S. Hart,

75, dies at his Horseshoe Ranch outside Los Angeles.

WILLIAM S. HART

JUNE 24

1716: First horse race in Texas staged by members of the Ramon Expedition.

1837: The steamboat *St. Peters* arrives at Fort Union in present Montana, loaded with goods to trade with the friendly Indian tribes. Also on board are several cases of contagious smallpox. The disease will devastate many tribes, including Mandans, Blackfoot, Crows, and Assiniboines.

1858: Fort Garland, a military post about 50 miles west of today's Walsenburg, established in Colorado's San Luis Valley.

1864: Colorado Gov. John Evans orders all friendly Indians to report to the reservation at Sand Creek because of recent tensions.

1889: Butch Cassidy pulls his first holdup in Telluride, Colorado.

1895: Future heavyweight champion William Harrison "Jack" Dempsey born in Manassa, Colorado.

1897: Cripple Creek miner from Scotland is arrested for indecent exposure for wearing his kilts on a public street.

1954: Colorado Springs, Colorado, chosen over 400 other locations as the site for the Air Force Academy.

JUNE 25

1874: Lawman Bill Tilghman and a group of buffalo hunters retrieve the body of fellow hunter Pat Congers from a saloon where he was slain in Petrie, Indian Territory, present-day Oklahoma. A fight breaks out with Congers' murderer, Blue Throat.

1876: The Battle of the Little Bighorn ~ "Ho-ka-hey!" yelled Crazy Horse, when he heard the soldiers were approaching. "It is a good day to fight! It is a good day to die!" And so it was. Lt. Col. George Armstrong Custer, in one of history's greatest military blunders, divides his command for an upcoming skirmish with Indians. Capt. Frederick Benteen and three companies are ordered to the west. Maj. Marcus Reno is ordered to cross the Little Bighorn, then mount his attack from the valley. Another company is sent back to the pack train. What Custer and his company run into is perhaps the largest congregation of tribes in history ~ 15,000 Sioux and Cheyenne. Reno's attack on the south end of the camp is repulsed. Custer and his 187 men are outnumbered by at least 1,500 warriors, probably more, and are completely wiped out in less than half an hour. How Custer died remains a mystery; indications show he may have committed suicide. The event itself will shock a country in the midst of its patriotic centennial celebration. No Native American on the continent will go unaffected. The solutions for the "Indian problem" will become more brutal, more swift.

1876: Unaware that their husbands have been slain that same day, the women of the 7th Cavalry meet at Fort Lincoln. The prayer meeting is conducted by Mrs. George A. (Libbie Bacon) Custer, and they sing "Nearer My God To Thee."

1892: Bob Ford's funeral is held at Creede, Colorado.

1900: In California's Yosemite National Park, Oliver Lippincott drives a sputtering automobile to the top of Glacier Point.

1921: Oil discovered at Signal Hill, Long Beach, California.

1965: USAF C-135 hits a mountain after a Los Angeles takeoff, killing 84.

JUNE 26

1804: Lewis and Clark expedition camps "at the upper point of the mouth of the river Kanzas."

1858: Anti-polygamy sentiment runs high as Federal troops march through Salt Lake City in a show of force but find that most of the Mormons have fled to Provo.

1876: Those members of the 7th Cavalry who were not with Custer remain pinned down. When the sun goes down, the Indians leave.

1927: San Francisco is linked to the Philippines by radio for the first time.

JUNE 27

1831: Chief Black Hawk agrees to move his Sauk Indians west of the Mississippi River in a prelude to the 1832 Black Hawk war.

1844: Mormon founder Joseph Smith and brother Hyrum are arrested and jailed at Carthage, Illinois for allegedly wrecking the printing press of the Nauvoo *Expositor*. Rumors of polygamy have the locals hopping mad. A mob forms, the men are pulled out into the street and lynched.

1874: The Battle of Adobe Walls ~ A group of 37 buffalo hunters, including a young Bat Masterson, holds off a charge by as many as 700 Comanche, Kiowa, and Cheyenne Indians, led by Chief Quanah Parker and Lone Wolf in the Texas panhandle. They are able to do so with new, long-range, rapid firing Sharps .50-caliber buffalo rifles that decimate the warriors' ranks. This action begins a three-day siege.

1876: The bodies of Lt. Col. George Armstrong Custer and his men are found mutilated at the Little Bighorn by Gen. Terry and Col. Gibbon. The only survivor on the American side is an Army steed called Comanche. This mount of slain Capt. Myles Keogh will never be ridden again, a living symbol of the brave who fell. He will live the good life at various posts, and enjoy an occasional bucket of beer. After his death in 1891, he will be stuffed and mounted for display at the University of Kansas in Lawrence.

1893: As the Panic of 1893 turns into a full scale depression, Colorado silver producers close their mines and smelters until they can obtain government support. Silver is now 77 cents an ounce. Railroads fail, as do 500 banks nationwide. Forces muster to repeal the Sherman Silver Purchase Act of 1890.

1903: Kid Curry escapes from jail in Knoxville, Tennessee and heads west.

1923: First mid-air refuelling of an airplane in the skies over Coronado, California.

1950: A small bear cub is found after a New Mexico forest fire, and is soon recognized internationally as Smokey the Bear, the symbol who echoes "Only you can prevent forest fires." He will be housed in a palatial bear cage in Washington D.C., where he will maintain his own personal zip code.

JUNE 28

1857: Author Emerson Hough (*The Story of a Cowboy, The Covered Wagon*) born in Newton, Iowa.

1866: Col. Carrington and a regiment aid two companies during a skirmish with Indians on the Powder River. The area will be secured and named Fort Reno.

1880: Texas Jack Omohundro, 33, dies of pneumonia in Leadville, Colorado, following an illustrious career in scouting and show business in which he was joined by William F. Cody.

1897: Kid Curry participates in his first bank robbery in Belle Fourche, South Dakota.

1927: Lieutenants Lester Maitland and Albert F. Hegenberger take off in a Fokker from Oakland, California, attempting to make history's longest over-water flight, just five weeks after Lindbergh crosses the Atlantic. Nearly 26 hours later, they will land in Hawaii, having covered 2,407 miles.

1930: Zane Grey's *The Border Legion* released by Paramount.

1946: Former Denverite Antoinette Perry dies in New York City. Broadway's Tony Awards, named in her honor, will begin the following year.

1965: Pecos National Monument established in New Mexico.

1982: San Francisco outlaws the private possession of weapons, the first large American city to do so.

JUNE 29

1541: Coronado's party crosses the Arkansas River in present Kansas in search of the fabled Seven Cities of Cibola.

1854: First territorial governor of Kansas appointed today, Andrew Reeder.

1874: The Battle at Adobe Walls ceases after a three-day siege.

1903: Following a train robbery at Parachute, Colorado, one of the cornered outlaws takes his own life rather than being taken by authorities. Pinkerton agents identify the body as that of Kid Curry, who has just escaped from jail in Knoxville, Tennessee. For Curry to participate in the robbery, he would have to have covered considerable distance. Rumors persist that the Kid joined other Wild Bunchers in Argentina, namely Butch Cassidy and the Sundance Kid.

1906: Mesa Verde National Park established in Colorado. It includes the best preserved pre-Columbian

cliff dwellings in the United States. It was home of the ancient Anasazi, and covers 52,074 acres.

1919: Actor Slim Pickens is born Louis Bert Lindley in Kingsberg, California.

1925: Santa Barbara, California receives heavy damage from an earthquake.

1928: Alfred E. Smith is the Democratic nominee for President, named today at the convention in Houston, Texas.

1930: *'Neath Western Skies* with Tom Tyler released by Syndicate.

1938: Olympic National Park established in Washington. A mountain wilderness extending to the seashore and covering 896,000 acres, it has the best remnant of a Pacific Northwest rain forest.

JUNE 30

1739: Paul and Pierre Mallet find stones with Spanish graffiti in present Ford County, Kansas.

1834: The Department of Indian Affairs is established.

1835: Col. William B. Travis captures the seaport of Anahuac during one of the early clashes for Texas independence.

1891: First passenger train scales Pikes Peak.

1894: John Wesley Powell resigns after 13 years as Director of the U.S. Geological Survey.

1905: An explosion at Union Pacific's Coal Mine Number One at Hanna, Wyoming, kills 169.

1918: The Ruff Building in Sioux City, Iowa collapses, killing 39.

1922: *The Village Street* by Frederick Faust (Max Brand) published by Putnam.

1924: In the Teapot Dome scandal, Fall, Sinclair, and Doheny are indicted on charges of conspiracy and bribery.

1930: Massive military complex Randolph Field opens near San Antonio, Texas.

1956: A TWA airliner, en route from Los Angeles to Kansas City, collides with a United plane on a Los Angeles to Chicago run, over the Painted Desert and the Grand Canyon. All passengers on both planes, 128 including crew members, perish in America's worst airline disaster to date.

1961: Inventor Lee De Forest dies at age 87 after registering over 300 patents, the most famous being the sound on film system in 1923.

1965: *Requiem for a Gunfighter* released by Embassy.

GREAT EVENT

Rail Road from Denver to Glenwood Springs

GRAND TOUR OF
CRAZY LEONARD'S GRASSROOTS TOURS & PHOTOGRAPHIC SAFARIS

Round Trip Passage on the

Rio Grande Zepher

Through the Moffat Tunnel and Gore and Glenwood Canyons

CHAMPANGE BRUNCH ABOARD THE ZEPHER

Accomodations at the Historic

HOTEL COLORADO

Admission to the Hot Springs Pool

VAPOR CAVES

DEPARTS

DENVER UNION STATION

July

JULY 1

1807: The Pike expedition is released by Spanish troops at Natchitoches, Louisiana, effectively ending its western journey.

1836: President Jackson turns down a Congressional resolution recognizing Texas.

1839: Johann August Sutter comes to San Francisco from Switzerland, where he will build Sutter's Fort and establish New Helvetia in the Sacramento Valley. In 1841, he will take over Fort Ross, ending Russian involvement in California.

1850: First overland mail service in the west is established between Salt Lake City, Utah and Independence, Missouri.

1858: Mormon leaders invite their followers to return to Salt Lake City after the federal troops have departed.

1862: President Lincoln signs Pacific Railroad Act, which begins a race between the Central Pacific and Union Pacific railroads to build this country's first transcontinental railroad.

1862: Congress directs antipolygamy legislation aimed at Utah's Mormons.

1882: "Frank James on the Trail" is published by *Morrison's Sensational Stories*.

1887: Clay Allison is killed when he falls under a wagon 40 miles from Pecos, Texas. His skull is fractured by a wagon wheel.

1895: San Francisco's Alcatraz Island designated a U.S. Disciplinary Barracks.

1898: Theodore Roosevelt leads his charge of Rough Riders up Cuba's Kettle Hill during the "splendid little" Spanish-American War. His group represents the last elite regiment of the United States Cavalry. The men make the charge on foot, although T.R. is on horseback.

1933: Temperature hits 114 degrees at Las Animas, Colorado.

1961: First community air raid shelter completed at Boise, Idaho.

1965: *Sons of Katie Elder* released by Paramount.

1965: *Cat Ballou* released by Columbia. Lee Marvin will receive the Oscar for a dual role as a drunken ex-gunfighter and a cold villain.

1979: July record snowfall at Stampede Pass, Washington -- 5.8 inches.

JULY 2

1809: Shawnee Chief Tecumseh pushes for defense of the western lands from white migration.

1849: State of Deseret draws up a petition to be admitted to the Union.

1855: Kansas legislature approves tough pro-slavery measures and expels anti-slavery legislators.

1859: Discovery of the Comstock Lode the previous June 10, announced in the Nevada City *Journal*.

1877: Troops under Lt. Col. Michael Sheridan rebury the enlisted men of the Little Bighorn massacre and remove the remains of officers for burial elsewhere.

1937: Last communication from Amelia Earhart in the South Pacific, as she attempts to fly around the world. Her take-off this day is from New Guinea, bound for Howland Island, 2,556 miles east.

1939: Dedication ceremonies honor the head of Theodore Roosevelt, the fourth and final President to appear on South Dakota's Mount Rushmore.

1961: Ernest Hemingway, 61, commits suicide at his home in Ketchum, Idaho.

JULY 3

1804: Lewis and Clark camp in present Atchison County, Kansas.

1827: Jedediah Smith returns with two of his original party, Silas Gobel and Robert Evans, to the Great Salt Lake rendezvous. The rest of his men he has left behind in California, with instructions to await his return within four months.

1852: U.S. Mint established in San Francisco.

1861: Pony Express arrives in San Francisco with letters from New York.

1865: Gen. Patrick E. Connor arrives at Fort Laramie in present Wyoming to protect the Overland Mail from Arapaho Indians.

1876: With the body of George Armstrong Custer and the surviving horse Comanche on board, the riverboat *Far West* begins a record-breaking journey. In 54 hours, it will travel 710 miles from the Little Bighorn to Bismarck, North Dakota.

1876: News of the Custer massacre first appears in print in Montana Territory's *Bozeman Times*.

1878: Billy the Kid and a group of Regulators have a long-range shoot out with rival cattle factions; no one injured.

1890: Idaho enters the Union as the 43rd state.

1897: Blues singer Blind Lemon Jefferson is born in Wortham, Texas.

1901: The last American robbery by the Wild Bunch occurs near Wagner, Montana. At 2:00 P.M., Butch Cassidy, Harry Longabaugh, Harvey Logan, and Camilla Hanks hold up a Great Northern train. Longabaugh, the Sundance Kid, kills passenger Sheriff Griffith of Great Falls, who starts shooting. An express car is then blown to smithereens with dynamite and the Bunch realizes a net profit of $65,000 in unsigned bank notes.

1950: Denver streetcars make their last runs.

1958: The state of Iowa is declared a disaster area as floods kill 21.

JULY 4

1804: From their keelboat, Lewis and Clark fire a celebration shot, and name "Fourth of July Creek" in present Kansas.

1817: Construction of the Erie Canal, a project to make the West more accessible, is begun at Rome, New York.

1838: Iowa Territory is formed from the old Wisconsin Territory. It contains present Iowa as well as portions of Minnesota, North Dakota, and South Dakota.

1854: Lawman-state senator-businessman William Matthew "Bill" Tilghman born in Fort Dodge, Iowa.

1854: The United States takes possession of the land obtained from

Mexico in the Gadsden Purchase following the Mexican War.

1858: Mormons return to their homes in Salt Lake City following their flight to Provo caused by the recent military scare.

1864: Due to labor shortages caused by the Civil War, Congress passes the Immigration Act which will enable companies like the Central Pacific railroad to import Chinese laborers.

1874: The largest arch bridge in the world opens in St. Louis, spanning the Mississippi River with tons of steel. Capt. James B. Eads engineered the construction, which took seven years, and assured the future of the city.

1876: First news of the Custer debacle of June 25 is reported in the eastern press. The *Helena Herald* also reports it on this day.

1876: First exhibition of electric light in San Francisco is performed by Father Joseph Neri from the roof of St. Ignatius College.

1878: The Seven Rivers gang lays siege to a group of Regulators, including Billy the Kid, at the South Spring River ranch during the Lincoln County War.

1882: Engineer Henry Arbuckle wins the "Little Emma" railroad engine during a crap game at Pueblo, Colorado. He will later use it to fight Indians.

1883: The first Wild West show is presented by William F. Cody (Buffalo Bill) in North Platte, Nebraska. His huge array of cowboys, Indians, settlers, trick riders, shooters, and a simulated buffalo hunt will become an international favorite.

1883: Pecos, Texas holds what it claims is history's first rodeo.

1884: On his 30th birthday, Bill Tilghman gets into a fight with and murders saloon keeper Ed Prather in Farmer City, Kansas.

1885: Flags flown at half-mast in Salt Lake City, a protest against U.S. policies toward Latter-day Saints.

1888: Prescott, Arizona Territory, holds what it claims is history's first organized rodeo.

1890: The cornerstone for the Colorado capitol is laid in Denver.

1891: Winfield Scott Stratton stakes his Independence claim on a vein of gold he has discovered near Cripple Creek, Colorado. The subject of Frank Waters' *Midas of the Rockies* will find his wealth to be a curse.

1896: "Wild Bill's Last Trail" by Ned Buntline published in *Diamond Dick Library Magazine*.

1898: Soapy Smith leads the Skagway, Alaska Fourth of July Parade as the Grand Marshal, on a white horse. It will be the last hurrah for this king of the con men.

1900: A Tacoma, Washington streetcar goes out of control; 41 die.

1903: President Theodore Roosevelt sends the first message by cable from San Francisco to Manila. Following that, he sends another message around the world in 12 minutes.

1910: "The battle of the century" takes place in Reno, Nevada. Jim Jeffries comes out of retirement, a "great white hope" to challenge flamboyant black champion Jack Johnson. Jeffries throws in the towel in the 15th round, then tells reporters it was not worth his winnings of $192,066 to take such a beating: "I could never have whipped Jack Johnson at my best. I couldn't have hit him in a thousand years."

1912: Heavyweight champ Jack Johnson defends his title with a ninth round knockout of Jim Flynn in Las Vegas.

1917: First indoor Indian rodeo takes place in Fort Worth, Texas.

1919: Jack Dempsey of Colorado decks Jess Willard of Kansas to win the World Heavyweight Championship on a scorcher in Dayton, Ohio.

1930: Dedication ceremonies are held for the giant bust of George Washington, first President to appear on Mount Rushmore.

JULY 5

1739: Near present Lamar, Colorado, Pierre and Paul Mallet meet friendly Comanches.

1810: Showman P.T. Barnum born in Bethel, Connecticut.

1843: Oregon settlers adopt Organic Laws, a constitution based on Iowa statutes.

1876: Twenty-seven women at Fort Lincoln, including Mrs. George Armstrong Custer, learn that they have been widowed by the Battle of the Little Bighorn.

1876: Custer massacre reported in the *Salt Lake Tribune*.

1876: Bismarck telegraph operator John Carnahan begins a 22-hour, $3,000 transmission of details to the east on the Battle of the Little Bighorn.

1891: Hailstorm kills 16 horses in Rapid City, South Dakota.

1899: Brazos River in Texas floods, killing 200.

1910: O. Henry, pen name of William Sydney Porter, creator of the "Cisco Kid," dies at age 47.

1920: James M. Cox named Presidential nominee by the Democratic National Convention meeting in San Francisco. Warren G. Harding will be the Republican's choice.

JULY 6

1862: Because it is a normal practice for newspaper writers to use pen names in wild Virginia City, young Samuel Clemens will begin writing as Mark Twain during the month of July. His first gig is with the *Territorial Enterprise*.

1876: First full account of the Battle of the Little Bighorn is carried in the *Bismarck Tribune*.

1876: Henry Wadsworth Longfellow, in *The Revenge of Rain-in-the-Face* echoes popular thought concerning the identity of Custer's killer:

> But the foemen fled in the night,
> And Rain-in-the-Face, in his flight
> Uplifted high in air
> As a ghastly trophy, bore
> The brave heart, that beat no more,
> Of the White Chief with yellow hair.

JACK DEMPSEY

1925: Singer Bill Haley ("Rock Around the Clock") born in Highland Park, Michigan.

1928: A 1.5-pound hailstone falls near Potter, Nebraska, the second largest in U.S. history.

1944: Annie Ralston James, widow of Frank, dies at age 91.

1956: *The Fastest Gun Alive* with Glenn Ford released by MGM.

1957: Thieves steal the 560-pound headstone of Wyatt Earp from the Hills of Eternity Memorial Park in Colma, California.

JULY 7

1540: Searching for the Seven Cities of Cibola, Coronado and his men take the Zuni pueblo Hawikuh and rename it Granada-Cibola.

1846: Cmdr. John Sloat occupies Monterey, declaring California belongs to the United States.

1875: On their way to Northfield, Minnesota, the James and Younger brothers steal $75,000 from a Missouri-Pacific express train near Otterville, Missouri.

1903: A train is robbed near Parachute, Colorado. Two days later, authorities have a gun battle with the suspects. One bandit commits suicide as he is being closed in on. Some say the dead man is cowboy Tap Duncan, but Pinkertons insist it is Harvey Logan. The book is closed on the outlaw, otherwise known as Kid Curry.

1911: Alphonso Steele, last survivor of the Battle of San Jacinto, dies.

1912: Jim Thorpe wins four of five pentathlon events at the V Olympiad in Stockholm.

1927: The Moffat Tunnel completed in Colorado. It is an $18 million, six-mile hole drilled through the Continental Divide to allow an east-west rail hookup.

1933: Zane Grey's *Life in the Raw* released by Fox.

1981: Ten inches of snow falls on Montana's Glacier National Park.

JULY 8

1828: Jedediah Smith's party reaches Oregon's Umpqua River.

1833: Stephen Austin arrives in Mexico City to negotiate the separate state of Texas.

1873: Editor W.J. Forbes, in the last issue of *New Endowment* says, "I'd like to publish it longer, but the fact is, I didn't bring enough money."

1892: *Science* magazine reports that diamonds have been discovered in a meteorite found in Canyon Diablo, Arizona.

1898: Soapy Smith is shot dead by Skagway City Engineer Frank Reid. The renowned con man was only 38, but had led a colorful, deceitful life which began in the mining fields of Colorado. Jefferson Randolph Smith got his nickname for a famous con he regularly pulled on the streets of Leadville and Denver. Here he wrapped bars of toilet soap in blue tissue paper, inserting choice bills in a few. The first miner to buy a $5 bar was always a plant, who waved a hundred dollar bill when he unwrapped his soap. This little trick enabled Soapy to finance larcenous operations wherever he went.

SOAPY SMITH

1900: Tom Horn rubs out cattle rustler Matt Rash, blasting him from cover with his rifle in Routt County, Colorado.

1950: The Nebraska 24-hour rainfall record is set at York with 13.15 inches.

1950: Statue of Milton Caniff's comic strip air ace Steve Canyon is unveiled at Idaho Springs, Colorado.

JULY 9

1846: The American flag is raised by Commander John B. Montgomery at Yerba Buena, future San Francisco.

1850: Asiatic cholera, reaching epidemic proportions in the United States claims its most famous victim, President Zachary Taylor.

1857: First stagecoach mail line from San Antonio to San Diego begins operation.

1907: San Francisco mayor Eugene Schmitz, convicted of corruption in office, sentenced to five years at San Quentin.

1922: Future movie Tarzan Johnny Weissmuller is the first swimmer to swim the 100 meter free style in under a minute, at Alameda, California.

1968: Author Vardis Fisher dies at age 73.

JULY 10

1700: Father Gabriel Marest, of the Kaskaskia mission writes of the Missouri River: "Its real name is the Pekitanou and the French call it the Missouri because this people is the first you meet there."

1824: Richard King, founder of the King Ranch in Texas, born in New York. His land holdings will eventually total 1.27 million acres, with 40,000 cattle, 1,200 sheep, and 6,600 horses.

1851: California Wesleyan College, future University of the Pacific, chartered at Santa Clara, California.

1863: Idaho is organized at Lewiston by Gov. William H. Wallace.

1865: The first rails on the transcontinental railroad are laid by the Union Pacific, building west from Omaha, Nebraska.

1881: The James brothers rob Riverton, Iowa's, Davis and Sexton Bank of $5,000.

1889: While working on a ranch outside Tombstone, Buckskin Frank Leslie gets into a quarrel with roommate Blonde Mollie Williams and shoots her dead. A ranch hand witnesses the killing. Buckskin gets 25 years.

1890: Wyoming, population 60,000, enters the Union as the 44th state. The women of Wyoming Territory had been granted voting privileges

July

in 1869. Wyoming thus becomes the first state in the Union to guarantee such rights.

1897: Silent film star John Gilbert born in Provo, Utah.

1908: Denver's first and only political convention nominates William Jennings Bryan as the Democratic standard bearer.

1913: Death Valley records the hottest temperature ever in the western hemisphere, 134 degrees.

JULY 11

1869: Cheyenne "Dog Soldiers" under Tall Bull are attacked by the 5th Cavalry in Colorado Territory. The Battle of Summit Springs will result in the deaths of Tall Bull and 52 warriors. The encampment was scouted by William F. Cody, who will work the battle into his future Wild West performances.

1878: During New Mexico's Lincoln County War, a posse under J.J. Dolan terrorizes the town of San Patricio.

1888: The hottest temperature ever recorded in Colorado is reached at Bennett, 118 degrees.

1892: Miners at Coeur D'Alene, Idaho, dynamite the Frisco Mill.

1954: The Mother Cabrini Shrine is dedicated west of Denver.

1954: Weather record keepers are skeptical over the 1888 report from Bennett, but there is no doubt that today the mercury climbs to 114 degrees at Sedgwick, Colorado.

JULY 12

1808: The first newspaper to be published west of the Mississippi River is the *Missouri Gazette* of St. Louis.

1834: Fur trapper Joe Walker's party, guiding the expedition of Capt. Benjamin Bonneville, arrives at the Bear River rendezvous.

1861: Wild Bill Hickok shoots it out with the McCanles Gang at Rock Creek Station, Nebraska where he is employed as a hand at the stage depot. Rancher David McCanles was irate because of a long-standing feud with the firm of Russell, Majors & Waddell and because Wild Bill was carrying on with his mistress, Sarah Shull. McCanles threatens to come after Hickok, whereupon Wild Bill tells him there will be "one less son of a bitch" if he tries. McCanles storms in; Hickok blows him away. In the ensuing fight, Hickok also wounds James Woods, who will be finished off by another employee. Hickok will be cleared of the murder. This incident is later wildly exaggerated in dime novels, with not a little help from Hickok himself, and will become a keystone in his reputation.

1870: Capt. C.B. McLelland and 6th Cavalry battle Kicking Bird's Kiowas on the Little Wichita in Texas.

1892: Ed O'Kelley sentenced to life in prison in Canon City, Colorado for the murder of Bob Ford. The man who killed the man who killed Jesse James will be released in 1902.

1899: Outlaw "Elzy" Lay is wounded by a posse following a train robbery with the Ketchum gang at Turkey Creek Canyon, New Mexico. The three robbers get away, after killing lawmen Tom Smith, Edward Farr, and W.H. Love.

1926: Evolutionary theory deleted from Texas school biology books.

1951: Kansas flooding kills 28, doing $935 million in damages.

JULY 13

1857: President Buchanan names Alfred Cumming to replace Brigham Young as Utah territorial governor.

1859: Horace Greeley's interview with Brigham Young appears in the *New York Tribune*.

1866: Construction begins on Fort Phil Kearny on the Tongue River, about 13 miles north of Clear Creek, Wyoming. A log stockade, it will be abandoned in 1868 and put to the torch by Sioux Indians under Red Cloud.

1869: Bloody anti-Chinese race riots rock San Francisco.

1886: Father Flanagan, future founder of Boys Town, Nebraska, born in Roscommon, Ireland.

1890: Explorer John C. Fremont dies at age 77. His glory days came before he was 40, when his rich narrations of the West made him a national celebrity.

1921: Christian Nelson shows his "I Scream Bar" to candy manufacturer Russell Stover in Omaha. Stover thinks the idea clever, but believes it will sell better if the treat is renamed "Eskimo Pie."

1930: *The Lone Rider* with Buck Jones is released by Beverly.

1937: Emmett Dalton, last surviving member of the notorious Dalton Gang, dies at age 66. In his life, he was an outlaw, a convict, a building contractor, and a Hollywood screen writer. He also penned the book *When the Daltons Rode*.

1950: The Ute Indians awarded $31,700,000 for tribal lands taken in Utah and Colorado from 1891-1938.

1953: Filming begins on the first feature to be shot in Denver, *The Glenn Miller Story*.

JULY 14

1776: Jemima Boone, 14-year-old daughter of Daniel, and two companions, are kidnapped by a small band of Shawnees and Cherokees near Boonesborough. Boone trails them north for two days, then leads a rescue.

1828: Kelawatset Indians attack a party of Jedediah Smith's trappers in Oregon. Smith is off scouting; 15 are killed.

1860: Author Owen Wister, who will create the modern Western with his 1902 classic *The Virginian*, born in Philadelphia, Pennsylvania.

1878: During the Lincoln County War, A.A. McSween and 60 supporters, including Billy the Kid, prepare for battle by reoccupying McSween's home.

1881: Billy the Kid murdered ~ William Bonney, aged 21, is shot dead by Pat Garrett at Fort Sumner, New Mexico. Returning from a dance, he enters the bedroom of Pete Maxwell where Garrett is sitting in the dark with his guns drawn. The Kid asks "Quien es?" and is blasted to kingdom come.

1882: Johnny Ringo found dead in Turkey Creek Canyon, Arizona Territory. Rumors he committed

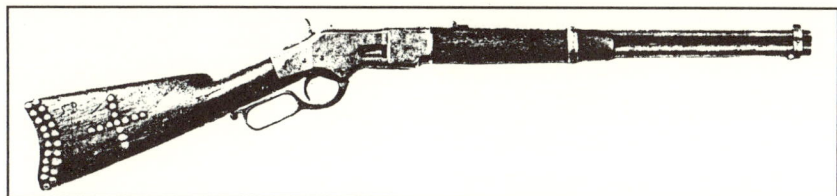

suicide don't hold much water, seeing as how this Shakespeare-quoting gunfighter had been scalped. Billy Claiborne said Buckskin Frank Leslie did it, but perhaps a more reliable source is Pony Deal, who blamed Johnny O'Rourke. The mystery is never solved.

1892: Martial law is called in the Coeur d'Alene mines after the dynamiting of an abandoned mill at Gem, in Idaho.

1901: Jim and Cole Younger are released from the Minnesota State Penitentiary after 25 years for their robbery attempt with the James boys at Northfield.

1912: Folk singer Woody Guthrie ("This Land is Your Land," "Oklahoma Hills") is born in Okemah, Oklahoma.

1912: Cherry Creek floods Denver.

1917: Author William Eastlake (*The Bronc People*) born in Brooklyn, New York.

1923: Actor Dale Robertson ("Tales of Wells Fargo") born in Oklahoma City, Oklahoma.

JULY 15

1806: Lt. Zebulon Pike begins his western expedition from Fort Belle Fountaine, near St. Louis. His strange journey, which some historians feel was in truth a spy mission for Gen. Wilkinson in an attempt to establish a new nation out West, will see him "discover" Pikes Peak in Colorado, and be captured by soldiers and taken to Mexico for interrogation.

1820: The first men to climb Pikes Peak, members of the Stephen Long expedition, are led by Edwin James.

1830: Sioux, Sauk, Fox, and other Indians sign a treaty giving the United States most of Iowa, Missouri, and Minnesota.

1878: First day of a five-day battle begins at A.A. McSween's home during the Lincoln County War. Only a horse and a mule are killed during the confrontation with the attack by the J.J. Dolan bunch.

1879: Although he may not have participated, Butch Cassidy is credited with robbing a train near Folsom, New Mexico of $70,000.

1881: The James boys rob the Chicago, Rock Island & Pacific railroad express near Winston, Missouri, killing the engineer and a passenger, and making off with $600. After this robbery, gang member Jim Cummins is considered not to be trustworthy.

1892: The Dalton Gang holds up a train of the Missouri, Kansas, and Texas line at Adair, Oklahoma Territory. One bystander is killed.

1913: Singer Lloyd "Cowboy" Copas ("Alabam") born in Muskogee, Oklahoma.

1923: Another golden spike celebration takes place at Nenana as President Harding presides at ceremonies honoring the completion of the Alaskan railroad.

1933: John Wayne's *The Man from*

Monterey released by Warner Brothers.

1982: Flooding of Colorado's Big Thompson Canyon kills three.

1983: William Foxley buys Denver's notorious Navarre Club, a former center of gambling and prostitution, for the purpose of turning it into The Museum of Western Art.

JULY 16

1808: The Missouri Fur Co. is incorporated by William Clark, Manuel Lisa, and Pierre Chouteau.

1866: First Sioux War begins in the Powder River region; Col. Carrington's horses are driven away.

1886: Pulp fiction writer Ned Buntline dies at age 62.

1936: Mary Elitch Long, who started Denver's Elitch Gardens, dies at age 80.

1938: Denver newspaper columnist Polly Pry, who played an instrumental part in the pardon of accused cannibal Alfred Packer, dies at age 80.

> **1945: The Atomic Age Begins** ~ First atomic bomb is tested in secret by scientists at Alamorgordo, New Mexico. The blast, which is detonated at 5:29:40 A.M. lights up the New Mexican skies, and is even "seen" by a blind person. Ground zero registers the hottest temperature ever recorded on earth, 100,000,000 degrees, some 10,000 times hotter than the surface of the sun. The official news release states that a munitions warehouse blew up. Scientist J. Robert Oppenheimer quotes the *Bhagavad Gita*: "I am become Death, the shatterer of worlds."

JULY 17

1763: John Jacob Astor born near Heidelberg, Germany. After arriving in New York City penniless in 1783, the young entrepreneur establishes the American Fur Company in 1808. His trading posts across the West make him the country's first millionaire.

1804: President Jefferson appoints Pierre Chouteau of St. Louis as Louisiana agent of Indian affairs.

1822: Trappers Hugh Glenn, Jacob Fowler, and John and Robert McKnight arrive in St. Louis to sell $4,499.64 worth of furs.

1870: A drunken Wild Bill Hickok takes on five besotted members of the 7th Cavalry in a saloon in Hays City, Kansas. Pvt. John Kile is killed, Pvt. Jeremiah Lanigan is wounded. Wild Bill leaves town shortly after the episode.

1878: Charlie Crawford wounded during the McSween/Dolan battle in the Lincoln County War. He will die in five weeks.

1881: Mountain man legend Jim Bridger, 77, dies near Westport, Missouri.

1893: The first of a dozen Denver banks to close in two days boards up its doors in the wake of the Panic of 1893, when the U.S. opts for a gold rather than a silver standard.

1944: Two munitions ships, the *E.A. Bryan* and the *Quinault Victory*, explode in San Francisco Bay's Port Chicago, killing 321.

1955: Disneyland opens in Anaheim, California.

1964: The GOP convention, meeting in San Francisco, nominates Arizona Sen. Barry Goldwater to run against President Johnson.

1981: Two suspended walkways in Kansas City's Hyatt Regency Hotel collapse, killing 111.

POLLY PRY

JULY 18

1857: Col. Albert Sidney Johnston and troops leave Fort Leavenworth in Kansas, headed for Brigham Young's Mormon empire. When the news reaches Utah, Salt Lake City is evacuated.

1867: Margaret Tobin, who will become famous as the "Unsinkable Molly Brown" aboard the *Titanic*, is born in Hannibal, Missouri.

1901: Hoping to bag his next victim, Tom Horn accidentally kills the son of target Kels Nickell, 14-year-old Willie. The boy was wearing his father's hat and coat, but that won't mean much in court. This is the crime for which Horn will hang.

1902: Actor Chill Wills born in Seagoville, Texas.

1914: Labor activist Joe Hill gets the death sentence for the murder of a Salt Lake City grocer and his son. The evidence was thin. Unionists think Hill's radical labor beliefs are behind the verdict. When asked how he wishes to die, Hill replies, "I'll take shooting. I'm used to that. I have been shot a few times in the past, and I guess I can stand it again."

1938: Douglas "Wrong Way" Corrigan of Texas sets out to fly from New York to California. He lands in Dublin instead.

1963: A crowd of 6,000 in Colorado Springs witness history's first all-rookie professional football game. The Denver Broncos beat the Houston Oilers 17-14.

1982: One-legged mountain climber Don Bennet plants a flag atop Washington's Mount Rainier.

JULY 19

1845: Robert, second son of Robert and Zerelda James, is born. The child born after Frank and before Jesse will die in infancy.

1871: The Hayden Expedition sees its first wonder in Yellowstone, Devil's Slide on Cinnabar Mountain.

1878: Sam Bass Gang member Seaborn Barnes is slain by Ranger Dick Ware in Round Rock, Texas.

1878: Dolan forces set fire to the home of Alexander McSween. Billy the Kid, Jim French, and Tom O'Folliard make a successful run for it, but Harvey Morris is killed in the attempt. A.A. McSween tries to surrender, but he and two others are slain in the confusion. Dolan's men set McSween's body on fire, then run wild through Lincoln, New Mexico.

1879: While Doc Holliday operates a saloon in Las Vegas, New Mexico, ex-scout Mike Gordon tries to get one of the dance hall girls to run away with him. She turns him down, Gordon stands in the street and begins firing his gun into the establishment. Holliday emerges and kills Gordon with one shot.

1881: Sitting Bull and 187 Sioux, back from four years in Canadian exile, surrender at Fort Buford, Dakota Territory.

JULY 20

1856: Handcart Migration of Mormons from Florence, Nebraska to Great Salt Lake begins. Thousands of Latter-day Saints will cross the prairies pushing their belongings in front of them in wheelbarrow-type vehicles.

1860: The first gold coins are produced in Colorado.

1878: A coroner's jury decides that A.A. McSween and the others killed during the battle at his home were resisting arrest.

1889: Cattle forces, mad over what they believe to be encroaching settlers, lynch James Averell and Ella Watson near Independence Rock in Wyoming Territory. Watson, known as "Cattle Kate," is the only woman ever hanged in Wyoming.

1920: Jack Johnson surrenders to authorities, having been convicted of violating the Mann Act. He is ordered to spend his sentence as athletic director at Leavenworth.

1924: Author Thomas Berger (*Little Big Man*) born in Cincinnati, Ohio.

1937: Possible death date of Butch Cassidy in Spokane, if we are to believe the historians who think Butch and the Kid evaded the military ambush in Bolivia.

1953: Twenty-two inches of hail reported at Dickinson, North Dakota.

JULY 21

1832: Henrietta Maria Morse Chamberlain, who, as the future widow of Richard King will build a cattle empire in Texas, is born in Boonville, Missouri.

1851: Outlaw Sam Bass born in Lawrence County, Indiana.

1865: The first western "duel" is fought, wherein the participants square off for a showdown on a main street. In this instance, Wild Bill Hickok and Dave Tutt meet at 6:00 P.M. on Market Square in Springfield, Missouri, after Tutt and Wild Bill have shown an interest in one Susanna Moore. A poker disagreement is the last straw. Tutt fires first, but Hickok fires best. He will be cleared of manslaughter charges. Soon after, Bill will make an unsuccessful run for mayor of Springfield.

1873: In their first train robbery, the James and Youngers derail a Rock Island train at Adair, Iowa, killing engineer John Rafferty and several passengers. They ride away with $2,000 amidst the wails of the injured.

1878: Sam Bass dies after a botched robbery at Round Rock, Texas. He is shot to death on July 19 by Texas Rangers, but holds on a couple of days until his 27th birthday.

1909: Bay City, Texas hurricane kills 41, does $2 million in damage.

1931: Pretty Boy Floyd blasts his way out of a trap set in Kansas City, Missouri, killing federal prohibition agent Curtis Burke.

1938: Author Owen Wister dies of a cerebral hemorrhage in Saunderstown, Rhode Island. As a memorial, a mountain in Wyoming's Grand Tetons is named for him.

JULY 22

1739: Party of Paul and Pierre Mallet reach Santa Fe, completing their western expedition.

1793: Alexander MacKenzie's party reaches the Pacific, completing the first continental crossing above Mexico, from Saskatchewan to Canada's Dean Channel.

1839: Railroad magnate David Moffat born in New York. In Colorado he will build the first railroad tunnel through the Continental Divide.

1846: Gen. Stephen Kearny arrives at Bent's Fort in southeastern Colorado.

1847: While an ill Brigham Young remains in a covered wagon, an advance party of 143 Mormons first set eyes on the land around the Great Salt Lake, dubbing it "the paradise of the lizard, the cricket and the rattlesnake."

1893: Educator Katharine Lee Bates, on holiday in Colorado, is inspired to write "America, the Beautiful," following a trip up Pikes Peak.

1916: A Preparedness Day parade in San Francisco ends in disaster when it is bombed by Warren Billings and Thomas Mooney. Ten are killed, 40 injured.

1918: A single bolt of lightning kills 504 sheep in Utah's Wasatch National Forest.

1920: The Prohibition Party, meeting in Lincoln, Nebraska, nominates Aaron Witkins for President.

JULY 23

1851: Treaty of Traverse des Sioux gives the United States Indian lands in Iowa and Minnesota.

1877: Angry workers, listening to speeches in San Francisco, go berserk and destroy several Chinese wash houses.

1892: Liquor sales on all Indian lands banned by Congress.

1911: *The Denver Post* announces "Greeley people live longer than any others in the world."

1921: Texas Klans claim responsibility for recent incidents of tarring and feathering.

1940: Author John Nichols (*The Milagro Beanfield War*) is born.

JULY 24

1766: Chief Pontiac surrenders to Sir William Johnson and the British at Oswego.

1832: Capt. Benjamin L.E. Bonneville leads 110 men and 20 wagons across the Continental Divide at South Pass in present Wyoming, the first wagons to make that crossing.

1846: Capt. John C. Fremont becomes a major in the newly formed California Battalion.

> **1847: The Mormons reach Utah ~** After many months on the trail, they reach their new home in Utah. Brigham Young reportedly signals the stopping point for his people at the Salt Lake valley, declaring, "This is the place."

1865: After a three-day march, Crazy Horse, Red Cloud, Young Man Afraid, Roman Nose, and others camp near Fort Casper in present Wyoming to plan their next battle.

1874: Floods at Eureka, Nevada kill 30.

1876: Explosion at the Black Diamond mine in Nortonville, California kills six.

1898: Aviatrix Amelia Earhart born in Atchison, Kansas. She will be the first woman to solo the Atlantic, and the first one to make the flight from Hawaii to California. She will disappear while attempting a round the world flight in 1937.

1907: Nine-year-old Amelia Earhart sees her first airplane at the Iowa State Fair in Des Moines.

1958: Jack Kilby, working for Texas Instruments in Dallas, draws the plans for the world's first silicone chip.

1977: Two thousand attend ceremonies at Ignacio, Colorado as Utes and Comanches settle a 200-year-old squabble over hunting rights.

JULY 25

1806: William Clark, on the Lewis and Clark expedition, carves his name at Pompey's Pillar, Montana.

1861: Confederate and Union troops in New Mexico have a brief skirmish.

1865: The two-day fight at Platte Bridge begins. Sioux Chief Crazy Horse leads a decoy party, but cavalry figure out the deception and get back to the fort before being caught by 3,000 warriors.

1868: Wyoming becomes a U.S. territory, created from Dakota Territory.

1871: Charles Richards of the Colt Firearms Company receives a patent to convert the Colt Army Model 1860 handgun to a cartridge loading design that will create the Peacemaker.

1877: As anti-Chinese riots continue in San Francisco, a lumberyard is burned. Firemen are detained by a mob from doing their job.

1878: Denver madame Mattie Silks puts $3,000 down on a house on Holliday Street, Denver's famed boulevard of ill repute, purchasing the house from the estate of Nellie French.

1882: With a postcard to a San Antonio newspaper, Roy Bean announces the first saloon west of the Pecos.

1887: Mormon Church president John Taylor, having conducted church affairs while on the lam for over two years, dies.

1895: Bannock Indians surround 250 settlers near Jackson Hole, Wyoming. They are upset over the ambush of their hunting party a month earlier. The 9th Cavalry is sent to disperse the Bannocks.

1901: Harvey Logan (Kid Curry) allegedly guns down Jim Winters for killing his brother Johnny Logan five years before. Curry waits in Winters' corral all night, then shoots his foe when he steps out on the front porch to brush his teeth.

1902: Frank Waters, author of *Masked Gods* and *Book of the Hopi* born in Colorado Springs, Colorado.

1939: Tuzigoot National Monument created in Arizona.

1974: Congresswoman Barbara Jordan of Houston delivers her "We, the people" speech concerning the impeachment of Richard Nixon.

JULY 26

1796: Artist George Catlin born in Wilkes-Barre, Pennsylvania. He will be among the first trained artists to capture Native Americans on canvas, thus providing a precious record of the Indian before the white man. His work will gain recognition, but when the government fails to purchase his collection, he will pack it up and go to Europe. When his exhibitions go deeply into the red, he will be forced to sell his collection to a Philadelphia magnate, and spend the rest of his days in poverty.

1827: Cherokees declare themselves a sovereign nation with a constitution heavily influenced by the United States Constitution.

1829: Ottawa, Chippewa, and Potawatomi Indians cede much of Michigan Territory to the United States.

1863: Sam Houston dies at age 70 in Huntsville, Texas. The man who played such a major role in the winning of Texas independence was convinced his life was a failure because of his state's secession from the Union during the Civil War. His last words are, "Texas, Texas! Margaret...."

JUDGE ROY BEAN

1865: Fight at the Platte Bridge ends as 3,000 warriors take only eight scalps; most of the troops remain inside the fort.

1878: Assistant Marshal Wyatt Earp helps put down a 3:00 A.M. disturbance by Texas cowboys in Dodge City, Kansas. He shoots gunman George Hoyt, who dies four weeks later from an infected wound. Hoyt will be the only man ever killed by Wyatt Earp in Dodge.

1885: Denver's Cherry Creek floods.

1895: Cherokee Bill murders prison guard Lawrence Keating at Fort Smith, Arkansas.

1943: Oklahoma heat record set at Tishomingo with 121 degrees.

JULY 27

1894: Horse thief Tom Smith wounds two and kills three U.S. marshals during a gun battle at

Muskogee, Oklahoma.

1931: Grasshoppers invade much of the West, causing widespread devastation in Iowa, Nebraska, and South Dakota.

1931: Oklahoma Gov. "Alfalfa" Bill Murray, quibbling with Texas over whether or not a Red River bridge should be toll free, extends his state's martial law to the Texas side, from Durant to Denison. A federal court steps in to put a stop to the "war."

1932: *Destry Rides Again* with Tom Mix released by Universal.

1959: *Last Train from Gun Hill* released by Paramount.

JULY 28

1849: The first clipper ship arrives in San Francisco from New York. The *Memnon* takes 120 days to complete the journey.

1862: Gold discovered at Grasshopper Creek, Montana. The town of Bannack springs up. Because of boundary confusion, the town was in Oregon in 1862, Idaho in 1863, Montana in 1864.

1864: Gen. Alfred Sully attacks Sitting Bull's camp at Killdeer Mountain, South Dakota.

1866: The U.S. 7th Cavalry is created by Congress.

1869: Explorer John Wesley Powell names Utah's Dirty Devil River.

1872: Editor C.W. Penrose of the Ogden, Utah, *Junction* is beaten senseless by a "pettifogging lawyer Keithly" who had received some bad press.

1881: A $10,000 reward is placed on the heads of Frank and Jesse James by Missouri Gov. Thomas Crittenden.

1922: Denver's Cherry Creek floods.

1923: During his western hiatus, President Harding contracts ptomaine poisoning.

1933: William Morris of Nueces County, Texas, receives the first government check for plowing under a crop, after he does so to his 47 acres of cotton.

1934: Hottest temperature ever in Idaho is recorded at Orofino: 118 degrees.

1943: Bill Bradley born in Crystal City, Missouri. He will play basketball for the New York Knicks before becoming a U.S. Senator from New Jersey.

1984: The XXIII Olympiad opens in Los Angeles, despite a boycott by the USSR and nations of the Eastern bloc.

JULY 29

1776: Escalante Expedition begins ~ Father Silvestre Velez de Escalante and Francisco Atanasio Dominguez will tour present Arizona, Utah, Colorado, and New Mexico and see, among other things, the Grand Canyon and the Great Salt Lake.

1842: Nevin Johnson Custer, George Armstrong's brother, is born.

1857: In the Battle at the Solomon River, Col. Edwin V. Sumner orders a saber charge against the Cheyenne.

1907: Big Bill Haywood is found Not Guilty of murdering former Idaho Gov. Frank Steunenberg.

1920: First transcontinental airmail arrives in San Francisco from New York.

1958: First cadets received at the Air Force Academy in Colorado Springs.

1986: Phoenix surpasses Denver as the largest city between St. Louis and the west coast. According to the U.S. Census Bureau, Phoenix ranks as the 21st most populated city with 1,846,600 people. Denver is 22nd with 1,827,100.

JULY 30

1923: Mass-murderer Roy Mitchell is the last person to be legally, publicly, hanged in Texas, before a crowd of 10,000 in Waco.

1934: *The Star Packer* with John Wayne is released by Lone Star/Monogram.

1946: First rocket to attain a 100-mile altitude is launched from White Sands, New Mexico.

1952: *High Noon* with Gary Cooper and Grace Kelly is released by United Artists.

JULY 31

1837: Civil War guerilla leader William Clarke Quantrill born in Canal Dover, Ohio.

1850: Territorial government established in Utah, formerly Deseret. Brigham Young is governor.

1855: President Pierce removes Andrew Reeder as Kansas governor, and installs pro-slaver Wilson Shannon.

1964: Singer Jim Reeves, 41, killed in a plane crash.

August

AUGUST 1

1770: Explorer William Clark who, with Meriwether Lewis will conduct the first major exploration of the Pacific Northwest, born in Caroline County, Virginia. William is the younger brother of George Rogers Clark, hero of western campaigns in the American Revolution.

1861: After defeating Union troops in New Mexico, Capt. John Baylor claims Arizona and New Mexico Territory for the Confederacy.

1867: The Hayfield Fight ~ Sioux, Cheyenne, and Arapaho Indians led by Dull Knife and Two Moon attack Second Lt. Sigismund Sternberg, eight troopers, and nine civilians in a Montana Territory hayfield. Though the battle can be seen from Fort C.F. Smith, no help is given. The Indians are finally scattered with Springfield rifles, but not before four are killed, including Sternberg.

1876: Colorado enters the Union as the 38th state. A territory since 1861, it has 200,000 inhabitants.

1903: Martha Jane Canary (Calamity Jane) dies at age 51 in a hotel room in Terry, near Deadwood, South Dakota. Her last request is to be buried next to her true love, Wild Bill Hickok.

1906: Over 30 years after the West's "Great Diamond Hoax," a real diamond mine, the only one in North America, is discovered by John Huddleston in Murfeesboro, Arkansas.

1917: I.W.W. agitator Frank Little, radical agitator for the Wobblies (International Workers of the World), is lynched near Butte, Montana.

1927: The Carter family is recorded for the first time. Their selections include, "Single Girl, Married Girl."

1931: Singer Ramblin' Jack Elliot born in Brooklyn, New York.

1941: Water is transported for the first time across the Mohave Desert and the San Bernardino Mountains to Los Angeles via the Colorado Aqueduct from Parker Dam in Arizona.

1947: Zane Gray's *Under the Tonto Rim* released by RKO.

1952: *The Big Sky* with Kirk Douglas released by Winchester/RKO.

1953: *Shane* with Alan Ladd released by Paramount.

1966: Charles Whitman murders his mother and his wife, then kills a total of 13 others with a high-powered rifle from his roost atop a tower on the University of Texas campus in Austin. He wounds another 31 before he is slain by police.

August

1976: On Colorado's 100th birthday, a flood on the Big Thompson River kills 139 while doing $30 million in damage. A 19-foot wall of water sweeps through Estes Park, wiping out several businesses.

1985: Wyoming's worst flash flood kills 12 and does $65 million in damage.

AUGUST 2

1832: Sauk and Fox Indians defeated in the Black Hawk War at the Bad Axe River in Wisconsin. After they surrender, several hundred are massacred by Illinois militia. Black Hawk escapes the slaughter.

1846: Gen. Kearny's army marches from Bent's Fort in Colorado toward New Mexico.

1862: First Idaho newspaper, the *Golden Age*, is published at Lewiston.

1862: Gold discovered at Boise Basin, Idaho.

> **1867: The Wagon Box Fight** ~ Red Cloud and Crazy Horse lead 1,000 Sioux against Maj. Powell and infantry guarding woodcutters near Fort Phil Kearny in Wyoming. Powell and his 30 men "circle the wagons," remove the wheels, and repulse three charges. Their secret is a .50 caliber Allin-Springfield rifles that offer rapid fire, a distinct innovation over the muzzle loaders Red Cloud believed the whites would have. Powell loses seven men and has another three wounded. Red Cloud counts 200 dead warriors.

1873: San Francisco's cable cars get a trial run, on the Clay Street Hill between Kearny and Jones, climbing a 307-foot grade.

> **1876: Wild Bill Hickok murdered** ~ Wild Bill sits down to his last game of poker in Deadwood Saloon No. 10. His requests to the other players to let him change seats so his back will not be to the door are scoffed at. At 4:15 P.M., W.B. is staring at a hand of aces and eights when a drunken Jack McCall stomps in, yells, "Take that, damn you," and puts a bullet in the back of his head. At the time of his death, Bill was carrying a .32 caliber Smith & Wesson Model No. 2 revolver.

1882: Roy Bean is appointed a justice of the peace by Texas Ranger Capt. T.L. Oglesby.

1905: Actress Myrna Loy, who will gain fame as Nora Charles in "The Thin Man" series, is born in Raidersburg, Montana.

1963: Author Oliver La Farge (*Laughing Boy*) dies at age 83.

1973: Famed Texas whorehouse "The Chicken Ranch" near La Grange closed down by authorities.

WILD BILL HICKOK

AUGUST 3

1859: Comanches officially expelled from Texas.

1866: Col. Henry B. Carrington sends two of his seven infantry companies from Fort Phil Kearny to establish Fort C.F. Smith on the Bighorn River.

1876: Wild Bill Hickok buried at Deadwood in Dakota Territory.

1877: Black Bart leaves his first poem after a California stagecoach robbery:
> *I've labored long and hard for bread*
> *For honor and for riches*
> *But on my corns too long you've tred*
> *You fine haired Sons of Bitches.*

He signs it, "Black Bart, the PO8." A series of headaches begins for Wells Fargo authorities.

1879: Body of Wild Bill Hickok moved to Mount Moriah.

1918: Casa Grande ruins in Arizona designated a national monument.

1933: The Castlewood Dam breaks, flooding Cherry Creek in Colorado.

1940: Football star Lance Allworth born in Houston, Texas.

1954: George Trendle sells the rights to the *Lone Ranger* to Jack Wrather for $3 million.

1970: Hurricane Celia, with winds of 180 MPH kills 11 Texans, doing $453 million in damage.

AUGUST 4

1706: Juan de Ulibarri of Santa Fe establishes relations with friendly Apaches in the surrounding area.

1837: The United States turns down a Texas petition for statehood.

1846: After three weeks among the Sioux, Francis Parkman leaves Fort Laramie on his return trip to the east. His emotions are high but he is a physical wreck, thanks to dysentery caused by too much dog stew.

1855: Free-state supporters meet in Lawrence, Kansas and call for their own constitutional convention.

1873: Custer and the 7th Cavalry are attacked during the Yellowstone Expedition, while guarding railroad surveyors.

1889: Fire levels much of the business section of Spokane, Washington.

1931: After seeing oil prices drop from a dollar to 22 cents a barrel in seven months, Oklahoma Gov. "Alfalfa" Bill Murray shuts down 3,106 oil wells until prices return to normal.

1932: Pretty Boy Floyd captures former Tulsa cop H.W. Nave, steals his clothes, and drives away howling with laughter.

1944: C-47 Army transport crashes outside Atkinson, Nebraska, killing 28.

AUGUST 5

1858: Julia Holmes, 20, is the first white woman to climb Pikes Peak.

1878: Billy the Kid and two other Regulators shoot it out with an Atanacio Martinez' posse. Martinez shoots one of his own men, and the murder is blamed on the Kid.

1863: Sioux wipe out 59 Pawnee at Massacre Canyon, Nebraska.

1893: In Indian Territory, the Osage tribe refuses to sell to the U.S., two million acres near the Cherokee Strip.

1914: Kansas City Southern head-on train crash kills 47 near Tipton Ford, Missouri.

1922: Train wreck at Sulphur Springs, Missouri kills 34.

1953: Lawman and former Texas Ranger Ira Aten dies at age 89 in Burlingame, California.

AUGUST 6

1874: Belle Starr's husband Jim Reed is killed near Paris, Texas.

August

1877: Winds reaching 75 MPH rip Denver.

1880: May Killeen weds Buckskin Frank Leslie in Tombstone, a few weeks after Leslie killed her first husband, Mike.

1892: Actor Hoot Gibson born. He will light up the screen in films such as *Spirit of the West* and *Sunset Range*.

1924: Ex Doolin-Dalton gang member Roy Daugherty (Arkansas Tom) is killed in a shoot out with Joplin, Missouri authorities.

1934: The move begins to transfer $3 billion in gold bullion from the San Francisco to the Denver Mint.

> **1945:** The first atomic bomb, developed and tested in the New Mexico desert, is dropped on Hiroshima, Japan. The blast equals 20,000 tons of TNT. Four square miles of the city are vaporized; at least 80,000 die.

AUGUST 7

1844: Explorer John C. Fremont returns to St. Louis following two expeditions in the West in 1842 and 1843. Guide Kit Carson had taken him as far as the mouth of the Columbia River in present Washington.

1877: Nine hundred Cheyenne, including Chief Little Wolf, arrive at the Darlington Agency in Indian territory, present Oklahoma.

1881: James brothers rob Chicago-Alton Express of $1,500, outside Glendale, Missouri.

1904: Steele's Hollow Bridge washes away in a flood, unknown to a Missouri Pacific train passing near Eden, Colorado; 96 are killed.

1913: Samuel F. Cody, the Texas native who went from being a European Wild West show performer to an aviation pioneer, is killed during an airplane demonstration at Aldershot, England, at age 52.

AUGUST 8

1814: Esther Hobart McQuigg Slack Morris is born in Tioga County, New York. She will be instrumental in giving Wyoming women the vote as well as becoming this country's first distaff judge, holding court in South Pass City, Wyoming. Her statue will one day stand in the U.S. Capitol's Statuary Hall.

1878: Hottest day ever recorded in Denver, 105 degrees.

1883: President Chester A. Arthur makes the first official visit by a President to western Indians en route to a fishing vacation at Yellowstone. He is the guest of Shoshone Chief Washakie.

1901: Physicist Ernest O. Lawrence, inventor of the cyclotron and recipient of the 1939 Nobel prize, born in Canton, South Dakota.

1922: Actor Rory Calhoun born in Los Angeles.

1923: President Warren G. Harding dies of ptomaine poisoning in San Francisco.

1932: Singer Mel Tillis born.

1967: The *San Francisco Chronicle* says "an Eastern crime syndicate is trying to gain control of LSD and marijuana traffic in Haight-Ashbury district."

AUGUST 9

1805: Lt. Zebulon Pike sets out on his northern voyage from St. Louis, presumably to locate the source of the Mississippi River.

1809: Future Alamo hero William Barret Travis born in Saluda County, South Carolina.

1850: The borders of Texas and New Mexico are adjusted, redefining borders established by the New Mexican convention. Boundary lines between New Mexico and Texas are changed.

1877: The two-day Battle of Big Hole in the Nez Perce War begins, near the present border of Idaho and Montana.

1898: The Spanish-American War ends with Spain's surrender. The 105-day war "to free Cuba" is over.

1903: Tom Horn's attempted escape from a Cheyenne jail is thwarted. While running away, his head is grazed by a bullet from the gun of townsperson O.M. Eldrich. Horn is hauled back to the jailhouse.

1936: Colorado Gov. E.C. Johnson formally declares 1,300 square miles of his state, located in the Rocky Mountains, to be a part of the United States. It had been left out of the original Louisiana Purchase.

1945: The plutonium atomic bomb developed in New Mexico is dropped on Nagasaki during World War II.

1965: The explosion of a *Titan-2* missile silo in Searcy, Arkansas kills 53.

1969: Actress Sharon Tate, 26, and four friends are found murdered in her rented home in Benedict Canyon, outside Los Angeles. The 26-year-old wife of director Roman Polanski is the victim of a cult slaying, carried out by members of the Charles Manson "family."

AUGUST 10

1821: Missouri, population just over 65,000, enters the Union as the 24th state with the capital at Jefferson City.

1823: The first major military action against western Indians takes place as troops attack an Arikara village on the upper Missouri River, in retaliation for an attack on white trappers in the area.

1825: Osage Indians cede more of their lands with a treaty signed today at Council Grove, Kansas.

1903: One of Colorado's worst labor conflicts begins as miners strike at Cripple Creek.

1927: President Coolidge dedicates Mount Rushmore, where Gutzon Borglum intends to carve massive busts of four Presidents, in South Dakota's Black Hills.

1932: The original Rin Tin Tin dies in Hollywood, with Jean Harlow at his side.

1972: Artist Christo unfurls a great curtain he has used to drape Colorado's Rifle Gap.

1987: Eight tourists die when Colorado Highway Department worker dislodges a boulder on Berthoud Pass. The huge rock smashes into a tour bus.

AUGUST 11

1873: Custer battles Sioux Indians at Yellowstone following the August 4 attack.

1956: Artist Jackson Pollock, born in Cody, Wyoming, is killed in an automobile accident in New York.

1965: Racial disturbances known as the Watts Riots begin in Los Angeles. In six days, 35 will die and $40 million in damage will be done.

AUGUST 12

1820: Fur trading magnate Manuel Lisa, 49, dies in St. Louis.

1821: At Bexar (future San Antonio) Texas, Stephen Austin arrives

August 121

to take the lands given to his late father by the Mexican government.

1840: The Battle of Plum Creek ~ Following a Comanche raid on Victoria and Linnville (coastal towns on Tavaca Bay) citizens escape by boat and watch while Comanches ransack the towns. Texas troops and soldiers track the Comanches to Plum Creek, get back much of the booty, and kill 80.

1842: Lawman David J. Cook born in Laporte County, Indiana. During his life he will arrest 3,000 outlaws in Colorado.

1853: A head, identified as that of bandit Joaquin Murieta, goes on a bizarre national tour, along with the hand of Manuel "Three-Fingered Jack" Garcia. They are a public curiosity, pickled in whisky. The head will be lost in the San Francisco earthquake of 1906.

1859: *Pike's Peak, or The Search for Riches* by F.H. Conway debuts in New York.

1860: Attorney/adventurer Temple Houston, son of Sam, born in Austin, Texas when his father is 67.

1890: The Brown Palace Hotel has its grand opening in Denver.

1896: The discovery of gold in Canada's Klondike Creek will set off yet another gold rush.

1919: The first flight over the Rocky Mountains goes from Glenwood Springs, Colorado to Denver.

1929: Singer Buck Owens ("Act Naturally," "I've Got a Tiger by the Tail") born in Sherman, Texas. He will also star on TV's "Hee-Haw."

1930: Singer Porter Wagoner ("The Cold Hard Facts of Life") born in West Plains, Missouri.

1936: Hottest day in Texas is recorded at Seymour -- 120 degrees.

1946: The Indian Claims Commission is established to handle all Indian claims against the United States regardless of where they occurred in history.

ANNIE OAKLEY
Born: August 13, 1860
Died: November 3, 1926
Markswoman

1866: Father dies; will be shuffled between foster homes, some good, some bad.
1872: Rejoins her mother, provides for the family by hunting.
1875: At 15, defeats Frank Butler at a shooting match at Cincinnati.
1882: Marries Frank Butler, who will manage her show business career.
1884: Tours with the Sells Brothers Circus at Columbus, Ohio.
1885: Joins Buffalo Bill's Wild West, in which she will star for 17 years.
1887: Defeats Grand Duke Michael of Russia during a British shooting match.
1889: Shoots a cigarette from the lips of Germany's Crown Prince Wilhelm.
1901: Critically injured in a train wreck near Lexington, Kentucky.
1903: Walks again after five operations. Resumes limited public exhibitions.
1912: Tours with Cody's farewell show.
1918: Demonstrates shooting technique for soldiers.
1922: Auto accident; never walks again.
1926: Dies at age 66.

1984: Closing ceremonies of the XXIII Olympiad in Los Angeles.

AUGUST 13

1846: Cmdr. Robert F. Stockton and the American fleet seize Los

Angeles, claiming California as a U.S. territory.

1860: Phoebe Ann Moses who, as Annie Oakley, will astound audiences of Buffalo Bill's Wild West with her incredible sharpshooting, is born in Darke County, Ohio.

1878: Billy the Kid, having escaped a posse, arrives at one of John Chisum's ranches. Before the month is out, he will demand $500 in back wages for his Regulators.

1912: Golfer Ben Hogan born in Dublin, Texas. He will win the U.S. Open in 1948, '50, '51, '53, the Masters in 1951 and 1953, and many other major tournaments. He is inducted into the PGA Hall of Fame in 1953.

1917: Author William Verne Athanas (*Maverick*) born in Cleft, Idaho.

AUGUST 14

1806: Davy Crockett marries Polly Finley in Jefferson County, Tennesse.

1831: Vigilante John Xavier Beidler born in Mountjoy, Pennsylvania. He will operate a saloon in Atchison, Kansas, then leave for Alder Gulch, Montana where he will participate in dozens of lynchings.

1842: Eight years of Indian wars in Florida end. Removal of native tribes begins immediately, but some Seminoles hold out in the Everglades.

1846: Francis Parkman passes through present Colorado.

1848: Territory of Oregon is created.

1862: City of Golden is approved as Colorado's territorial capital.

1903: Jim Jeffries whips Gentleman Jim Corbett in San Francisco.

WILL ROGERS

1923: Frontier Mine in Kemmerer, Wyoming, explodes killing 99.

1959: The American Football League, which will put professional teams in Houston, Dallas, Denver, Los Angeles, and Oakland, is formed in Chicago.

AUGUST 15

1805: Lewis and Clark reach the Continental Divide.

1806: John Colter leaves the Lewis and Clark expedition to trap beaver with two mountain men in the Yellowstone country.

1824: Cattleman John Simpson Chisum, a key figure in New Mexico's bloody Lincoln County War, born in Madison County, Tennessee.

1846: Gen. Kearny declares New Mexico part of the United States.

1846: *The Californian*, the state's first newspaper, is published in Monterey.

1850: Territory of New Mexico is created in Congress on the fourth anniversary of its declaration as a U.S. possession.

1870: Kansas Pacific crews join rails linking Denver with the east near Strasburg, Colorado.

1887: Edna Ferber, author of *So Big* and *Cimarron* born in Kalamazoo, Michigan.

August 123

1912: Cooking expert Julia Child born in Pasadena, California.

1935: A plane crash in Alaska claims the lives of pilot Wiley Post and humorist Will Rogers.

WILL ROGERS
Born: November 3, 1879
Died: August 15, 1935
Humorist

1880s: Attends six schools, including a military academy.
1898: Quits school to be a cowboy in Texas.
1901: Gaucho in Argentina. Tours Africa in a Wild West show.
1903: Tours Australia and New Zealand.
1904: Tells his family he will stay in show business.
1905: Madison Square Garden debut.
1908: Marries Betty Blake.
1913: Appears in Ziegfield's "Midnight Frolic" review.
1916: Star of Ziegfield Follies.
1919: First of 15 motion pictures: *The Roping Fool*. First of seven books: *The Peace Conference*.
1920s: Regularly heard on radio.
1922: Begins weekly column in *New York Times*, which will subsequently be syndicated nationally, and will be written until his death, over a thousand columns.
1930s: Aids disaster victims in Florida, Mississippi, and Nicaragua.
1934: #1 motion picture box office attraction.
1935: Killed in Alaskan plane crash at the height of his career.

AUGUST 16

1826: Jedediah Smith sets out on the first expedition overland from Utah to California. His party will travel from the Great Salt Lake through Cajon Pass.

1856: Texan Gail Borden patents a milk concentrating process that will evolve into the creation of condensed milk. He gets the idea from mothers' long trips with their children at sea.

1878: Family quarrel breaks out at Henry Beckwith's ranch near Seven Rivers, New Mexico. Beckwith does away with son-in-law William Johnson in one blast from his shotgun.

1889: Outlaw Bob Younger dies of tuberculosis at the Minnesota State Prison.

1896: Discovery of gold in the Klondike region finds many western prospectors heading north.

1909: This will be the last day it rains in San Bernardino County, California until May 6, 1912.

1915: A tropical storm floods Waco, Houston, Galveston, and Taylor, Texas, killing 101.

1925: Actor Fess Parker, who will gain fame in the 1950s as Walt Disney's Davy Crockett, born in Fort Worth, Texas.

1930: Actor Robert Culp, star of TV's "Trackdown", born in Oakland, California.

1986: The last of Colorado's nine Neusteters stores closes in Denver, ending 75 years in the retail business in that city.

AUGUST 17

1786: David Crockett born in Greene County, Tennessee. Arguably the first western hero, he will battle Indians with Andrew Jackson, serve in the U.S. House of Representatives, and die fighting at the Alamo. In addition to being an authentic American hero, he will be known for his backwoods wit, and win many political battles by making his opponents look ridiculous. His popularity will become even stronger after his death and more than 100 years after the fact, he will become a television pop phenomenon.

> **DAVY CROCKETT**
> **Born:** August 17, 1786
> **Died:** March 6, 1836
> **Indian fighter, Congressman, Alamo defender**
>
> **1813:** Enlistment runs out during the Creek War. He returns home for a Christmas break.
> **1814:** Re-enlists to fight the Creek Indians.
> **1817:** Becomes Justice of the Peace of Lawrence County, Tennessee.
> **1818:** Becomes town commissioner of Lawrenceburg, Tennessee.
> **1821:** Resigns to run for the Tennessee legislature.
> **1824:** State political career ends when the Tennessee house adjourns.
> **1827:** Elected to U.S. House of Representatives.
> **1833:** First fictional exploits appear.
> **1834:** Has speaking engagements throughout the east.
> **1835:** After being voted out of Congress, tells voters: "You can all go to hell. I'm going to Texas!"
> **1836:** Dies at the Battle of the Alamo.

1805: Lewis and Clark meet Sacajawea's brother, a chief of the Shoshones, as they approach the Bitterroot Mountains.

1833: The Mexican Congress decides to secularize missions, which will take four years to complete.

1846: Cmdr. Stockton annexes California to the United States, sets up a government, and makes himself governor.

1854: High Forehead, a Miniconjou Sioux, creates a tense situation after he kills an aging Mormon cow with an arrow on the Oregon Trail near Fort Laramie. Two days later, a confrontation will result.

1877: Billy the Kid shoots his first victim, Frank "Windy" Cahill, after Cahill calls him a "son of a bitch." Cahill will take one day to expire.

1896: George W. Carmack becomes the first to discover gold in Alaska, on the Klondike River.

FESS PARKER AS DAVY CROCKETT

1954: Walt Disney releases *The Vanishing Prairie*. He is surprised when it becomes his first banned film. New York censors take the action because the film depicts the birth of a buffalo.

1978: Three New Mexicans become the first to cross the Atlantic in a balloon. They cover 3,100 miles in five days, 17 hours, and six minutes, from Maine to France.

1981: The skeleton of a Tyrannosaurus Rex, buried 65 million years, is found in Haystack Butte, South Dakota, the sixth such skeleton to be discovered on earth.

AUGUST 18

1774: Explorer Meriwether Lewis

August

born in Albemarle County, Virginia. In addition to leading the famous expedition with William Clark, he will serve as a private secretary to President Jefferson from 1801-1803, and become the first governor of Louisiana Territory from 1807-1809.

1846: Gen. Stephen Kearny occupies Santa Fe after an 800-mile march from Leavenworth.

1856: Kansas Territorial Governor Shannon resigns, to be replaced by pro-slaver Daniel Woodson.

1862: Santee Sioux Indians in Minnesota under Chief Little Crow, angry because government supplies have not arrived, begin a six-week massacre of some 350 whites. Over 600 male Indians will be arrested for the outbreak; 38 will be hanged.

1870: An era ends as the last overland stagecoach arrives in Denver.

1877: Frank "Windy" Cahill expires, thus becoming the first man to be killed by Billy the Kid.

1895: Fire at Denver's Gumry Hotel kills 22.

1913: Jack London's Wolf House, his San Francisco home, burns.

1925: A severe hailstorm wipes out many Iowa farms.

1937: Actor Robert Redford born in Santa Monica, California. His Western roles will include Harry Longabaugh in *Butch Cassidy and the Sundance Kid*. He will also direct, and be known for his active support of western environmental issues.

1939: Singer Molly Bee born in Oklahoma City, Oklahoma.

1983: Hurricane Alicia hits Texas, killing 21 and doing $1.6 billion in damage in the Houston and Galveston areas.

AUGUST 19

1782: Battle of Blue Ticks, the last battle of the American Revolution and the last organized Indian attack in Kentucky, is fought. Wyandots and British officers inflict heavy casualties on pursuing settlers, including 23-year-old Israel Boone, who dies in his father Daniel's arms.

1804: The only casualty of the Lewis and Clark expedition, Sgt. Charles Floyd, becomes ill. He dies the following day, of "Biliose Chorlick," akin to a ruptured appendix.

1846: Gen. Zachary Taylor begins his advance on Monterey during the Mexican War.

1848: The *New York Herald* reports the California gold discovery.

> **1854: The Grattan Fight** ~ Lt. John L. Grattan, looking for a reason to teach local Sioux a lesson following High Forehead's August 17 murder of a Mormon cow, orders his men to fire into a camp of Brules. Chief Conquering Bear is killed. Oglalas and Brules swoop down on Grattan's forces and kill all 30 infantry men. This is the first armed confrontation between the U.S. Army and the Teton Sioux.

1872: In Wyoming, the *Laramie Daily Independent* reports on "The Great Diamond Fields of America." Two Kentucky cousins, Philip Arnold and John Slack, have salted a secret mesa in Colorado with uncut diamonds purchased in Europe. The scam will reach dizzying proportions, and involve some very influential people before it is exposed by future U.S. Geological Survey head Clarence King.

1895: Outlaw John Wesley Hardin, 41, is shot to death in the Acme Saloon in El Paso, Texas by John Selman.

1906: Inventor Philo Taylor Farnsworth born on a sheep ranch in Beaver, Utah. One of the fathers of television, he will eventually hold 165 registered patents, covering a variety of video applications including power, focusing, contrast, scanning, and synchronization.

1931: Jockey Willie Shoemaker born in Fabens, Texas.

AUGUST 20

1794: Gen. Mad Anthony Wayne claims to defeat 2,000 Ohio Indians at the Battle of Fallen Timbers, ending hostilities in that area.

1846: Francis Parkman's party, returning to the East, reaches the Pueblo in present Colorado, on the Arkansas River.

1871: A bloody shoot out in Newton, Kansas: Cowboy Hugh Anderson avenges the death of friend, William Bailey, by blasting Mike McCluskie in Perry Tuttle's saloon. A huge fight breaks out wherein four die and three are wounded, including Anderson.

1905: Jazzman Jack Teagarden born in Vernon, Texas.

1910: Fires in drought-stricken Idaho end, taking 85 lives and three million acres. Smoke from the blazes spreads a third of the way around the world.

1923: Singer Jim Reeves ("Welcome to My World") born in Galloway, Texas.

1923: Al Spencer robs his first and only train at Okesa, Oklahoma.

1971: Texas Instruments introduces the world's first pocket calculator, priced at $149.

AUGUST 21

1863: The Raid on Lawrence occurs at dawn as Quantrill's Raiders, a group of 450 irregular Confederates, thunder into the Kansas town, an abolitionist stronghold. In three hours, they level the city, burning many buildings and homes, and slaughtering 150 male residents. With Quantrill are future wild west figures Frank James and Cole Younger.

1877: Dodge City trigger man George Hoyt dies of gunshot wounds received from Wyatt Earp on July 26.

1883: The trial of Frank James begins in Gallatin, Missouri. To accommodate the crowds, it is held in an opera house. James will be acquitted.

AUGUST 22

1828: Napoleon Boone, grandson of Daniel, is the second white child and first white boy born in present Kansas, at the Kansa Agency. The first was Lucia F. Pixley in 1826 or 1827, but the exact date cannot be determined.

1891: An electric street railway system begins operations in Boise, Idaho.

1911: President Taft vetoes Arizona statehood because of its constitution which provides for the recall of judges.

1923: During a gasoline war in Los Angeles, prices drop to six cents per gallon.

1986: The Kerr-McGee Corporation agrees to pay Karen Silkwood's estate $1.38 million, ending a ten-year-old contamination lawsuit. The settlement concludes a long, bitter struggle that began when employee Silkwood, attempting to report Kerr-McGee irregularities, was mysteriously killed in an auto accident.

AUGUST 23

1872: The first Japanese commercial vessel to arrive in San Francisco carries a cargo of tea.

1877: Brigham Young, 76, dies of peritonitis in the Mormon Utah he founded. His $2.5 million estate will be divided among 17 wives and 48 children.

1877: With no legal authority to operate in Florida, Ranger John Armstrong arrests John Wesley Hardin on a train in Pensacola. Armstrong kills Jim Mann and pistol whips Hardin unconscious. He then arrests Hardin's three suite mates and hauls them back to Texas.

1883: President Chester A. Arthur visits Yellowstone.

1897: The first Cheyenne Frontier Days celebration is held in Wyoming.

1899: First ship-to-shore wireless telegraph message is sent from a lightship to the Cliff House in San Francisco.

1930: Actress Vera Miles born in Boise City, Idaho.

1933: Cedar Breaks National Monument is created in Utah.

1945: Lawman Elfego Baca, age 80, dies in Albuquerque, New Mexico.

1947: Presidential daughter Margaret Truman makes her singing debut at the Hollywood Bowl.

AUGUST 24

1821: Mexico, which at this time includes the province of New Mexico, gains her independence from Spain.

1869: When inebriated soldier John Mulrey resists arrest, Hays City Sheriff Wild Bill Hickok blasts him with his .45. Mulrey dies the next morning.

1873: William Henry Jackson becomes the first man to photograph Colorado's elusive Mount of the Holy Cross. Rumored about for years, the mountain is secluded among other peaks in the Rockies near Leadville. Thousands of years of erosion have left deep ravines crossing at a 90-degree angle that have filled with snow. To get the perfect dawn exposure, Jackson's party camps overnight on Notch Mountain without food or shelter. Jackson is not to be disappointed.

1930: *Spurs* with Hoot Gibson released by Universal.

AUGUST 25

1540: Hernando de Alarcon leaves Acapulco to explore the Sea of Cortes, the future Gulf of California.

1829: Mexico turns down a request from President Jackson to buy Texas for the U.S.

1836: Author Bret Harte born in

Albany, New York. In 1868 he will become editor of San Francisco's *Overland Monthly* where many of his most famous stories, including "The Luck of Roaring Camp" and "The Outcasts of Poker Flat" will see print for the first time.

1863: Twenty thousand are left homeless in Kansas City, Kansas, following Quantrill's Lawrence raid, as Union officials go on an anti-guerilla search-and-seize procedure. In four Missouri counties, Order No. 11 is in effect, driving all residents from their homes.

1877: History's first duel between women happens on the main streets of Denver. Madam Mattie Silks is none too pleased with the advances Kate Fulton has been making toward her beau, Cort Thomson. The two choose their pistols, square off, and fire. They miss each other, but Thomson receives a flesh wound in the neck. No one is sure from which gun the shot came. A fistfight breaks out between the ladies. Kate gets a broken nose and leaves town the next day.

1896: Outlaw Bill Doolin killed by a posse in Oklahoma. Bill Dunn puts 21 holes in him with one shotgun blast.

1933: Zane Grey's *Man of the Forest* with Randolph Scott released by Paramount.

AUGUST 26

1806: The Pike party abandons boats to begin its trip across the Great Plains.

1873: Inventor Lee De Forest born in Council Bluffs, Iowa. In addition to inventing the first electronic sound amplification system in 1906, he will develop the process for putting sound on film and revolutionize the movie industry in 1923.

1879: Rancher John Beckwith is slain by rustler John Jones during a cattle argument in Lincoln County, New Mexico.

1891: A rain making experiment works in Midland, Texas, which hadn't seen a drop since 1888.

1907: Underwater at San Francisco's Aquatic Park, Harry Houdini escapes from chains in 57 seconds.

1930: Actor Lon Chaney, 47, dies in Los Angeles.

AUGUST 27

1832: Black Hawk surrenders, turned over to the U.S. by the Winnebagos with whom he was living. After a year in jail, he will return to his family, and die in 1838.

1872: Flathead Indians cede their Montana lands to the United States.

1875: Financier William Ralston, major San Francisco executive, drowns in San Francisco Bay shortly after the board of directors of his bank requests his resignation. Whether his death is accidental or a suicide is never determined.

1915: Wife of Gen. John Pershing and three of his children die in a fire in San Francisco.

1916: Actress Martha Raye born in

August

Butte, Montana.

1954: A B-36 bomber crashes while attempting a landing at Ellsworth AFB in San Diego, California, killing 24.

1958: Cyclotron inventor Ernest O. Lawrence dies at age 57.

AUGUST 28

1857: Fort Abercrombie, a military outpost, established in Dakota Territory.

1869: Seneca Howland, O.G. Howland, and William H. Dunn separate from John Wesley Powell's first exploration party down the Colorado River, having endured enough danger for one summer. They climb the north rim of the Grand Canyon, where they are met and killed by Paiute Indians.

1872: Wild Bill Hickok lends his fame to a Grand Buffalo Hunt at Niagara Falls. It will be a financial failure. Wild Bill's take is larger than the gate receipts.

1908: Lyndon Baines Johnson, 36th U.S. President, born near Stonewall, Texas.

1934: Writer Upton Sinclair wins the California Democratic gubernatorial nomination. He will lose by a small margin in November.

1963: Potash mine explosion in Moab, Utah kills 18.

AUGUST 29

1839: Samuel Colt receives patent on his famed "Walker" model pistol, a larger revolver with new innovations.

1877: John Tunstall establishes the Lincoln County Bank.

1881: "The True Life of Billy the Kid" is published in *The Five Cent Wide Awake Library*.

1891: Joyce Clyde Hall, who will found Hallmark Cards Inc. in 1913, born in David City, Nebraska.

1966: The Beatles play their last live concert in San Francisco's Candlestick Park.

AUGUST 30

1856: Violence over the slavery question continues in Kansas. At Osawatomie, John Brown and 40 backers are driven out by Kansas militia.

1861: Maj. Gen. John C. Fremont, in charge of the western department and stationed in St. Louis, declares martial law in Missouri when unscrupulous characters add to his troubles there. President Lincoln will remove him from command shortly after he confiscates Missouri lands and pronounces all slaves emancipated.

1868: Maj. George A. "Sandy" Forsyth and "50 first-class hardy frontiersmen" march toward Fort Wallace, near present Wallace, Kansas, on a search for Indians that will culminate in the Battle of Beecher's Island.

1869: Maj. John Wesley Powell and five others complete the first journey down the Green and Colorado Rivers, emerging at the mouth of the Virgin River in Arizona. All hope for their survival had been abandoned; Mormon rescuers were fishing with nets for the crew's remains.

1869: The first shipment of tea overland arrives in San Francisco from Chicago. Williams, Butters, and Co. imported 90 baskets.

1870: An "all-Pullman" palace-car excursion leaves St. Louis for Denver.

1874: Gen. Nelson A. Miles battles

mixed forces of Southern Cheyennes, Comanches, and Kiowas in the Palo Duro Canyon of Texas in the first battle of what will become the Red River War to force Indians onto the reservation.

1918: Singer Kitty Wells ("It Wasn't God Who Made Honky Tonk Angels") born in Nashville, Tennessee.

1919: Author Mari Sandoz divorces Wray Macumber in Nebraska, citing "extreme mental cruelty."

1931: Martial law declared in portions of Idaho due to arsonists setting forest fires.

1936: The second Presidential head to be unveiled at Mount Rushmore is that of Thomas Jefferson.

1984: A dozen separate fires in Montana burn some 250,000 acres, jumping such natural barriers as the 100-yard wide Missouri River.

AUGUST 31

1803: Lewis and Clark descend the Ohio River, the first leg of their western journey.

1901: Great Northern train wreck near Nyack, Montana kills 34.

1903: First automobile to complete a cross-country trip under under its own power, a Winton, arrives in New York from San Francisco in 63 days.

1928: Actor James Coburn born in Laurel, Nebraska. Among his westerns will be *Pat Garret and Billy the Kid*, *Major Dundee*, and *Magnificent Seven*.

1933: Denver's Cherry Creek floods.

1964: California has the highest population of any state in the nation, according to statistics released today by the Census Bureau.

1965: Alibates Flint Quarries in Texas is designated as a national monument.

1973: Western movie director John Ford dies in Palm Desert, California.

THE POWELL EXPEDITION

September

SEPTEMBER 1

1821: Trade along the Santa Fe Trail is initiated as William Becknell leads a wagon train out of St. Louis toward New Mexico.

1836: The Whitman Party, the first group to make the overland crossing with several women, arrives in Walla Walla, in present-day Washington. The wagon train of missionaries was led by Dr. Marcus Whitman through South Pass.

1838: Explorer William Clark of the Lewis and Clark expedition dies at age 68.

1870: The day Calamity Jane claimed that she was married to Wild Bill Hickok in a ceremony on the prairie performed by two itinerant ministers.

1877: Fearing an uprising while Crazy Horse is in captivity following his surrender, Gen. Phil Sheridan wires Gen. George Crook: "I think your presence more necessary at Red Cloud Agency than at Camp Brown and wish you to get off at Sidney and go there."

1893: U.S. deputy marshals shoot it out with the Doolin Gang at Ingalls, Oklahoma in the Cherokee Strip. They tell Doolin's bunch to come out of the Ransom and Murray Saloon, but Bill Doolin tells them to go to hell. Three of 13 marshals are killed. Roy "Arkansas Tom" Daugherty is arrested. Doolin escapes.

1894: Fire, whipped by a hurricane, wipes out Hinckley, Minnesota, killing 500.

1933: Singer Conway Twitty born Harold Lloyd Jenkins in Friars Point, Michigan.

1957: *3:10 to Yuma* with Glenn Ford is released by Columbia.

1959: *The Oregon Trail* released by 20th Century Fox.

1972: Mexican American political group La Raza Unida founded at El Paso, Texas.

SEPTEMBER 2

1846: The Donner Party moves across the alkali flats south of the Great Salt Lake on its ill-fated journey to California.

1885: Anti-Chinese riots in Rock Springs, Wyoming claim 28 lives.

1901: Basketball coach Adolph Rupp born in Halstead, Kansas. At Kentucky University, he will earn a niche in the Basketball Hall of Fame for his record 879 wins from 1930-1977.

1919: Employee Orville Harrington takes home his first gold bar from the Denver Mint. In the days of minimum security, Harrington will slip more than 80 such bars in his wooden leg (one every night or so) before he is nabbed by authorities.

SEPTEMBER 3

1806: Zebulon Pike expedition begins the overland portion of its exploration, entering southeast Kansas.

1851: The London *Morning Chronicle* criticizes California's "Committee of Vigilance."

> **1855: The Battle of Blue Water** – Brig. Gen W.S. Harney and soldiers attack Little Thunder's Brule Sioux, camped on the Bluewater River north of the North Platte River in Nebraska, in retaliation for an earlier raid. Of 250 Indians, 86 are killed and 70 women and children are captured. A teenaged Crazy Horse returns to the camp from a hunt and witnesses a new kind of brutal warfare.

1863: Lawman Ira Aten born in Cairo, Illinois.

1868: U.S. Army captures a Santee Sioux village at White Stone.

1913: Actor Alan Ladd born in Hot Springs, Arkansas. In 1953, he will play the ultimate drifter in *Shane*.

1964: The National Wilderness Preservation System is created.

1970: Largest recorded hailstone in U.S. history falls on Coffeyville, Kansas. It weighs one and three-eighths pounds and has a circumference of 17.5 inches.

SEPTEMBER 4

1781: Los Angeles is founded.

1802: Missionary Marcus Whitman born in Rushville, New York. He will lead settlers to the Pacific Northwest before meeting an untimely end at the hands of Cayuse Indians.

1877: After Lt. William Clark offers $100 to anyone at Camp Rogers who will murder Crazy Horse, 400 Indians and eight cavalry companies leave for the chief's lodge, six miles distant. At the Spotted Tail Agency to receive medical treatment for his wife, he is persuaded to go back home.

1878: General Lew Wallace is appointed governor of New Mexico by President Hayes, in hopes of putting down the bloody Lincoln County War. While in New Mexico, he will do the majority of his work on his Biblical epic, *Ben Hur*.

> **1886:** Geronimo surrenders to Gen. Nelson A. Miles at Skeleton Canyon in Arizona Territory. He will be kept a prisoner of war in Fort Marion, Florida, then will be moved to Oklahoma, where he will remain until his death in 1909.

1917: The first American officer to be killed in World War I is 1st Lt. William Fitzsimmons of Kansas. An army hospital in Denver will be named in his honor.

1951: President Truman's address at the Japanese Peace Treaty Conference in San Francisco is the nation's first transcontinental television broadcast.

1970: Worst flood in Arizona's history sweeps cars as far as 40 miles and kills 23.

1972: The first horse race with a $1 million purse is run at the All-American Futurity in Ruidoso, New Mexico.

SEPTEMBER 5

1847: Outlaw Jesse Woodson James born in Missouri. His exploits as a daring Robin Hood are largely a rural fantasy. In fact he robs from everyone, keeps the money, and kills plenty of people in the process. The most famous gunslinger of the Old West, Jesse was bad to the bone. In the end, he will be assassinated and will take his place in history as the most charismatic of the border thugs.

1867: First railroad shipment of cattle bound for the east coast leaves Abilene, Kansas.

JESSE JAMES
Born: September 5, 1847
Died: April 3, 1882
Outlaw

1864: Participates in Bloody Bill Anderson's raid on Centralia, Missouri.
1866: Robs first bank, the Clay County Savings & Loan of Liberty, Missouri.
1867: Robs Richmond, Missouri bank, killing three.
1868: With Frank and Youngers, robs the Southern Bank of Kentucky at Russellville.
1871: Robs Corydon, Iowa bank of $4,000.
1872: Robs the Columbia Kentucky Deposit Bank, kills a teller. Robs Savings Association Bank of $4,000. Steals gate receipts from Kansas City Fair.
1873: First train robbery; James and Youngers derail a Rock Island train at Adair, Iowa, killing engineer, John Rafferty and several passengers.
1874: Robs Concord Stage at Malvern, Arkansas. More train and bank robberies.
1875: Pinkertons bomb Samuel home.
1875: Robs a Texas stagecoach of $3,000. Steals $75,000 from a Missouri-Pacific Express train near Otterville, Missouri.
1876: Great Northfield Minnesota Bank Raid.
1879: Robs the Chicago and Alton Express outside Glendale, Missouri of $35,000.
1881: Robs Riverton, Iowa bank of $5,000. Robs train near Winston, Missouri; kills engineer and passenger; $10,000 reward placed on his head.
1882: Assassinated by Robert Ford at his home in Missouri.

1877: Chief Crazy Horse is murdered as he is being led to a cramped cell at Fort Robinson, Nebraska. When he sees the tiny quarters, he bolts and resists. Soldier William Gentles stabs him with a bayonet. Crazy Horse lies in agony in the adjutant's office, while his parents are kept outside and prevented from seeing their son. At 11:40, the Strange Man of the Oglalas dies. He was approximately 36 years old.

1881: Denver's Tabor Grand Opera House has its grand opening. The Opera House is a monument of sorts, erected by Silver King Horace Tabor. His kingdom goes bust when the silver market fails. Barely a decade later, he is found sitting in the balcony sobbing, his opera house having gone into receivership.

1925: During a wild party in San Francisco, actress Virginia Rappe dies after accusing movie comic Roscoe "Fatty" Arbuckle of viciously raping her. Arbuckle will be acquitted after three trials, but his film career is destroyed.

SEPTEMBER 6

1844: Second Fremont expedition sees the Great Salt Lake for the first time," stretching in still and solitary grandeur."

1873: David Roberts shoots and kills Peter Welsh and George Summer in front of Cy Goddard's saloon in Hays City, Kansas.

1877: Dispatch from Camp Robinson, Nebraska: "Crazy Horse died at midnight. His people took his body, and all is quiet this morning."

1895: A posse led by Bill Tilghman captures Doolin gang member Little Bill Raidler on a ranch near Elgin, Kansas.

1939: California floods claim 45.

1950: UPI reports that J. Frank Dalton, 102 and still claiming to be Jesse James, is ill in an Austin hospital.

1966: Birth control leader Margaret Sanger dies in Tucson.

1975: Assassination attempt on President Ford is thwarted in Sacramento as authorities apprehend former Manson gang member Lynette "Squeaky" Fromme.

1984: Singer Ernest Tubb dies at age 70.

SEPTEMBER 7

1778: Nearly 400 Shawnees and French Canadian allies surround and lay siege to Boonesborough, but withdraw after negotiations, fire arrows, and tunneling fail to capture it.

> **1876: The Great Northfield, Minnesota Bank Raid** ~ The James and Younger brothers attempt to rob the First National Bank of Northfield, Minnesota. Cashier Joseph Heywood is shot when he refuses the robber's demands. The citizens rally and trap the gang, killing Clell Miller and William Stiles. A posse kills Charlie Pitts. Cole, Jim, and a wounded Bob Younger are eventually captured and given life sentences in the state penitentiary. Frank and Jesse James are wounded, but not seriously.

1936: Rock singer/composer Buddy Holly born Charles Hardin Holley in Lubbock, Texas.

1936: Hoover/Boulder Dam begins operation. The construction, begun in 1931, included the diversion of the Colorado River by moving 3.5 million tons of earth. At peak production, 6,000 were employed for the construction. The dam, which measures 727 feet high and 1,244 feet across, weighs 88 million pounds.

1943: Fire at Houston's Gulf Hotel kills 55, injures 32.

1971: Actress Spring Byington, 77, dies in Los Angeles.

SEPTEMBER 8

1810: The *Tonquin* sails out of New York for Oregon, carrying 33 members of Astor's Pacific Fur Company. After a stopover in Hawaii, they will reach the Columbia River and establish Astoria.

1832: Miriam Young, first bride of Brigham Young, dies of tuberculosis.

1865: The U.S. Cavalry battles Sioux, Arapaho, and Cheyenne forces at Dry Fork on the Powder River in Wyoming.

1883: A northern transcontinental railroad between Duluth, Minnesota and Portland, Oregon is completed.

1897: Singer Jimmie Rodgers, "The Singing Brakeman," the acknowledged "father of country music" born in Meridian, Mississippi.

1900: This country's worst hurricane occurs in Galveston, Texas as a 20-foot tidal wave destroys half the city's homes, drowns 6,000 residents, and does $100 million in damage.

1907: Neiman-Marcus opens in Dallas.

1932: Singer Patsy Cline ("Crazy," "Sweet Dreams") born in Winchester, Virginia.

1965: "Don't eat grapes," becomes a rallying cry as Cesar Chavez and his National Farm Workers Union strike against California grape growers.

SEPTEMBER 9

1850: New Mexico and Utah become U.S. territories.

1850: California enters the Union as the 31st state. The state is in the second year of a four-year boom during the gold rush that will see her population mushroom from 15,000 to 250,000.

1876: Oglala Sioux Chief American Horse (Wasechuntashunka) is killed by the U.S. Army under the command of Gen. George Crook at the Battle of Slim Buttes during retaliatory attacks against the Indians following the Little Big Horn. The Chief surrenders after a severe stomach wound, and dies while Army surgeons operate.

1878: Chiefs Dull Knife and Little Wolf lead 335 Cheyenne from their agency located in Indian Territory. Their desire is to return to their northern homelands. Their epic exodus will be the subject of Mari Sandoz' book *Cheyenne Autumn*.

1899: Deputies Burt Alvord and Billy Stiles and members of their gang are arrested after holding up a Southern Pacific train near Cochise, Arizona.

1909: Railroad magnate Edward Harriman dies at age 71.

1967: Snippy the horse is found dead near Alamosa, Colorado. Many believe he was killed by a flying saucer.

SEPTEMBER 10

1873: Isabella Bird arrives in Colorado for a tour of the Estes Park region, as well as other points of interest. Her account, *A Lady's Life in the Rocky Mountains*, will be a priceless observance from a well-educated yet dispassionate reporter.

REWARD!
- DEAD OR ALIVE -
$5,000.00 will be paid for the capture of the men who robbed the bank at
NORTHFIELD, MINN.
They are believed to be Jesse James and his Band, or the Youngers.
All officers are warned to use precaution in making arrest. These are the most desperate men in America.
Take no chances! Shoot to kill!
J. H. McDonald,
SHERIFF

1923: The old Pony Express record from St. Joseph, Missouri to San Francisco is broken by a group of 75 riders, taking 42 hours off the record for 2,180 miles. They average 13.75 MPH as opposed to the Express time of just over 10 MPH.

1961: Actor Leo Carrillo, Pancho in the "Cisco Kid" series, dies at age 81.

SEPTEMBER 11

1842: Mexican forces invade Texas and occupy San Antonio.

1847: First performance of Stephen Foster's "Oh, Susanna," soon to be a gold mining favorite, is heard in a Pittsburgh saloon.

1853: The first electric telegraph is operated, connecting San Francisco's Merchant Exchange with Point Lobos.

1857: The Mountain Meadows Massacre ~ History still clouds what happened to the 150 members of the California bound Fancher wagon train at Mountain Meadows, Utah. The belief is that Mormon zealot John D. Lee persuaded Paiutes to help his men carry out the dirty work, but it is never proven. Under a white flag, Lee tells the Fancher party that they can appease the Indians. The men are separated from the women and children, then murdered. While the Indians kill the women, the Mormons finish off the sick. The children are whisked away to Salt Lake City homes. Twenty years later, Lee is the only person brought to trial. He is shot for the atrocity.

1862: William Sydney Porter born in Greensboro, North Carolina. As novelist O. Henry he will create such characters as "The Cisco Kid."

1902: Jimmy Davis born in Quitman, Louisiana. In addition to being two-time Louisiana governor (1944 and 1960), Davis will record a string of hits including "Where the Old Red River Flows" while he is in office in 1962. He will be elected to the Country Music Hall of Fame.

1921: A five-day flood kills 51 in San Antonio, Texas.

1928: Transcontinental bus service begins between Los Angeles and New York.

SEPTEMBER 12

1818: Pirate Jean Lafitte's fleet of ships is caught in a Galveston hurricane, losing much of its loot.

1893: Idaho State Medical Society organized at Boise.

1912: Rodeo champ Paul Carney born in Galeton, Colorado.

1931: Singer George Jones born in Saratoga, Texas. Hits will include "The Race Is On" and "White Lightning."

1935: Howard Hughes sets a world land-speed record of 352.46 MPH.

1958: Texas Instruments' Jack Kilby demonstrates the first use of an integrated circuit.

1964: Canyonlands National Park, 257,000 acres next to the Colorado and Green Rivers, is established in Utah.

1972: Actor William Boyd, "Hopalong Cassidy", dies at age 77.

SEPTEMBER 13

1847: Maj. Gen. Winfield Scott's army takes the Chapultepec Palace outside Mexico City during the Mexican War.

1859: California Supreme Court Judge David S. Terry kills his political opponent, Sen. David C. Broderick, in a duel at Lake Merced.

1911: Bluegrass master Bill Monroe born in Rosine, Kentucky. His hits will include "Uncle Pen" and "Mule Skinner Blues."

1918: Rin Tin Tin born in a foxhole in Fleury, France during World War I. He will be found and adopted by American pilot Lee Duncan, then come to America for a lucrative film career. His first feature is *Where the North Begins*.

1954: The first national security meeting outside Washington is held in Denver, in President Eisenhower's hospital room at Fitzsimmons Army Medical Center.

1982: A merger of the Western Pacific, Missouri Pacific, and Union Pacific railroads is authorized by the Interstate Commerce Commission, linking the West by a single system.

HOPALONG CASSIDY & TOPPER

SEPTEMBER 14

1712: A monopoly on the western fur trade is secured by Sieur Antoine Crozat. The area reaches from the Carolinas to present-day New Mexico; the governor is the founder of Detroit, Antoine de la Mothe Cadillac.

1816: Author Hamlin Garland born in West Salem, Wisconsin. A writer of short stories and novels that deal with mid-western farm life, he will win the 1922 Pulitzer Prize for *A Daughter of the Middle Border*.

1847: Maj. Gen. Winfield Scott enters Mexico City during the Mexican War, and flies the American flag over the National Palace, the Halls of Montezuma.

1869: Catherine McCarty, Billy the Kid's mother, allegedly buys a town lot in Wichita, Kansas. Today, historians believe that this was a case of mistaken identity, that this was really another woman with the same name, and that Billy's mother was in New York during this period.

1889: Robert Younger, serving a life prison sentence for his part in the Northfield, Minnesota bank robbery, dies of tuberculosis at age 32.

1899: James Warner Bellah who, along with Willis Goldbeck, will write the screenplay for *The Man Who Shot Liberty Valance* born in New York City.

1901: Theodore Roosevelt is sworn in as President after William McKinley dies from an assassin's bullet. More than any President so far, he will work to protect the western environment.

1905: Warrior Rain-in-the-Face dies. On his deathbed he is asked about his part in the killing of George Armstrong Custer, another persistent rumor, by missionary Mary Collins. Rain replies, "Yes I killed him. I was so close to him that the powder from my gun blackened his face." It is also rumored that Rain cut out Custer's heart and ate it during the Battle of the Little Bighorn.

1914: Actor Clayton Moore, star of television's "The Lone Ranger," born in Chicago.

SEPTEMBER 15

1806: On the trip home, Lewis and Clark pass the mouth of the Kansas River near present Kansas City while descending the Missouri.

1850: A fire in San Francisco burns 1,500 buildings and does $4 million in damage.

1857: President Brigham Young forbids United States troops to enter Utah.

1858: The Overland Mail Company begins business, delivering the first mail overland from the East to the West Coast.

1896: A head-on train wreck is staged by the Missouri, Kansas, and Texas railroad as a publicity stunt near Waco, Texas. Two of the 50,000 spectators are killed when the trains collide at 90 MPH.

1903: Roy Acuff born in Maynardsville, Tennessee. His classic songs will include "Wabash Cannonball" and "Great Speckled Bird."

1908: Tumacacori National Monument created in Arizona.

1923: The governor of Oklahoma declares martial law, citing a "state of rebellion and insurrection" because of increased Ku Klux Klan activities.

1923: Barely a month into a life of crime, Al Spencer is killed near Bartlesville, Oklahoma.

1923: *The Long, Long Trail* by George Owen Baxter, a pen name of Max Brand, is published by Chelsea.

1934: Zane Grey's *Wagon Wheels* released by Paramount.

SEPTEMBER 16

1857: John Butterfield and Waterman L. Ormsby obtain a government contract for their Butterfield Overland Mail to run from St. Louis to San Francisco.

1858: First Butterfield Overland Mail leaves St. Louis for San Francisco.

1874: Catherine Antrim, Billy the Kid's poor mother, dies at age 34 in Silver City, New Mexico.

1875: Dry goods tycoon J.C. Penney born in Hamilton, Missouri. He will live 95 productive years, start from the bottom with one store in Kemmerer, Wyoming and finish with 1,660 outlets nationwide.

> **1893: The Cherokee Strip,** or Outlet is opened for settlement. A 6.5 million acre tract of land is opened on a first come first serve basis on a sweltering hot day in north central Oklahoma. A total of 50,000 people claim land during this, the largest of the Oklahoma land runs.

1921: El Paso bans Ku Klux Klan masked parades.

SEPTEMBER 17

1776: The Presidio of San Francisco is founded.

1846: Santa Anna is given control of the Mexican Army during the Mexican War.

September

1848: Francis X. Aubrey breaks his own record for the 780-mile Santa Fe Trail for the second time in one year. He makes the ride in an incredible five days, 16 hours. The record by the 23-year-old "skimmer of the plains" is never broken.

1864: John Dolan is hanged in Virginia City for stealing $700 from a friend.

> **1868: The Battle at Beecher's Island** ~ 500 Sioux and Cheyenne warriors attack 50 volunteers under Maj. George A. Forsyth and Lt. Frederick Beecher. The men hold a sandbar in the Arikaree Fork of the Republican River in eastern Colorado; hence, the "island." Cheyenne war chief Roman Nose is killed in the attack at 6:00 P.M. The battle rages for five days. Forsyth counts 35 wounded, and five dead. The Indians suffer 70 killed and an unknown number wounded.

1899: American educator Milton S. Eisenhower, brother of the future President, born in Abilene, Kansas.

1923: Singer Hank Williams born Hiram King Williams in Georgiana, Alabama. His classic songs will include "Your Cheatin' Heart" and "Lovesick Blues."

1923: A fire in Berkeley, California kills 24 and does $10 million in damage.

1930: Boulder Dam construction begins.

1935: Future author Ken Kesey (*Sometimes a Great Notion*, *One Flew Over the Cuckoo's Nest*) born in La Junta, Colorado.

1937: Bust of Abraham Lincoln, the third President to be carved on Mount Rushmore, is dedicated in South Dakota.

1948: *Red River* with John Wayne and Montgomery Clift is released by United Artists.

1965: Worst September snow storm in Wyoming dumps 20 inches at Lander.

SEPTEMBER 18

1846: Charles Stanton and William McCutchen leave the Donner Party to attempt to reach Sutter's Fort in California for provisions.

1900: The country's first primary for elective officials is held in Minnesota.

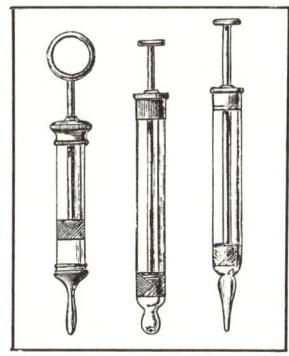

1925: Silver Dollar Tabor, the star-crossed daughter of one-time silver millionaire Horace Tabor, scalded to death in Chicago. Hypodermic needles and morphine are found at the death scene.

1964: Author J. Frank Dobie dies.

1975: Kidnapped newspaper heiress Patricia Hearst is captured by the FBI in San Francisco after a 19-month search.

SEPTEMBER 19

1827: Jim Bowie disembowels banker Morris Wright with a knife, not long after Wright turns down his loan request.

1877: Sam Bass and company rob a Union Pacific train at Big Springs, Nebraska of $60,000 in gold coin.

1900: First appearance of the Ringling Brothers Circus in San Francisco.

1959: Soviet Premier Nikita Khrushchev begins his tour of the western United States. Highlights will include a visit to a movie set, a tour of an Iowa farm, and a refusal of admittance into Disneyland.

1968: First baby born on the Golden Gate Bridge.

SEPTEMBER 20

1806: Lewis and Clark pass the French village of La Charette on the Missouri River (in present-day Missouri) on their return trip. This is the first white settlement they have seen in two and a half years.

1858: Camp Walbach is established to protect settlers passing through Cheyenne Pass, between Nebraska and Wyoming.

1921: The University of Nebraska bans student KKK membership.

1967: Hurricane Beulah does $1.5 million in damage and kills 13 in Texas.

SEPTEMBER 21

1805: Lt. Zebulon Pike reaches the mouth of the Minnesota River on his northern voyage.

1832: Sauk and Fox Indians agree to live west of the Mississippi River.

1873: Custer's command arrives at Fort Abraham Lincoln on the Missouri River, opposite Bismarck, North Dakota.

1876: Brothers Jim, Robert, and Cole Younger are arrested for the Northfield, Minnesota bank robbery they staged with the James brothers, and are given life sentences. Jim and Cole will receive pardons after 25 years. Robert will die in prison in 1889.

1904: Chief Joseph of the Nez Perce tribe dies in exile in Washington. Agency officials term the cause of his death as "a broken heart."

CHIEF JOSEPH
Born: 1840
Died: September 21, 1904
Chief (Nez Perce)

1861: Becomes a chief of the Nez Perce in Oregon.
1863: Wallowa Valley opened for white settlement.
1877: Agrees to move his people to a reservation in Idaho. During the move, young Nez Perce warriors murder several settlers. Troops are sent against him. He leads more than 600 of his people, fewer than 200 of them fighting men, in a running battle in an attempt to reach Canada. Surrenders after battle of Bear Paw Mountains.
1885: Transferred to Colville Reservation in Washington.
1904: Dies at age 64.

1950: Skies over Denver seem to light up with UFO's. Sightings come from all corners of the city, as the strange objects are tracked at 500 MPH.

1983: Interior Secretary James Watt makes the famous bonehead remark that will cost him his job. While discussing a committee to study Interior coal-leasing policies, he comments on how balanced a makeup it has saying the committee includes "a black, a woman, two Jews, and a cripple."

SEPTEMBER 22

1554: Explorer Francisco Vasquez de Coronado, 44, dies in Mexico.

1711: The Tuscarora War begins with a massacre of settlers in North Carolina.

September

1784: First Russian settlement in Alaska is established at Three Saints Bay on Kodiak Island.

1846: Gen. Stephen Kearny establishes law in New Mexico and appoints Charles Bent as governor.

1869: The Cincinnati Red Stockings arrive in San Francisco for some baseball after traveling overland.

1891: Sauk, Fox, and Potawatomi lands, some 900,000 acres, are opened for settlement in Oklahoma under a proclamation issued today by President Harrison.

1951: Jacob Horner, last white survivor of the Little Bighorn (he and a few others were left behind because there weren't enough horses) dies at age 96. The last surviving Indian chief of that battle, Iron Hail, dies in 1955 at age 98.

1975: President Ford escapes the second attempt on his life in less than a month, both in California. Sara Jane Moore is arrested in San Francisco.

CRAZY HORSE

SEPTEMBER 23
(American Indian Day)

CRAZY HORSE
Born: 1842
Died: September 5, 1877
War Chief (Oglala Sioux)

1855: As a teen, witnesses the Battle of Blue Water as soldiers attack Little Thunder's camp.
1865: Begins service under Red Cloud during war on whites.
1866: The Fetterman Massacre, near Fort Phil Kearny in Wyoming. Crazy Horse decoys an attack force to its death.
1867: The Wagon Box Fight ~ 1,000 Sioux attack infantry guarding woodcutters near Fort Phil Kearny, Wyoming.
1868: Attacks Horsecreek Station.
1876: At the Battle on the Rosebud, attacks Gen. Crook and 1,000 troopers with columns of mounted Sioux and Cheyenne.
1876: One of the field marshals at the Battle of the Little Bighorn.
1877: Surrenders at the White River Valley in Nebraska.
1877: Murdered while being led to a cramped cell at Fort Robinson, Nebraska.

1806: Lewis and Clark return to St. Louis following their historic western expedition. They log 7,689 miles during a journey that lasts two years, four months, ten days. The expedition costs the government $38,722.25, slightly higher than President Jefferson's estimate of $2,500.

1839: France becomes the first European country to recognize Texas' independence.

1872: In a daring daylight robbery, Jesse and Frank James and Cole Younger grab the gate receipts of the Kansas City Fair, $978. In the scuffle, a bullet ricochets, hitting a little girl in the leg.

1875: Henry McCarty, soon to be dubbed Billy the Kid, is arrested for the first time after a practical joke in which he is left holding a bag of stolen laundry in Silver City, New Mexico.

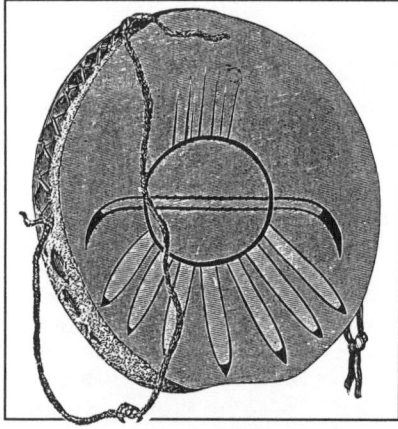

1878: With federal troops in pursuit, Cheyennes attempting to return to their homelands cross the Arkansas and Santa Fe tracks east of Dodge City, Kansas.

1899: U.S. Supreme Court associate justice Thomas Campbell Clark, who will write the opinion upholding the 1964 Civil Rights Act, born in Dallas, Texas.

1902: Explorer John Wesley Powell dies at age 69 in Haven, Maine.

SEPTEMBER 24

1870: First Colorado Central train arrives in Denver.

1890: The Manifesto is issued in Utah by Mormon Church president Wilford Woodruff, stating that Mormons will obey federal law which officially outlaws plural marriages.

1905: Four thousand of Louis Gantz' 7,000 sheep are shot or clubbed to death by cattlemen in Basin, Wyoming. No prosecution occurs because of the dominant cattle concerns.

1906: Wyoming's Devils Tower is designated as the first national monument by President Theodore Roosevelt.

1930: Astronaut John Young born in San Francisco. He will make three ventures into space with the Gemini and Apollo programs.

1955: President Eisenhower suffers a heart attack at his in-laws' home in Denver. During his convalescence, the country will be run from this city's Fitzsimmons Army Medical Center.

1972: Korean war F-86 Supersabre, judged unsafe for flying, crashes into an ice cream parlor while trying to take off from Sacramento, killing 22.

1976: Kidnapped heiress-turned-revolutionary Patricia Hearst, is sentenced to seven years for her bank robbing escapade with the Symbionese Liberation Army.

SEPTEMBER 25

1751: Illinois commandant La Jonquiere notes the war going on in the area between Pawnee and Osage Indians.

1806: The Zebulon Pike party is met by 300 friendly Pawnees in present Kansas.

1846: Gen. Kearny leaves Santa Fe, headed for California to oversee the newly established American government.

1867: Cattle pioneer Oliver Loving of the famous Goodnight-Loving Trail, dies of gangrene at Fort Sumner, New Mexico, from wounds suffered in an Indian battle.

ASTORIA
WASHINGTON IRVING

1873: According to her account, Calamity Jane gives birth to the illegitimate daughter of Wild Bill Hickok in a cave.

1875: Henry McCarty, *aka* Billy the Kid, escapes from jail in Silver City, New Mexico.

1893: A state wool growers association is started at Mountain Home, Idaho.

1908: Northern Pacific train kills 23 in a head-on collision near Young's Point, Montana.

1919: President Wilson suffers a stroke and collapses during a speech at Pueblo, Colorado.

1920: *Riders of the Silences* by John Frederick, *aka* Max Brand, published by H.K. Fly.

1926: Coldest September reading in the U.S. recorded at Yellowstone National Park, where it reaches -9 degrees.

SEPTEMBER 26

1811: Indiana Territorial Governor and future President William Henry Harrison leads a 1,000-man force against Shawnee Chief Tecumseh. Harrison led his army against the Shawnee center near the confluence of the Tippecanoe and Wabash Rivers, because he knew Tecumseh was absent from the area.

1820: After a long, adventurous life, Daniel Boone dies quietly in his sleep at the home of his son, Nathan, just five weeks short of his 86th birthday. Nathan's home was near present-day Defiance, Missouri, west of St. Louis on the Missouri River.

1823: Author Francis Parkman (*The Oregon Trail*) born in Boston, Massachusetts.

1846: Francis Parkman returns to Westport, Missouri after four-and-a-half months along the Plains and Front Range area of the Rockies.

1862: William H. Antrim, Billy the Kid's stepfather, honorably discharged from the Indiana Volunteer Infantry.

1888: Author/historian J. Frank Dobie (*A Vaquero of the Brush Country, Coronado's Children*) born in Live Oak County, Texas.

1925: Singer Marty Robbins ("El Paso") born in Glendale, Arizona.

1935: Cowboy/author Andy Adams dies at age 76 in Colorado Springs, Colorado.

1947: Singer Lynn Anderson ("Rose Garden") born in Grand Forks, North Dakota.

SEPTEMBER 27

1832: Author Washington Irving's western tour begins at Independence, Missouri.

1864: Bloody Bill Anderson's Confederate guerillas, including 17-year-old Jesse James, raid Centralia, Missouri. After much looting and shooting, they hold up a train as it comes into town and execute 20 unarmed Union soldiers.

1867: First appearance of Wild Bill Hickok in a dime novel is "Wild Bill the Indian-Slayer" in De Witt's *Ten Cent Romances*.

1868: Seventy black troopers under Col. L.H. Carpenter arrive to give aid at the Battle of Beecher's Island in Colorado. The battle is over, but the field ambulance they bring is badly needed.

1869: Samuel Strawhim leads a pack of drunken teamsters in busting up a saloon in Hays City, Kansas on the night of September 26. Sheriff Wild Bill Hickok arrives on the scene after midnight, orders the party stopped, and all hell breaks loose. Hickok blows Strawhim's head off, and the trouble stops immediately.

1870: The impoverished Henry Comstock, discoverer and seller of the original Comstock Lode, commits suicide.

1872: At the Kansas City Exposition, Wild Bill Hickok refuses to let the band play "Dixie," upsetting the Texans in attendance.

1894: Groundwork is laid by the Bureau of Indian Affairs to school Indian children with white children in public schools.

1909: President Taft designates three million acres for conservation, including Wyoming's Teapot Dome.

1915: A gasoline tanker explodes in Ardmore, Oklahoma, killing 44.

1930: *Santa Fe Trail* with Richard Arlen released by Paramount.

1936: Twenty-two inches of snow falls in Denver.

1956: Woman athlete of the half-century, Babe Didrikson Zaharias, 45, dies of cancer.

SEPTEMBER 28

1542: Joao Rodrigues Cabrillo sails into San Diego Bay. Cabrillo, a Portuguese in service to Spain, sails into the Bay during his exploration of the coast of California.

1814: After a long Christmas break, Davy Crockett re-enlists to fight the Creek Indians.

1864: At a meeting at Camp Weld in Colorado, Black Kettle and White Antelope are accused of numerous attacks by Cheyenne and Arapaho in the area. The Indians blame the Sioux. They are moved to Sand Creek in southeastern Colorado, where they are promised safety.

1867: William T. Sherman writes to John Sherman: "Whether right or wrong, those railroads will be built, and everybody knows that Congress, after granting the charts and fixing the routes, cannot back out and surrender."

1874: Col. Ranald Mackenzie orders the slaughter of 2,000 Comanche ponies in the Palo Duro Canyon of Texas. A 200-mile forced march of captured Indians to Fort Sill, Oklahoma follows.

1914: Singer Bill Boyde born in Fannin County, Texas.

1917: Kellyville, Oklahoma train wreck claims 23 lives.

1920: Max Brand's *The Ten-Foot Chain or Can Love Survive the Shackles* published by Reynolds.

1926: Country comic Jerry Clower born in Liberty, Michigan.

1930: *Shadow Ranch* with Buck Jones released by Beverly.

1937: The Bonneville Dam on Oregon's Columbia River is dedicated by President Franklin D. Roosevelt.

SEPTEMBER 29

1857: Cowboy and suspected rustler Nathan D. Champion is born in

Williamson County, Texas.

1879: The Meeker Massacre in Colorado occurs at the Ute's White River Agency, as Indian agent Nathan Meeker and several others are slaughtered. In the northwestern section of the territory, fighting breaks out between Utes and soldiers under Maj. Thomas Thornburgh at Milk Creek. Twelve soldiers, including Thornburgh, are slain in five days of fighting; 37 Utes perish. For these two actions, the Utes will be forced to move to Utah and their 12 million acres will be opened for settlement.

1907: Singer, actor, executive, baseball team owner Gene Autry born in Tioga, Texas.

1912: Author Henry Wilson Allen who wrote under the names Will Henry and Clay Fisher, (*Where the Sun Now Stands*; *McKenna's Gold*; *I, Tom Horn*) born in Kansas City, Missouri.

1934: Zane Grey's *The Dude Ranger* released by Principle/Fox.

SEPTEMBER 30

1830: Choctaw Indians give the United States eight million acres east of the Mississippi in exchange for land in present Oklahoma.

1830: Jim Bowie granted Mexican citizenship, a formality for doing business in Texas.

1855: Gov. Brigham Young proposes to have his followers come to Utah using handcarts instead of covered wagons.

1860: Gold discovered in Idaho that will lead to the founding of Pierce.

1878: The new governor of New Mexico, Gen. Lew Wallace, arrives in Santa Fe and relieves former governor Samuel Axtell of his duties.

1889: Wyoming becomes the first state to grant equal voting rights to women.

1931: Actress Angie Dickinson, best known for her performance in *Rio Bravo*, born in Kulm, North Dakota.

1932: Zane Grey's *Heritage of the Desert* released by Paramount.

1935: President Franklin D. Roosevelt dedicates Boulder Dam in Nevada.

October

OCTOBER 1

1800: Under a secret treaty, Napoleon reacquires Louisiana from Spain, which had gotten it from France 37 years earlier.

1804: William C. Claiborne becomes governor of the Territory of Orleans, covering much of the western U.S., thus inaugurating American government in the former French territory.

1876: Sgt. John Armstrong of the Texas Rangers attacks an outlaw camp at midnight near Carrizo, Texas. Of the four badmen, three die, and the other is shot four times.

1881: "Billy the Kid" Claiborne (not to be confused with Mr. McCarty/Antrim) kills James Hickey in Charleston, Arizona.

1890: Yosemite National Park is dedicated in California. Mountains, glacial formations, beautiful gorges, three redwood groves, and this country's highest waterfall grace 761,320 acres.

1896: U.S. Post Office begins Rural Free Delivery.

1897: Al and Frank Jennings rob a Rock Island train, getting away with $300 and a pocket watch.

1899: Author Ernest James Haycox, Jr. (*Deep West, Canyon Passage*) born in Portland, Oregon.

1910: An explosion at the *Los Angeles Times* building kills 21 people. J.B. and J.J. McNamara will later be convicted.

1910: Bonnie Parker, who will join Clyde Barrow for a reign of criminal terror in the 1930s, is born in Rowena, Texas.

1921: Violence breaks out during a KKK rally in Lorena, Texas; ten are wounded.

1922: Idaho's Philo Farnsworth opens his lab in San Francisco where he will begin his television transmission experiments.

1925: Gutzon Borglum places a flag on Mount Rushmore in South Dakota's Black Hills, where he will carve giant heads of four Presidents.

OCTOBER 2

1835: First shots of the Texas revolution fired at the Battle of Anahuac on the Gulf of Mexico. In other developments, Mexican troops attempt to steal a cannon for colonists in Gonzales. Many are killed by the cannon. The attempt is unsuccessful.

1841: Legendary lawman "Texas" John Slaughter born in Sabine Parish, Louisiana.

1871: Brigham Young and other Mormon leaders are arrested on charges of "lascivious cohabitation," (polygamy). Lower courts will convict them, but the Supreme Court will overturn the decisions citing a lack of jurisdiction.

1877: Colorado voters reject women's suffrage.

1919: Utah ratifies the 19th amendment concerning women's suffrage.

1924: Wyoming Gov. William B. Ross dies of a ruptured appendix. He will be succeeded in the upcoming election by his wife, Nellie Tayloe Ross, the first American female governor.

1935: President Franklin D. Roosevelt observes a mock invasion preparation in San Diego as 50,000 men attack using 129 warships and more than 400 airplanes.

1968: Redwood National Park is established in California, 56,201 acres that house America's tallest redwood, 367 feet high. On the same day, North Cascades National Park is established in Washington, 504,781 acres covered with glaciers, mountains, and lakes.

1970: An airline carrying the Wichita State football team crashes in the Rocky Mountains near Silver Plume, Colorado, killing 30 on board.

OCTOBER 3

1842: Marcus Whitman leaves Oregon for a trip to Boston and Washington, where he will drum up interest in the new country.

1859: The first school in Colorado opens in Auraria, present Denver.

1873: Captain Jack and three other Modocs are hanged in Oregon for murder.

1880: Writer Damon Runyon is born in Manhattan, Kansas. His family will move to Pueblo, Colorado when he is very young. As a young man, he will write for both *The Denver Post* and the *Rocky Mountain News*, before relocating to Manhattan, New York. His tough guy fiction, which will include *Guys and Dolls*, will become a favorite.

1892: The University of Idaho opens in Moscow.

1900: Tom Horn takes care of another cattle rustler, "Nigger Isom" Dart, in Routt County, Colorado. Horn positions himself 200 yards from Dart's cabin with a .30-.30 rifle. Isom emerges to go to to his corral and is killed instantly with a blast to the head.

1912: Rain falls in Bagdad, California for the last time until November 8, 1914.

1956: *Tension at Table Rock* released by RKO.

1967: Folk singer Woody Guthrie, 55, dies of Huntington's chorea in Queens, New York.

OCTOBER 4

1859: Kansas voters ratify the Wyandotte constitution, an anti-slavery measure.

1861: Artist Frederic Remington born in Canton, New York. His Western paintings and bronzes will make him one of the region's major artists.

FREDERIC REMINGTON
Born: October 4, 1861
Died: December 26, 1909
Artist

1878: Enrolls in Yale School of Fine Arts. First published drawing is of a football player.
1880: Drops out of college, goes to work as a clerk in the New York governor's office.
1881: Vacations in Montana.
1882: After another year in Albany, vacations in Kansas. First published illustration, *Cowboys of Arizona*, appears in *Harper's Weekly*.
1884: Marries Eva Caten. Makes frequent trips West.
1889: Top illustrator in the country; travels with Mexican army.
1895: Begins casting his art in bronze. First one is *The Bronco Buster*.
1909: Dies at age 48 of appendicitis.

CHIEF JOSEPH

1869: Wells Fargo officials agree to pay Lloyd Tevis $5 million for exclusive railroad express rights in a closed door meeting in Omaha.

1876: Texas A&M University chartered in Bryan.

1915: Dinosaur National Monument established in Colorado and Utah.

1981: Body of alleged Presidential assassin Lee Harvey Oswald is exhumed in Dallas for positive identification. Authorities determine it is the body of Oswald, disproving the theory that it was really that of a Russian secret agent.

OCTOBER 5

1813: Chief Tecumseh of the Shawnee tribe killed in the Battle of the Thames during the War of 1812, fighting against William Henry Harrison at Ontario, Kansas. Tecumseh's death effectively ended Indian resistance in the Old Northwest.

1871: While putting down a disturbance by 50 Texas cowboys, Abilene sheriff Wild Bill Hickok shoots Phil Coe, who will die in three days. A colleague of Hickok's, Mike Williams, breaks through the crowd to see what is happening and Wild Bill, thinking a Texan is about to get him, puts two bullets in his friend's heart. Hickok takes the mistake badly. He closes the town and never fires a shot at another man.

1877: Chief Joseph surrenders his Nez Perce tribe after a 1,700-mile, 115-day attempt to escape to Canada. Following the Battle of Bear Paw, he turns over his people in Montana, just 60 miles from the border. Joseph was a civil chief rather than a war chief, but he was the only chief left alive to surrender. His image as a brilliant strategist and military leader came primarily from the press. His words of surrender, possibly enhanced by an interpreter, are stirring:

> *"I am tired of fighting. Our chiefs are killed. Looking Glass is dead. Toohoolhoolzote is dead. The old men are all dead. It is the young men who say yes or no. He who led on the young men (Ollokot) is dead. It is cold and we have no blankets. The little children are freezing to death. My people, some of them, have run away to the hills, and have no blankets, no food; no one knows where they are ~ perhaps freezing to death. I want to have time to look for my children and see how many of them I can find. Maybe I shall find them among the dead. Hear me, my chiefs! I am tired; my heart is sick and sad. From where the sun now stands I will fight no more forever."*

1882: Six months after brother Jesse's murder, Frank James surrenders his guns to Missouri Gov.

October

Thomas Crittenden. Says Frank, "I want to hand over to you that which no living man except myself has been permitted to touch since 1861, and to say that I am your prisoner." He will soon be acquitted of all his crimes, and spend the rest his remaining 32 years in a variety of odd jobs that include bouncer and shoe salesman. At 70, he will stand outside the old James residence, charging four bits a tour.

1892: The Daltons Raid Coffeyville, Kansas in one of the biggest blunders of the Old West. The Dalton Gang, brothers Emmett, Bob, and Grat, accompanied by Bill Powers and Dick Broadwell decide to make their mark on history by robbing two banks at the same time. Authorities are tipped in advance; instead of riding out of the First National and C.M. Condon banks, they are pinned down by gunfire. Many of the town's residents have armed themselves from local stores, who gladly opened their gun cases to accommodate the emergency. Four corpses become the centerpiece of a macabre town celebration. The only survivor, Emmett, recovers from 20 bullet wounds to serve a 14-year prison sentence. When he is released, he will go to Hollywood to become a screen writer.

1899: First car in Texas driven approximately 50 miles from Dallas to Terrell by Ned Green.

1908: Broadway producer Josh Logan of *Paint Your Wagon* fame born at Texarkana, Texas.

1917: Hottest October day on record in Arizona. At Sentinel, the mercury hits 116 degrees.

OCTOBER 6

1840: New Mexican businessman and politician Thomas Benton Catron born near Lexington, Missouri.

1845: Brigham Young's 11th wife, Olive Grey Frost, 29, dies only eight months after they are wed.

1846: Gen. Stephen Kearny, en route to California from Santa Fe, runs into Kit Carson on the trail, who tells him of American success in that region. Kearny sends 200 of his men back to Santa Fe and continues on with 100.

1863: Quantrill's Raiders defeat cavalry at Baxter Springs, Kansas during the Civil War.

1866: America's first train robbery takes place in Jackson County, Indiana, as brothers Simeon and John Reno relieve the Ohio and Mississippi railroad of $13,000.

1955: United DC-4 crashes into a mountain near Laramie, Wyoming, killing 66.

OCTOBER 7

1854: Andrew H. Reeder appointed first territorial governor of Kansas.

1870: A lynch mob led by Clay Allison hangs accused murderer Charles Kennedy in Elizabethtown, New York. Allison decapitates the body and displays the head in a saloon.

1878: President Hayes declares New Mexico's Lincoln County, in the throes of a bitter cattle war, to be in a state of insurrection.

1879: Union martyr Joe Hill born Joel Hagglund in Gavle, Sweden.

1879: After a three-year hiatus following the botched raid on Northfield, Minnesota, Frank and Jesse James rob the Chicago and Alton Express outside Glendale, Minnesota of $35,000.

1894: Temple Houston kills Ed Jennings and wounds John Jennings, brothers of Al, during a brawl in a Woodward, Oklahoma bar.

1905: Actor Andy Devine, "Jingles" on TV's "Wild Bill Hickok," is born in Flagstaff, Arizona.

1907: Samuel F. Cody of Birdville, Texas flies the first airplane over British soil.

OCTOBER 8

1838: A force of 300 Kickapoo Indians attacks a party of 25 surveyors at Battle Creek, Texas. There will be only seven surviving surveyors.

1860: First telegraph line between San Francisco and Los Angeles is opened.

1910: Starkville, Colorado mine explosion kills 56.

1932: *The Big Stampede* with John Wayne is released by Warner Brothers.

OCTOBER 9

1776: Mission Dolores founded in present San Francisco.

1832: Washington Irving journeys to present Oklahoma, arriving at Fort Gibson.

1858: Overland Mail stage from west to east reaches St. Louis from San Francisco after 23 days, four hours.

1891: College of Idaho opens in Caldwell.

1836: First generators turned on at Boulder Dam, Nevada, sending electricity 260 miles to Los Angeles.

1959: At 22, Bobby Darin is the youngest entertainer ever to head the bill at the Sands Hotel's Las Vegas Copa Room.

1983: Secretary of the Interior James Watt resigns.

OCTOBER 10

1805: Lewis and Clark discover the Snake River, the first they have encountered which flows west.

1858: First Butterfield Overland Mail, from east to west, reaches San Francisco from St. Louis covering 3,000 miles in 23 days, 23 hours.

1867: Outlaw Cullen Baker holds up a government supply wagon in Cass County, Texas, killing the driver.

1869: Wild Bill Hickok prevents a lynching in Hays, Kansas.

1877: The funeral for George Armstrong Custer is held at the U.S. Military Academy Chapel at West Point.

1904: Head-on train crash at Warrensburg, Missouri kills 29.

1961: Underground nuclear explosion test is held in Nevada.

1971: London Bridge, recently moved from Great Britain to the desert of Lake Havasu, Arizona, is dedicated.

1973: Record flooding in northern Oklahoma; 20 inches fall on Enid in 13 hours.

OCTOBER 11

1806: Gen. James Wilkinson receives a dispatch from Aaron Burr suggesting a war between Spain and the U.S. might help their scheme to set up a new country Out West.

1809: Explorer Meriwether Lewis, of Lewis and Clark fame, dies at age 35. It was never proven whether he was murdered or committed suicide.

1877: Outlaw Exterminator Clay Calhoun guns down mass-murderer John Allman among cliff dwellings, and turns in the body at Holbrook, Arizona. Allman has four aligned bullet holes in the mouth, chest, stomach, and groin.

1878: Texas outlaw/cattle thief "Wild Bill" Longley is hanged five days short of his 27th birthday, for the murder of Wilson Anderson. Anderson was an old friend who had murdered Longley's cousin, Cole Longley, on April 1, 1875.

OCTOBER 12

1907: Colorado becomes the first state to declare Columbus Day a holiday, thanks to a nationwide campaign begun by Italians in the city of Pueblo.

1930: *The Girl of the Golden West* is released by First National.

1933: Alcatraz Island designated a federal prison.

DWIGHT D. EISENHOWER

1940: Tom Mix is killed in a one-car automobile accident near his ranch in Florence, Arizona. His list of 400 films includes *The Last Trail* and *Destry Rides Again*.

1974: The Texas Big Thicket, 85,850 acres is designated a national preserve.

OCTOBER 13

1753: Twenty-one year old surveyor George Washington is ordered to the Wild West ~ Ohio.

1832: Washington Irving embarks

on a 400-mile tour of present Oklahoma with a company of mounted rangers.

1890: Author Conrad Richter (*The Sea of Grass, The Light in the Forest*) born in Pine Grove, Pennsylvania.

1920: Actress Laraine Day born in Roosevelt, Utah. She was best known for the *Dr. Kildare* series of films in the 1940s.

1936: Lake Mead National recreation area is established in Arizona and Nevada.

OCTOBER 14

1832: Blackfoot Indians attack a party of American Fur Company trappers near Jefferson River in Montana, killing William H. Vanderburg.

1832: Chickasaws agree to give up all their lands east of the Mississippi River.

1890: Dwight David Eisenhower born in Denison, Texas. He will spearhead World War II's D-Day before becoming the 34th President of the U.S. from 1953-1960.

1901: Annie Rogers is arrested in Nashville for being an accomplice of Harvey Logan, alias Kid Curry.

1913: Cabrillo National Monument established on San Diego Bay in California. The 123-acre monument honors Juan Rodriguez, who discovered the state.

1922: Timpanogos Cave in Utah becomes a national monument.

1947: Chuck Yeager breaks the sound barrier for the first time in the skies over present Edwards AFB in California.

1955: Buddy Holly is discovered while opening a Lubbock, Texas concert for Bill Haley and the Comets.

OCTOBER 15

1863: The San Francisco and San Jose railroad is opened.

1880: Chiricahua Apache leader Victorio, perhaps the tribe's best military strategist, is killed after he and his followers have been tracked down by a combined force of U.S. and Mexican troops near the Tres Castillos mountains south of El Paso. Accounts vary on who did it. Some say it was an Indian scout with the Mexicans; others say he committed suicide.

1892: Montana Crow lands totalling 1,800,000 acres are opened for settlement by President Harrison.

1893: Business executive John Jay Hopkins born in Santa Ana, California. As head of General Dynamics, he will oversee the building of the *Nautilus*, the first nuclear-powered submarine.

1899: The luxurious "Overland Limited" begins its first run from Chicago to Oakland.

1905: The Lewis and Clark Centennial Exposition, commemorating the 100th anniversary of the famous explorers' trip, closes in Portland, Oregon.

1921: *Free Range Lanning* by George Owen Baxter, *aka* Max Brand, published by Chelsea.

October   153

1955: Film version of *Oklahoma* released by Magna Corporation.

1955: Elvis Presley plays Lubbock, Texas. His opening act is Buddy Holly, accompanied by Bob Montgomery. Unknown to either of them, 13-year-old Mac Davis is in the audience.

1956: Colorful Oklahoma Gov. "Alfalfa" Bill Murray dies at age 86.

1966: Guadalupe Mountains in Texas becomes a national park. Mountains and earth faults along the most extensive Permian limestone fossil reef in the world comprise the 81,077 acre park.

1966: Tornado in Belmond, Iowa wipes out 100 homes, 75 percent of the city's businesses, and does $11 million in damage.

OCTOBER 16

1808: Kansa Indians banned from Fort Clark because of "insolent and violent conduct."

1851: Gunfighter William Preston "Wild Bill" Longley born in Austin County, Texas.

1884: Marshal Bill Tilghman blazes away with pistols and his Winchester, convincing a group of drunken cowboys to get out of Dodge.

1891: Sarah Winnemucca dies at age 47 after a life spent crusading for Paiute rights. After scouting for the U.S. Army in 1878, she conducts a lecture series, drawing the attention of thousands to the plight of the Native American.

1903: "Black Friday" in Aberdeen, Washington as fire destroys 140 buildings.

1931: Arizona nurse Winnie Ruth Judd shoots two of her friends, dismembers the bodies, then packs them and ships them in two trunks and a suitcase to Los Angeles.

1938: Aaron Copland's ballet *Billy the Kid* opens in Chicago.

OCTOBER 17

1835: First resolution creating the Texas Rangers is drawn up.

1893: Actress Spring Byington, best known for her TV series "December Bride," born in Colorado Springs, Colorado.

1909: Denver's most beautiful madame, Jennie Rogers, dies.

1913: Coal mine owners fire machine guns from a specially designed armored car called the "Death Special" into the tents of striking miners' families at Forbes.

1920: Actor Montgomery Clift born in Omaha, Nebraska. His films include *Red River*, *Raintree Country*, and *The Misfits*.

OCTOBER 18

1806: After six weeks on the plains, the Zebulon Pike party reaches the Arkansas River near Great Bend, in present-day Kansas.

1846: The starving Donner Party circles its wagons at Truckee Meadows, having lost many of its provisions in a six-day crossing of the desert.

1895: First Denver "Festival of Mountain and Plain" is held.

1930: *Billy the Kid* with Johnny Mack Brown released by MGM.

1982: Former First Lady Bess Truman, 97, dies in Independence, Missouri.

OCTOBER 19

1842: Monterey is seized by Thomas Catesby Jones of the Navy, who raises the American flag, thinking America and Mexico are at war.

Two days later he apologizes and leaves.

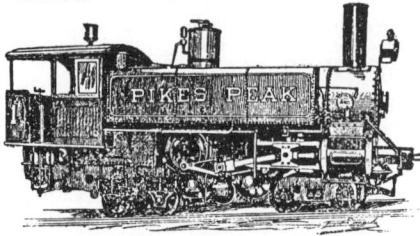

1846: Charles Stanton returns to the Donner Party with provisions and two Indian guides.

1901: Jim Younger puts a bullet through his brain three months after completing a 25-year sentence for the botched Northfield, Minnesota bank raid.

1936: The first high school to fingerprint students does so in Watertown, South Dakota.

1984: Odem, Texas gets 25 inches of rain in a three and one-half hour downpour.

OCTOBER 20

1859: First marriage in Denver takes place between John Atkins and Lydia Allen.

1890: The Pikes Peak railroad is finished.

1981: Playwright Mary Coyle Chase, whose *Harvey* won the 1945 Pulitzer Prize, dies in her hometown, Denver.

OCTOBER 21

1805: The date Davy Crockett is supposed to marry Margaret Elder. She will jilt him for another.

1806: Gen. James Wilkinson sends a note to President Jefferson, informing him of Aaron Burr's "wicked conspiracy" to set up a new country in the western territories.

1810: A 40-man advance party for John Jacob Astor's Pacific Fur Co. starts up the Missouri River.

1860: William F. "Billy the Kid" Claiborne (not to be confused with William Bonney, the true Kid), born in Yazoo County, Michigan.

1868: Earthquake rocks San Francisco.

1876: Gen. Nelson A. Miles battles Sitting Bull while the Indian Chief is retreating to Canada.

1921: *The Seventh Man* by Max Brand published by Putnam's.

1937: Actor Michael Landon ("Bonanza," "Little House on the Prairie") born in New York City.

1939: Author Zane Grey dies of a heart attack at age 69, shortly after completing *Western Union*.

1972: Hohokam Pima National Monument created in Arizona to preserve the remnants of Hohokam culture, a farming people who existed until 1400 A.D.

OCTOBER 22

1812: John "Grizzly" Adams born in Medway, Massachusetts. His fame will come after he relocates to San Francisco and opens a menagerie. Some say his favorite bear, Benjamin Franklin, was the model for the California state flag.

1824: Davy Crockett's state political career ends when the Tennessee house adjourns.

1836: Sam Houston is sworn in as the first president of Texas.

1853: Minister James Gadsden is given the go-ahead to negotiate a purchase of land south of the Gila River. His deal will come to be known as the Gadsden Purchase.

1870: Greeley, Colorado lyceum debating society organized.

1902: Former train robber Camilla Hanks of the Wild Bunch slain in a San Antonio saloon brawl.

1903: Ten thousand Montana workers are laid off as Amalgamated Copper shuts down operations in a show of power.

1903: Geneticist George W. Beadle born in Wahoo, Nebraska. He will receive the 1940 Nobel Prize for his work concerning gene functions in the production of enzymes.

1934: Oklahoma's Pretty Boy Floyd killed by Melvin Purvis and FBI agents on a farm in Ohio.

1934: *The Trail Beyond* with John Wayne released by Lone Star/Monogram.

1949: *She Wore a Yellow Ribbon* with John Wayne released by Argosy/RKO.

OCTOBER 23

1813: Astoria, J.J. Astor's fur trading enterprise, is turned over to the British Northwest Company, when the traders learn that British forces are on the way.

1855: Kansas free-soilers hold their own convention in Topeka and outlaw slavery.

1908: Last bubonic plague-carrying rat is caught in San Francisco.

1913: Three are killed when police fire into a crowd of striking miners in Trinidad, Colorado.

1914: San Antonio floods kill 20.

1924: Listeners on the west coast hear the first national radio network broadcast, a speech by President Coolidge from Washington.

1962: San Francisco's Candlestick Park becomes a boxing ring for the first time, for the Gene Fulmer vs. Dick Tiger bout.

1970: New land speed record is set on the Bonneville Salt Flats Utah as Gary Gabelich travels 622.4 MPH in his rocket sled.

1972: Fossil Butte National Monument created in Wyoming.

OCTOBER 24

1859: Residents of the year-old cities of Denver and Auraria meet to decide who will have authority in each area.

1861: After the link is made in Salt Lake City, the first transcontinental telegraph signal is sent from San Francisco to Washington D.C. over a line that is longer than 3,500 miles.

1861: The Pony Express suspends operations after 18 months. Completion of the Overland Telegraph line has made it obsolete.

1871: Riots in Los Angeles claim 22 Chinese.

1926: Artist Charles M. Russell, 62, dies in Great Falls, Montana.

CHARLES M. RUSSELL
Born: March 19, 1864
Died: October 24, 1926
Artist

1880: Quits school to head out West to be a cowboy. Sketches scenes by campfire.
1888: Lives on the Blood Indian Reservation in Montana.
1895: Decides to make a living from art.
1896: Marries Nancy Cooper. Works in studio in Great Falls, Montana.
1911: First New York showing.
1920: A quarter-century of work produces financial success.
1924: Tours Europe.
1926: Dies of a heart attack.

1930: *The Big Trail* with John Wayne released by Fox.

1947: A United DC-6 crashes at Bryce Canyon, Utah, killing 52.

1960: John Wayne's lavish production *The Alamo* released by United Artists. Richard Widmark is Jim Bowie, Laurence Harvey is Travis, and Wayne plays Davy Crockett.

OCTOBER 25

1832: The Asiatic cholera epidemic breaks out in New Orleans, where 6,000 will die in the next two weeks.

1860: Grizzly Adams dies of an infected head wound, suffered while scuffling with Fremont, one of his bears. He is in New York at the time, working for P.T. Barnum.

1921: Bat Masterson, 67, dies of a heart attack while writing his sports column for the New York *Morning Telegraph*.

1923: Carlsbad National Monument is established in New Mexico. Several companies have mined the tons of bat guano out of these mysterious caverns for two decades. Now the area is under official protection.

1923: The U.S. Senate begins its investigation of the Teapot Dome incident.

1926: The future University of California is dedicated at Los Angeles.

1929: Albert Bacon Fall is convicted of taking a bribe in the Teapot Dome affair.

1933: Folk singer Woody Guthrie marries Mary Jennings in Pampa, Texas.

1939: "Trunk murderess" Winnie Ruth Judd escapes from the Arizona Hospital for the Insane for the first time. She is recaptured five days later.

1949: Effigy Mounds National Monument is established in Iowa.

1962: John Steinbeck wins the Nobel Literature Prize for his combined output.

OCTOBER 26

1804: Touissant Charbonneau is hired as an interpreter by the Lewis and Clark expedition as it passes through a Mandan village on the upper Missouri.

1825: The water route to the West, the Erie Canal, opens between New York City and Lake Erie.

1832: George Catlin is present at Castor Hill, outside St. Louis, as William Clark, then Superintendent of Indian Affairs, works out a treaty with the Shawnees and Delawares.

1860: Western adventurer Frank Eaton, who will earn notoriety as Pistol Pete, born in Hartford, Connecticut.

1864: Civil War guerilla leader "Bloody Bill" Anderson is slain by Union soldiers near Richmond, Missouri.

> **1881: The Gunfight at the OK Corral** ~ A feud that has been brewing for some time, explodes in 30 seconds of raw violence near Tombstone's most famous livery stable. Wyatt Earp, his brothers Morgan and Virgil, and their friend Doc Holliday, open fire on the Clantons and McLaurys. Billy Clanton, Frank McLaury, and Tom McLaury are killed; Holliday, Virgil Earp, and Morgan Earp are wounded. Ike Clanton runs away, and Wyatt Earp is left without a scratch. Virgil, not Wyatt as is widely supposed, was marshal of Tombstone.

1901: Explosion at the Diamondville Mine in Wyoming kills 22.

1974: John Day Fossil Beds in Oregon become a national monument.

1984: The heart of a baboon in implanted in 15-day-old "Baby Fae" at Loma Linda University Medical Center in California.

OCTOBER 27

1804: Lewis and Clark camp for the winter near the mouth of the Knife River in present-day North Dakota, having covered some 1,600 miles in less than six months. They call their log stockade Fort Mandan.

1835: James Bowie and an advanced guard attack a detachment of Mexican troops near Concepcion Mission, San Antonio. Surviving Mexicans take refuge behind the walls of the Alamo.

1873: Joseph Glidden applies for a patent on his invention, barbed wire.

1873: Dance hall owner Red Beard of Delano, Kansas goes on a drunken rampage, wounding prostitute Anne Franklin. He and competitor Joe Lowe, owner of Rowdy Joe's Bar, get into a quarrel. Lowe mortally wounds Beard. During that fight, gunfighter William Anderson is blinded when a bullet passes behind his eyes.

1876: Mountain man Joseph R. Walker dies at age 77 in Martinez, California.

1881: Reporting yesterday's Gunfight at the OK Corral, the *Tombstone Epitaph* headline reads: "Three Men Hurled into Eternity in the Duration of a Moment."

1901: Artist Herndon Davis who will paint the famed *Face on the Barroom Floor* in Central City, Colorado is born in Wynnewood, Oklahoma.

1929: *The Long, Long Trail* with Hoot Gibson is released by Universal.

1930: Wheatley Mine in McAlester, Oklahoma explodes, killing 30.

1933: Pianist Floyd Cramer born in Shreveport, Louisiana.

1972: Two national recreation areas are established at Glen Canyon in Arizona and Utah, and Golden Gate in California.

OCTOBER 28

1805: Zebulon Pike's construction of a stockade is completed at the mouth of the Swan River on his northern expedition to find the source of the Mississippi.

1834: The United States demands that Seminole Indians vacate Florida.

THE ALAMO

1835: A detachment under Col. James Bowie and Col. Jim Fannin raises the flag over San Antonio following yesterday's battle.

1866: Roy Bean, the future "Law West of the Pecos judge," marries Virginia Chavez in San Antonio, Texas.

1880: While he is being arrested for public intoxication in Tombstone, Curly Bill Brocius' pistol goes off, killing Marshal Fred White. The other peace officer on hand, Virgil Earp, hears White say it was an accident before he dies; Curly Bill will be acquitted of murder.

1895: F.G. Bonfils and Harry H. Tammen purchase the *Evening Post* in Denver for $12,500. Soon, the renamed *Denver Post* will be the most powerful newspaper in the West.

1901: Annie Oakley is critically injured in a train wreck while touring with Buffalo Bill's Wild West near Lexington, Kentucky. Doctors believe she will never walk, much less shoot, again. She proves them wrong.

1931: Zane Grey's *Riders of the Purple Sage* is released by Fox.

FIFTEEN BULLETS MOW FLOYD DOWN

Federal Agent Who Got Dillinger Kills Pretty Boy as He Runs From Under Corn Crib on Ohio Farm; Bandit Doesn't Use His Two Guns.

(CRIME NEVER PAYS)
East Liverpool, O., Oct. 23.—(A. P.)—Charles Arthur (Pretty Boy) Floyd, infamous outlaw whose bullets blazed a crimson path over a dozen midwestern states, is dead.

1934: Twenty thousand attend the funeral of Charles Arthur "Pretty Boy" Floyd in Sallisaw, Oklahoma. An armed robber by trade, he became a Robin Hood figure when he got into the habit of tearing up mortgages during bank jobs. A Woody Guthrie ballad about Floyd claims:

As through this life you ramble
As through this life you roam
You will never see an outlaw
Drive a family from their home.

1965: The 630-foot Gateway Arch is completed in St. Louis.

OCTOBER 29

1796: The first American ship to explore California's coastline is Ebenezer Dorr's *Otter*, which sails into Monterey Bay today.

1831: Agent John Dougherty reports on the smallpox epidemic among Pawnees. In four Kansas villages, "no one under 33 years of age escaped the monstrous disease."

1858: The first store opens in Denver.

1917: Coldest October day in U.S. history occurs when the mercury at Soda Butte, Wyoming hits -33 degrees.

1953: San Francisco plane crash kills 19, including concert pianist William Kapell.

1978: James Schelich is the first $275,000 slot machine winner in Las Vegas.

OCTOBER 30

1838: The Haun's Hill Massacre – In the name of religion, Nehemiah Comstock and 200 men attack a Mormon camp in Missouri, slaughtering 20 men, women, and children. After plundering the camp, they toss the bodies down a well. This follows Gov. Lilburn Boggs' edict that "the Mormons must be treated as enemies and must be exterminated or driven from the state."

1864: Town of Helena, Montana is organized.

1866: The James and Youngers rob the Alexander Mitchell Bank of Lexington, Missouri of $2,011.50.

1868: Work begins on the Atchison, Topeka, and Santa Fe railroad at Topeka, Kansas.

1875: Clay Allison participates in the lynching of Cruz Vega in Colfax County, New Mexico.

1961: *The Comancheros* with John Wayne released by 20th Century Fox.

OCTOBER 31

1848: Boston Custer, George Armstrong's brother, is born.

October

1863: Outlaw Tom "Black Jack" Ketchum born in San Saba County, Texas.

1864: Nevada enters the Union as the 36th state. Though the 40,000 population is too low to meet legal guidelines, President Lincoln okays the measure to help his 13th Amendment against slavery. The text of its constitution is telegraphed to Washington, running up a bill of $3,416.

1880: A riot occurs in Denver's Hop Alley, that city's Chinatown.

1912: Actress Dale Evans born in Uvalde, Texas.

1944: Singer Kinky Friedman born in Rio Duckworth, Texas.

November

NOVEMBER 1

1832: Lyne Barret, driller of the first Texas oil well, born in Virginia.

1836: Seminole Indians, led by Osceola, go on the warpath in Florida as a protest to Indian removal.

1844: Voters in Iowa, hoping for statehood, adopt a constitution.

1855: A bridge collapses near Gasconade, Missouri. Unaware of the situation, a Pacific railroad of Missouri train comes full speed ahead and plunges into the river, killing 22 on board.

1873: In De Kalb, Illinois, the first barbed wire is manufactured by Joseph F. Glidden.

1875: Clay Allison guns down Pancho Griego in New Mexico.

1887: The first train arrives in Aspen, Colorado.

1889: The Apache Kid and seven other Apache Indians are sent to Yuma Prison on a trumped up charge of murdering a whiskey peddler.

1924: Marshal Bill Tilghman, at age 71 a legend as a lawman of the Old West, is murdered by Wiley Lynn, an intoxicated prohibition agent in Cromwell, Oklahoma.

1925: Lava Beds National Monument created in California.

1929: Albert Bacon Fall is sentenced for his part in the Teapot Dome scandal.

1932: Pretty Boy Floyd robs the Sallisaw, Oklahoma State Bank of $2,500. Says the local newspaper of the relaxed heist: "It was like the hometown performance of a great actor who has made good on Broadway."

1944: Denver playwright Mary Coyle Chase's smash hit *Harvey* opens on Broadway.

1955: John Gilbert Graham plants a bomb in his mother's suitcase at Denver's Stapleton International Airport. The plane explodes over Longmont, Colorado, killing her and 43 others. Graham is convicted of the first act of aerial sabotage in the United States. He had recently taken out a great quantity of insurance on his mother. He will be executed.

1966: Warmest November day in Los Angeles, 100 degrees.

1979: Former First Lady Mamie Doud Eisenhower dies of a massive stroke at age 82.

NOVEMBER 2

1734: Daniel Boone born in Berks County, Pennsylvania. An early explorer of the Wild West (at that time Kentucky) Boone will become one of the first famous backwoodsmen. He will found Boonesborough in 1775, braving the perils of the wild as well as the natives. After a brief political career, he will move even further west, into Missouri.

> **DANIEL BOONE**
> **Born:** November 2, 1734
> **Died:** September 26, 1820
> **Frontiersman**
>
> **1734:** Born in Berks County, near Reading, Pennsylvania.
> **1753:** Moves to North Carolina.
> **1755:** Participates with General Braddock's campaign against French.
> **1769:** Explores Kentucky.
> **1775:** Opens the Wilderness Road from the Cumberland Gap, establishes Boonesborough.
> **1778:** Captured by Shawnee Indians.
> **1779:** Political career begins.
> **1786:** Elected to Kentucky legislature. Loses Kentucky holdings; relocates in West Virginia.
> **1798:** Moves from West Virginia to Missouri, becomes district magistrate.
> **1820:** Dies in Missouri.

1805: Lewis and Clark reach the Cascade Mountains.

1856: Grizzly Adams makes his theatrical debut at San Francisco's Union Theatre.

1869: Wild Bill Hickok loses the election he needed to succeed himself as the sheriff of Ellis County, Kansas, 114-89.

1870: Bear River Tom Smith is shot and killed near Abilene, Kansas.

1880: Pat Garrett is elected sheriff of Lincoln County, and charged with the task of bringing in Billy the Kid.

1889: North Dakota and South Dakota enter the Union as the 39th and 40th states, respectively.

1897: Edward Harriman takes charge of the Union Pacific railroad.

1902: The first fingerprinting at a federal penitentiary takes place in Leavenworth, Kansas.

1912: Last cattle from the fabled Texas XIT ranch are sold. At its peak, the XIT was the largest ranch in the world, running 160,000 head of cattle on three million acres in the Texas panhandle.

1982: Peter MacDonald is unseated as Navajo tribal chairman following accusations of official improprieties. He is replaced by Peterson Zah.

NOVEMBER 3

1762: France secretly cedes Louisiana west of the Mississippi plus Isle d'Orleans, to Spain.

1793: Texas founding father Stephen Fuller Austin born in Virginia.

> **STEPHEN AUSTIN**
> **Born:** November 3, 1793
> **Died:** December 27, 1836
> **Colonizer of Texas**
>
> **1793:** Born in Virginia.
> **1821:** Following the death of father Moses Austin, goes to Texas to claim the lands the government of Mexico had given his father.
> **1823:** Mexico confirms settlement of Texas.
> **1832:** 8,000 live in his colonies.
> **1834:** Arrested by Mexican authorities for inciting Texans to rebel.
> **1835:** Leads Texas forces against Mexicans in San Antonio, seeks recognition of Republic of Texas in Washington.
> **1836:** Dies at age 43.

1804: Sauk and Fox Indians cede over five million acres of present Wisconsin to the United States.

1813: Davy Crockett participates in Andrew Jackson's raid on the Creek

Indian settlement of Tallussahatchee, Alabama.

1853: The William Walker expedition, on a mission to stop Apaches from raiding in southern California, lands its ship at La Paz, seizes the Mexican government there, and names the area the Republic of Southern California.

1883: Black Bart pulls his last stagecoach robbery near Copperopolis, California. A shotgun wielding youth scares him off, but he leaves behind a telltale handkerchief. Authorities will check over a hundred San Francisco laundries before finding its owner.

1883: Native Americans are declared aliens and dependents of the government by the United States Supreme Court.

1885: Anti-Chinese riots in Tacoma, Washington force 200 from their homes.

1899: Bob Curry passes five bank notes from the Wilcox robbery at the Stockman's Bank in Montana.

1926: Annie Oakley dies at age 66.

1954: Linus Pauling receives the Nobel Chemistry Prize for his work on proteins and molecules at California's Institute of Technology.

1961: The first member elected to the Country Music Hall of Fame is Jimmie Rodgers.

NOVEMBER 4

1854: Lighthouse on Alcatraz Island, California completed.

1856: John C. Fremont is defeated in his Presidential bid by James Buchanan.

1856: Future Texas Ranger James Buchanan Gillett born in Austin, Texas.

PAT GARRETT

1862: Fort Sumner established in New Mexico.

1870: Central Pacific train is robbed of $40,000 in gold at Verdi, Nevada. Outlaw Jack Davis is arrested.

1879: Humorist Will Rogers born in Indian Territory, near what will become Oolagah, Oklahoma.

1891: A cage falls in the Anaconda Mine in Montana, killing 17.

1958: A nuclear-bomb-laden B-47 catches fire in the skies over Texas and crashes. The bomb does not detonate.

NOVEMBER 5

1846: Cmdr. Stockton is ordered to turn over California governorship to Gen. Kearny after Mexicans retake all the southern California coastal towns except San Diego.

1862: Three-hundred-three Santee Sioux sentenced to death following an outbreak in Minnesota. President Lincoln will commute all but 39 of the sentences.

1867: Wild Bill Hickok loses the election as sheriff of Ellsworth County, Kansas to Capt. E.W. Kingsbury.

1905: Actor Joel McCrea born in Los Angeles. In 1944, he will star in *Buffalo Bill*. Other Westerns will include *The Virginian* and *Gunfight at Dodge City*.

1911: First transcontinental flight ends in Pasadena, California after an 82 hour, 4 minute flight from New York. Pilot C.P. Rogers has many stops along the way.

1912: Leonard Slye, who will grow up to become Roy Rogers, born in Cincinnati, Ohio.

1920: *The Night Horseman* by Max Brand published by Putnam's.

1933: Speak-easy celebrity Texas Guinan dies.

1960: Singer Johnny Horton, 33, is killed in a Texas car crash. His last performance was at the Skyline in Austin, site of Hank Williams' last show. Horton's widow, Billy Joe, was also the widow of Hank Williams.

NOVEMBER 6

1528: Sailing from Florida, Cabeza de Vaca is washed ashore at Galveston Island, becoming the accidental discoverer of Texas.

1862: Telegraph communication between San Francisco and New York established.

1874: Julia and Adelaide Germain, the six- and four-year-old daughters of John Germain, who had been kidnapped from their wagon train by Cheyenne Indians in Kansas the previous spring, are rescued by troops under Lt. Frank Baldwin.

1882: Lily Langtry, future heartthrob of Judge Roy Bean, makes her American debut at New York's Fifth Avenue Theatre in Shakespeare's *As You Like It*.

1891: Comanche, the U.S. Army horse that survived the Battle of the Little Bighorn, dies at Fort Riley, Kansas.

1910: Doolin-Dalton gang member Roy Daugherty (Arkansas Tom) is paroled from prison at Lansing, Michigan.

1938: First "Red Ryder" Sunday comic strip appears. Fred Harman's creation is a tough, clean, square-jawed straight-shooter who, with his faithful Indian companion Little Beaver, will sell thousands of Daisy BB guns.

1960: Denver's Cooper Theater opens, the nation's first cinerama house.

FACE ON THE BARROOM FLOOR

NOVEMBER 7

1805: Lewis and Clark Corps of Discovery believe they have reached the Pacific Ocean. They have actually arrived at the Columbia River.

1811: Gov. William Henry Harrison's troops resist a surprise Indian attack at the Battle of Tippecanoe in Indiana Territory. When Harrison makes his successful bid for the Presidency in 1840, his slogan will be "Tippecanoe and Tyler too," referring to this battle and his Vice-Presidential choice.

1848: Mexican War hero Zachary Taylor is elected President.

1876: With the arrest of Johnny Ringo and George Glidden, the "Hoodoo War" in Texas comes to an end. The conflict, a bloody struggle that involved a lot of rustling and shooting, had begun in February, 1875. Hoodoos were masked vigilantes who took suspected rustlers from jails and lynched them.

1893: Colorado grants voting rights to women.

1960: *North to Alaska* with John Wayne released by 20th Century Fox.

1962: Artist Herndon Davis, most famous for his *Face on the Barroom Floor* in Central City, Colorado, dies while completing a mural in Washington D.C.

NOVEMBER 8

1887: John Henry "Doc" Holliday, 35, dies of tuberculosis in Glenwood Springs, Colorado. Barefoot, his last words are, "This is funny," noting that he will not be "dying with his boots on." He gulps down whiskey and expires.

1889: Montana enters the Union as the 41st state.

1893: Historian Francis Parkman dies at age 70. Best known for *The Oregon Trail*, he also authored *The Conspiracy of Pontiac* and the multi-volume *France and England in North America*.

DOC HOLLIDAY
Born: 1852
Died: November 8, 1887
Gambler, gunfighter, dentist

1868: Involved in a plot to blow up a federally occupied courthouse.
1872: Graduates from the Pennsylvania College of Dental Surgery.
1873: Tuberculosis diagnosed.
1874: Opens practice in Dallas, Texas. Gambles frequently.
1875: Jailed for wounding a saloon keeper. Kills another who accuses him of cheating at faro.
1877: Travels to Fort Griffin, Texas. Lives with prostitute Big Nose Katie Elder. Meets Wyatt Earp. Disembowels Edward Bailey following another cheating accusation. Moves to Dodge City.
1880: Arrives in Tombstone, Arizona. Reunited with Earp and Elder.
1881: May have robbed the Benson-Tombstone stage.
1881: Helps the Earps at the Gunfight at the OK Corral.
1882: Aids Wyatt's trail of revenge against the men who shot Virgil.
1883: Gambles in Deadwood.
1884: Shoots a Leadville bartender over a five dollar loan.
1886: *New York Sun* reports that he has killed 30 men. When asked about it he replies, "I claim to have been a benefactor to the country."
1887: Checks into a sanitorium in Glenwood Springs, Colorado. Dies at age 35.

1904: Theodore Roosevelt elected President.

1914: First rain in Bagdad, California since October 3, 1912.

1976: Smokey the Bear dies at age 70 (bear years) in his home in Washington D.C.

NOVEMBER 9

1848: First post office in San Francisco opens at Pike and Clay streets.

1875: Sioux followers of Sitting Bull and Crazy Horse are labeled hostile by Indian Inspector E.C. Watkins.

1888: Mine disaster at Frontenac, Kansas kills 40.

1894: Cherokee Bill kills Ernest Melton in Lenapah, Oklahoma.

1924: Nellie Tayloe Ross elected governor of Wyoming, becoming the first woman in U.S. history to hold that job.

1929: *The Virginian* with Gary Cooper released by Paramount.

1960: Actor Ward Bond, 57, best known for his role of Seth Adams on TV's "Wagon Train," dies of a heart attack in Dallas, Texas.

NOVEMBER 10

1602: Sebastian Vizcaino sails into San Miguel Bay and renames it San Diego de Alcala, present-day San Diego.

1808: Osage Indians cede Missouri and Arkansas lands to the United States in return for a reservation in Oklahoma.

1832: Washington Irving's Oklahoma expedition ends after a 400-mile trek through a "part of the Pawnee hunting grounds where no party of white men had yet penetrated."

1926: Queen Marie of Rumania pays a state visit to Denver.

1934: Former Butch Cassidy accomplice "Elzy" Lay, formerly with the Wild Bunch, dies in Los Angeles, California.

1970: Peter MacDonald is the first college graduate to lead the Navajos. He is chosen chairman of the nation's largest tribe.

1978: Badlands National Park established in South Dakota. The 170-square mile area had been a national monument since 1929.

NOVEMBER 11

1806: The Zebulon Pike expedition enters present Colorado.

1842: Gunslinger Ben Thompson born in Knottingly, Yorkshire, England.

1885: Leland Stanford Junior University is founded by the railroad magnate as a memorial to his deceased son at Palo Alto, California.

1889: Washington, with a population of 350,000, enters the Union as the 42nd state.

1911: Oklahoma City sets its record high and low for this date on the same day, 83 degrees and 17 degrees.

1921: Doolin-Dalton gang member Roy Daugherty, *aka* Arkansas Tom, is released from prison after serving eight years for bank robbery.

1933: A dust storm rages in South Dakota; in a couple of days, the dirt will be in the air over Albany, New York.

1955: President Eisenhower is released from Fitzsimmons Army Hospital in Denver 49 days after his heart attack.

1955: The Cowboy Hall of Fame is dedicated in Oklahoma City.

NOVEMBER 12

1867: A conference is held at Fort Laramie, in southeastern Wyoming, to discuss "Indian Problems."

1880: *Ben Hur*, an epic work of fiction by former New Mexico Gov. Lew Wallace, is published. Wallace worked on his Biblical tale in his spare time, when he wasn't dealing with the Lincoln County war and Billy the Kid.

1906: The warmest November day in U.S. history is registered at Craftonville, California ~ 105 degrees.

1916: Astronomer Percival Lowell dies in Arizona.

1916: Rodeo champ Fritz Truan born in Ceile, California.

1934: Cult family leader Charles Manson born in Cincinnati, Ohio.

1936: The San Francisco-Oakland Bridge, the longest over navigable waters, is dedicated.

1951: *Paint Your Wagon* opens on Broadway.

1971: Arches National Park is established in Utah. Sandstone arches and other natural formations including a 100-foot tall bridge are included on 82,953 acres.

NOVEMBER 13

1833: Joe Walker's party becomes the first group of white men to camp in the Yosemite Valley.

1833: A meteor shower beginning the evening of the 12th, wows the West. Missionary Jotham Meeker notes, "The Indians are much alarmed by it;" it is dubbed "The Night the Stars Fell."

1863: First and only woman to be legally hanged in Texas is Chipita Rodriguez, charged with the murder of John Savage.

1878: Gen. Lew Wallace's amnesty proclamation for most participants in the Lincoln County War is issued in New Mexico. Billy the Kid is not included.

1916: Actor Jack Elam born. His westerns will include *Gunfight at the OK Corral* and *The Comancheros*.

1963: *McLintock!* with John Wayne released by United Artists.

1974: Twenty-eight year old Karen Silkwood dies in an Oklahoma auto crash en route to meet with a *New York Times* reporter to discuss nuclear improprieties. The safety problems were with her employer, the Kerr-McGee Cimarron Plutonium Plant near Crescent, Oklahoma.

1955: Historian, essayist, conservationist Bernard DeVoto dies.

NOVEMBER 14

1882: Buckskin Frank Leslie guns down "Billy the Kid" Clairborne in a Tombstone shoot out.

1896: Future First Lady Mamie Doud born in Cedar Rapids, Iowa. When she is ten, her wealthy 36-

year-old father will retire to Denver. She will meet Dwight David Eisenhower while visiting her summer home in San Antonio where he is stationed.

1931: *The Cisco Kid* with Warner Baxter released by 20th Century Fox.

NOVEMBER 15

1806: Pikes Peak discovered near present Las Animas, Colorado. Zebulon Pike first sees the mountain that will one day bear his name. He says Pikes Peak appears "like a small blue cloud."

1844: Californios revolt; Governor Micheeltorena abdicates.

1869: Free postal delivery begins in San Francisco.

1872: The mayor of San Francisco exchanges a message with the mayor of Adelaide, Australia, in ceremonies honoring the completion of the telegraphic route to Australia via Europe.

1887: Artist Georgia O'Keeffe born in Sun Prairie, Wisconsin. After teaching art in the public schools in Amarillo, Texas, she has her first one-woman show in 1917 in New York City. She marries photographer Alfred Stieglitz in 1924. After a visit to Taos in 1929, she will permanently relocate there. Her art will reflect the haunting themes of the parched southwest.

1934: *In Old Santa Fe* with Ken Maynard released by Mascot.

1959: Coldest November day in United States history is recorded at Lincoln, Montana: -53 degrees.

NOVEMBER 16

1821: William Becknell and his traders arrive in Santa Fe. The route they used will soon be known as the Santa Fe Trail.

PIKE'S PEAK

1846: Gen. Taylor captures Saltillo during the Mexican War.

1907: Oklahoma enters the Union as the 46th state. Voters had chosen the name "Sequoyah" for their new state, after the inventor of the Cherokee alphabet, but they were turned down by Congress.

1907: New Mexico's Gila Cliff Dwellings are designated a national monument.

1934: Leopold Stokowski conducts the premiere performance of Harl McDonald's *First Symphony*, also called *The Santa Fe Trail*.

1955: Walt Disney airs "Davy Crockett and the Great Keelboat Race."

1958: Tucson, Arizona gets 6.4 inches of snow.

1961: Texan Sam Rayburn, a member of Congress for 48 years and Speaker of the House for 17 nonconsecutive years, dies at age 79.

NOVEMBER 17

1817: Davy Crockett's political career begins as he becomes justice of the peace of Lawrence County, Tennessee.

1821: The Tennessee House adjourns. Davy Crockett goes home and explores the Obion River country in western Tennessee with sons John Wesley and Abram Henry.

1856: Fort Buchanan in southeastern Arizona is the first post to be set up in the Gadsden Purchase area.

1878: Public administrator Grace Abbott born in Grand Island, Nebraska. As director of the U.S. Children's Bureau, she will aid the fight to get passage of a child labor amendment.

1882: Cornerstone laid for the University of Texas at Austin.

1889: Union Pacific begins daily service between Chicago and Portland, Oregon.

1929: Alexander Martin, an Old West photographer whose plates had a habit of revealing ghosts of the dearly departed in portrait shots, dies in Denver.

1981: Kathryn Jean Whitmire, elected the first woman mayor of Housston.

NOVEMBER 18

1805: Members of the Lewis and Clark expedition kill a California condor.

1846: First Thanksgiving observed in San Francisco.

1856: Ohio Representative John Bingham sends a letter to Secretary of War Jefferson Davis nominating George Armstrong Custer to West Point.

1865: Mark Twain's "The Celebrated Jumping Frog of Calaveras County" is published by *Saturday Press*.

1867: The Denver Pacific Railroad and Telegraph Co. incorporates with a stock of $2 million. Backers such as John Evans and David Moffat want to link Denver to Cheyenne by rail, thus insuring the survival of the city by access to the transcontinental railroad.

1883: At noon, railroads operating in this country adopt four time zones, the dividing lines coming at the 75th, 90th, 105th, and 120th meridians.

1923: The first photographs of New Mexico's Carlsbad Caverns appear in the *New York Times*.

1959: Robert Frank, only child of Frank James, dies at age 81.

1966: At Edwards AFB in California, Maj. William Knight sets an X-15 record with a speed of 4,233 MPH.

NOVEMBER 19

1854: Sam Houston is baptized in the Baptist church at age 61 to please his wife Margaret. When told that his sins have been washed away, he replies, "Lord, help the fish down below."

1905: Author Jack London takes his second bride, Charmian Kittridge of Berkeley, California at ceremonies in Chicago.

1907: Jack Schaefer, author of *Shane* born in Cleveland, Ohio.

1908: Author Frederick Dean Glidden, who under the pen name of Luke Short will write such works as

King Colt and *A Man Could Get Killed*, is born in Kewanee, Illinois.

1915: Labor martyr Joe Hill, convicted of the murder of a Salt Lake City merchant, a crime which he possibly did not commit, is executed at 5:00 A.M. by a Utah firing squad. His last words are "Fire ~ go on and fire!"

1915: Biochemist Earl Wilbur Sutherland, winner of the 1971 Nobel Prize for his work with enzymes, born in Burlington, Kansas.

1919: Zion National Park is established in Utah. The gorge of the Virgin River and many colorful formations fill 147,034 acres.

1943: Gunsight inventor John Hill Redfield dies in Denver.

1985: Largest civil judgement in American history, $10.53 billion, is awarded the Pennzoil Company which charged Texaco with undermining its own agreement in an attempt to purchase the Getty Oil Co.

NOVEMBER 20

1809: Trading party of Joseph McLanahan, Reuben Smith, James Patterson, and Manuel Lisa leave Missouri for a business outing to New Mexico. Here they are arrested, taken to Chihuahua, and thrown in jail for two years.

1843: Trading post at Blacksnake Hills is renamed St. Joseph, Missouri, as the new town grows rapidly.

1889: Astronomer Edwin P. Hubble born in Marshfield, Missouri. With his 1929 discovery that nebulae are receding at a speed proportionate to their distance, we first learn about the expanding universe.

1903: Tom Horn, the accused murderer of Willie Nickell, is hanged in Cheyenne, Wyoming one day before his 43rd birthday. He will be buried in Boulder, Colorado.

TOM HORN
Born: November 21, 1860
Died: November 20, 1903
Scout, lawman, hired gun

1863: Moves to Ohio with parents.
1874: Runs away from home; may have met Billy the Kid in New Mexico.
1877: Stagecoach driver for Overland Mail.
1883: Scouts during wars with Apache Indians in the southwest.
1886: Joins hunt for Geronimo into Mexico.
1887: Serves as deputy sheriff of Yavapai County, Arizona.
1888: Wins steer roping competition at an Arizona rodeo.
1891: Becomes range detective for private cattle firm.
1895: May have been hired to assassinate a Wyoming rancher.
1896: Another mysterious murder while employed by Iron Mountain Ranch.
1898: Serves in Spanish-American War; contracts yellow fever.
1899: Returns to Iron Mountain Ranch.
1900: Slays suspected rustler Matt Rash.
1901: Kills the son of target Kels Nickell, 14-year-old Willie.
1903: Escape attempt.
1903: Hanged in Cheyenne, Wyoming.

1906: An Oklahoma statehood constitutional convention convenes at the territorial capital of Guthrie.

1969: Eighty-nine Indians from 20 tribes claim Alcatraz Island in San Francisco Bay "by right of discovery."

NOVEMBER 21

1860: Tom Horn, a scout during the Apache wars, a Pinkerton agent, and an enforcer against cattle rustling in the twilight of the Old West, born in Memphis, Missouri.

1869: Controversial Oklahoma Gov. William Henry "Alfalfa" Bill Murray born in Toadsuck, Texas.

1921: First educational radio station in the United States is WOI at Iowa State College in Ames.

1922: A Supreme Court suit is initiated in Kansas to ban KKK activities in that state.

1934: Latest first snow of the season hits Denver.

1948: Clay Calhoun, the last surviving member of the Outlaw Exterminators, a group of Arizona lawmen, dies at age 87.

1959: Prize fighter Max Baer dies.

1980: Fire at the MGM Grand Hotel in Las Vegas kills 84, injures hundreds.

NOVEMBER 22

1899: Aviator Wiley Post born in Grand Saline, Texas. He will make the first round the world flight in 1933.

1916: Writer Jack London, 40, commits suicide at Glen Ellen, California.

1924: First football game to draw 100,000 is played in Memorial Stadium at Berkeley as Stanford plays the University of California; 76,000 are in the stadium, another 24,000 are strategically positioned on Tight Wad Hill.

1931: Denver native Paul Whiteman premieres Grofe's *Grand Canyon Suite* in Chicago.

1934: *Lawless Frontier* with John Wayne released by Lone Star/Monogram.

> **1963:** President John F. Kennedy is assassinated while riding in a motorcade through the streets of Dallas, Texas. His death shocks the nation. Most Americans begin a four-day vigil around their television sets. His accused murderer, Lee Harvey Oswald, will be killed before he can be brought to trial. Many important questions regarding the event will go unanswered.

1982: One hundred MX missiles are called on for deployment near Cheyenne, Wyoming by President Reagan.

NOVEMBER 23

1828: Marshal Ashmun Upson, ghost writer for Pat Garrett's *Authentic Life of Billy the Kid*, is born in Connecticut.

1850: The day the action begins in Bret Harte's *The Outcasts of Poker Flat*, when gambler John Oakhurst notices a change in the moral climate of Poker Flat.

1852: Waters of Lake Merced near San Francisco sink 30 feet following an earthquake-like shock.

1858: Enterprising trader Jim Sanders becomes the Denver postal service, offering to carry letters to Wyoming for 50 cents apiece.

1859: William Bonney, who will become the notorious Billy the Kid, born in the slums of New York City. A punk in every sense of the word, he will be a murderous influence on New Mexico's Lincoln County War, though it is doubtful he killed one man for each of his 21 years.

> **BILLY THE KID**
> **Born:** November 23, 1859
> **Died:** July 14, 1881
> **Outlaw**
>
> **1859:** Born in New York City.
> **1873:** Moves with mother to New Mexico, where she marries William Antrim.
> **1874:** Mother Catherine Antrim dies in New Mexico.
> **1875:** Arrested for the first time in Silver City, New Mexico; escapes from jail.
> **1877:** Kills his first man.
> **1878:** Active participant in the Lincoln County War.
> **1880:** Avoids a trap set by Pat Garrett in Fort Sumner, New Mexico.
> **1881:** Convicted of murder, sentenced to hang.
> **1881:** Escapes from the Lincoln County Jail.
> **1881:** Murdered by Pat Garrett at Fort Sumner, New Mexico.

1902: Murderer Augustine Chacon hanged in Solomonville, Arizona.

1903: Troops are called to Cripple Creek, Colorado during riots by striking miners.

1926: Marksman Frank Butler dies in Detroit, 20 days after the death of his wife, Annie Oakley.

NOVEMBER 24

1601: New Mexico Gov. Don Juan de Onate returns from an expedition in the northeast in which he and a party of 230 set up the first Spanish settlement in the southwest, San Gabriel, near the pueblo of San Juan on the Rio Grande.

1806: Near present Pueblo, Colorado, Zebulon Pike announces that he will walk to Pikes Peak, climb it, and be back before dinner. Pike was a terrible judge of distance and height. The mountain was 45 miles away and over 14,000 feet high. He returns a week later, having failed in the attempt to scale the mountain, and states flatly that it would be humanly impossible to climb it.

1835: Texas Rangers created by the provisional government of Texas.

1852: Cmdr. Matthew Perry sails from San Francisco on the *Susquehanna*, bound for Japan. The journey will open trade with the Far East.

1864: In a series of actions during the Civil War, conducted on the pretense of protecting settlers, Gen. Kit Carson and 400 men attack a Kiowa/Comanche village near Adobe Walls, Texas.

1868: Composer Scott Joplin, creator of ragtime, born in Texarkana, Texas.

1870: Susan James marries Allen H. Palmer, formerly of Quantrill's raiders, against her brother Jesse's wishes.

1874: Illinois farmer Joseph Glidden is granted a patent on his invention, barbed wire.

1956: *Giant* released by Warner Brothers. A modern Western of Texas oil, the film will be remembered for the classic image of James Dean stretched out in his convertible, a solitary Texas house on the horizon.

1963: Accused Presidential assassin Lee Harvey Oswald is shot to death before a national television audience during a move from police headquarters to the Dallas County Jail. Striptease club owner Jack Ruby is arrested.

1973: John Niehardt, author of *Black Elk Speaks*, dies.

NOVEMBER 25

1835: Texas navy established.

1846: Carry Amelia Moore, who will grow up to be saloon smasher and prohibitionist champion Carry Nation, is born in Kentucky.

1863: Alphonso Jackson Jennings, the worst train robber in history, as well as an actor in many "B" Westerns, is born in Tazwell County, Virginia.

1864: Kit Carson and 400 volunteers hold off 3,000 attacking Indians at Adobe Walls in the Texas panhandle. In this, the high point of his military career, Carson's command will count only 25 fatalities.

1868: William Ellsworth "Elzy" Lay, the "educated" member of the Wild Bunch, born in McArthur, Ohio.

1876: Cheyenne Chief Dull Knife's village on the Powder River is destroyed by Ranald Mackenzie's troops in the wake of the Little Bighorn massacre. Over 200 lodges are burned, and to make matters worse, 7th Cavalry souvenirs are found in the rubble.

1895: Cornerstone for Leadville's Ice Palace is laid.

1971: A skyjacker calling himself D.B. Cooper bails out of an airplane flying over the Pacific Northwest with thousands of marked dollars. No trace of him or the money is ever found.

1983: Denver's Thanksgiving blizzard leaves 30 inches of snow.

NOVEMBER 26

1849: Susan James, only sister of Frank and Jesse, born in Kearney, Missouri.

1853: William Barclay "Bat" Masterson born Bartholomew Masterson in Henryville, Quebec, Canada. He'll hunt buffalo as a young man, then drift into police work and gambling. Sometimes he will shoot his foes; other times he'll bat them over the head with his cane, necessary because a jealous soldier put a bullet in his leg. After a stint as a fight promoter, Bat will become a sportswriter for the New York *Morning Telegraph*.

BAT MASTERSON
Born: November 26, 1853
Died: October 25, 1921
Gambler, lawman, sports writer

1867: Moves with parents to Wichita, Kansas.
1872: Leaves home, labors in Dodge City.
1874: While a buffalo hunter, participates in the Battle of Adobe Walls in Texas panhandle.
1875: Scouts for Gen. Nelson Miles.
1876: Kills Sergeant King in Texas saloon gunfight. Leaves for Dodge City; becomes a peace officer.
1877: Wins sheriff election of Ford County, Kansas.
1878: Revenges brother Ed's killing in Dodge City.
1879: Appointed deputy U.S. marshal. Later defeated in sheriff election.
1881: Goes to work for Wyatt Earp at the Oriental Saloon in Tombstone.
1882: Serves as town marshal of Trinidad, Colorado, then promotes sporting events.
1891: Manages a large gambling hall in Denver.
1902: Moves to New York City, goes to work as a sports columnist for the *Morning Telegraph*.
1921: Dies while working at his desk.

November

1855: More free state/slave state problems for Missouri and Kansas as the two-week long Wakarusa War begins near Lawrence. Free-staters battle 1,500 Show Me State thugs.

1861: Politician and Teapot Dome scandal figure Albert Bacon Fall born in Kentucky.

1868: First baseball game in San Francisco to be played on an enclosed field.

1872: The "Great Diamond Hoax" is exposed in the San Francisco *Evening Bulletin* under the heading "The Diamond Chimera." Bank of America's William Ralston returns $80,000 each to 25 investors while the men who started the scam, Philip Arnold and John Slack, escape for greener pastures with $600,000 to divide.

1894: Mathematician Norbert Wiener, who will found the science of cybernetics, born in Columbia, Missouri.

NOVEMBER 27

1806: After spending the night in a cave on Cheyenne Mountain, Zebulon Pike gives up the idea of climbing the mountain that will be named for him. He writes, "I believe no human being could have ascended to its pinical."

1826: Jedediah Strong Smith and his fellow trappers reach Mission San Gabriel, becoming the first white Americans to make the overland trip to California.

1862: George Armstrong Custer meets his future bride, Elizabeth Bacon, at a Thanksgiving party.

1868: At the Battle on the Washita, Custer destroys a Cheyenne village in Indian Territory, killing Black Kettle, his wife, and 101 other Cheyenne at dawn on a bitter, snowy morning. Custer reports 19 soldiers killed in action.

1876: Trial of Jack McCall, murderer of Wild Bill Hickok, begins in Yankton, Dakota Territory. He is found guilty.

1886: Rodeo champ Lewis Bowman born in Weed, New Mexico.

1887: U.S. Marshal Frank Dalton, "the only good Dalton" and one of "Hanging Judge" Isaac Parker's marshals, is killed while trying to apprehend a Kansas bootlegger.

1892: Custer's father, Emanuel, dies.

1907: Federal troops are called to deal with striking miners at Goldfield, Nevada.

1942: Rock guitarist Jimi Hendrix born Johnny Allen Hendrix in Seattle, Washington.

1952: Winnie Ruth Judd escapes from the Arizona State Insane Hospital for the sixth time, only to be recaptured two days later.

1953: *Hondo* with John Wayne released by Warner Brothers.

1978: Disgruntled ex-supervisor Dan White shoots to death San Francisco Mayor George Moscone and city supervisor Harvey Milk.

His "Twinkie defense" will claim he was provoked to the violence by too much junk food.

NOVEMBER 28

1872: Fighting breaks out in Oregon between Modoc Indians led by Captain Jack and American soldiers because the Modocs have not moved on to Oregon's Klamath Reservation. The Modocs retreat into California, killing a dozen settlers on the way.

1873: Oil magnate Frank Phillips, who will participate in the founding of the Phillips Petroleum Co. in 1917, born in Scotia, Nebraska.

1925: Nashville's Grand Ole Opry, the home of country and western music, broadcasts the first in a series of Saturday night hoedowns over WSM radio.

1942: Fire at Boston's Coconut Grove kills 498, including matinee cowboy idol Buck Jones.

NOVEMBER 29

1777: First pueblo in California established, San Jose de Guadalupe.

1831: Revolt in California occurs when Pio Pico, Jose Carrillo, and Juan Bandini lead an insurrection against Mexican Gov. Manuel Victoria, who will resign.

> **1847: The Whitman Massacre ~** Cayuse Indians raid a mission near Walla Walla, in present Washington state, convinced that missionary Marcus Whitman and his settlers have brought a plague of measles. Whitman is killed in his kitchen. In the attack, 13 whites are slain including Whitman's wife, Narcissa.

> **1864: Massacre at Sand Creek ~** Col. John M. Chivington and 600 U.S. Cavalrymen slaughter over 100 Cheyenne and Arapaho men, women, and children at Black Kettle's camp in Colorado Territory. White soldiers scalp the dead. These trophies, including pubic hair scalps from several Indian women, are displayed a few days later during intermission at a Denver theatre. Chivington claims 500 killed. Chief White Antelope dies in the attack, but Black Kettle escapes. Most of Chivington's command was composed of the 3rd Colorado Volunteers, not U.S. soldiers. The 3rd was a short-term, poorly organized, poorly disciplined outfit, recruited from the riffraff of Denver's saloons and mining camps. They were the ones who committed the atrocities. Several Congressional and military committees condemned Chivington's actions, but he had left the Army soon after Sand Creek, and so escaped punishment.

1872: Horace Greeley dies in Pleasantville, New York, 24 days after losing the Presidential election to Ulysses S. Grant.

1876: Nellie Tayloe, future first American woman governor, born in St. Joseph, Missouri.

1880: Billy the Kid and "Billy

SAND CREEK MASSACRE

Wilson" (D.L. Anderson) elude a posse of eight near White Oaks, New Mexico, though they lose their horses in the gun battle.

1949: American Airlines DC-6 crashes in Dallas, killing 28 including Swiss violinist Julio Cochard.

1951: First underground atomic bomb test in Nevada.

1974: Oil tycoon H.L. Hunt dies at age 85.

1975: Record New Mexico 24-hour snowfall is set with 34 inches at Red River.

1976: Nellie Tayloe Ross celebrates her 100th birthday by reading greeting cards from Wyoming school children.

NOVEMBER 30

1806: The Pike party travels 15 miles up the Arkansas River in a blinding snowstorm.

1835: Author Samuel Clemens, who will start calling himself Mark Twain while writing for a Nevada newspaper in the gold rush days, is born in Florida, Missouri.

1837: Texas revolutionary Erastus "Deaf" Smith dies.

1884: Elfego Baca arrests a cowboy in Frisco, New Mexico for disturbing the peace. When riders come to teach him a lesson, Baca slays the foreman with his Colt. The worst will come the next day.

1902: Harvey Logan (Kid Curry) is sentenced to 20 years hard labor and fined $5,000 for his part in a recent train robbery.

1944: Albert Bacon Fall, key figure in the Teapot Dome scandal, dies in El Paso, Texas.

1951: Winnie Ruth Judd escapes the Arizona State Insane Hospital for the fourth time.

December

DECEMBER 1

1842: William Antrim, Billy the Kid's stepfather, born in Huntsville, Indiana.

1863: Construction begins on the Union Pacific railroad in Omaha, Nebraska. It will build westward and eventually join the Central Pacific at Promontory Point, Utah, completing the nation's first transcontinental railroad.

1879: The Earp brothers arrive in Tombstone, Arizona.

1884: Elfego Baca takes refuge in a *jacal* as 80 irate cowpokes surround him for the kill. They will fire some 4,000 bullets into the flimsy structure, sure they have killed the upstart. The next morning, they wake up to the smell of beef stew and tortillas as Elfego prepares his breakfast. When the episode is finally over, Baca emerges without a scratch, having wounded five and killed three of the cowboys.

1896: Temperatures in Kipp, Montana rise 30 degrees in seven minutes.

1904: Louisiana Purchase Exposition closes after seven months in St. Louis.

1913: Denver's worst blizzard begins. It will dump 45.7 inches of snow over the next five days.

1913: Actress/singer Mary Martin of *Peter Pan* fame born in Weatherford, Texas.

1917: Father Edward Flanagan founds Boys Town in Nebraska.

1919: Author Clifton Adams (*Desperado, Two Gun Law*) born in Comanche, Oklahoma.

1934: *The Westerner* with Tim McCoy released by Columbia.

1957: Buddy Holly and the Crickets make their live TV debut on "The Ed Sullivan Show."

DECEMBER 2

1832: Former Tennessee Gov. Sam Houston, 39, crosses the Red River from Oklahoma after a visit among the Cherokees, and steps on Texas soil for the first time.

1863: Mohave Chief Irataba arrives for a visit to San Francisco.

1873: Train robber / actor / horse thief Henry Starr born at Fort Gibson, Indian Territory.

1905: Diamondville Mine in Wyoming explodes, killing 18.

1913: The Brazos River floods, drowning 177 Texans.

1952: Gordon Kerr becomes the first to have his birth televised. The event takes place in Denver, over KOA-TV.

DECEMBER 3

1806: The Pike expedition camps

December

between present Pueblo and Canon City, Colorado.

1888: Richard Wetherill discovers the Cliff Palace at today's Mesa Verde National Park in southwestern Colorado.

1927: Singer Ferlin Husky born in Flat River, Missouri. His hits will include "Wings of a Dove."

1932: Zane Grey's *The Golden West* released by Fox.

1939: Winnie Ruth Judd escapes the Arizona State Insane Hospital for the second time. She will be recaptured 12 days later.

DECEMBER 4

1674: French explorer Father Marquette sets up a mission at the present city of Chicago.

1842: Many historians believe this to be the birth date of Crazy Horse, the Sioux warrior who will be one of the great field marshals of the Indian Wars.

1844: James Knox Polk elected President. He heavily favors the annexation of Texas, California, and Oregon.

1867: The Grangers, the Patrons of Husbandry, founded in Washington D.C.

1902: Gold discovered on Columbia Mountain in Nevada.

1972: Temperature in Livingston, Montana drops 34 degrees in 20 minutes.

1976: Colorado rock star Tommy Bolin dies of a drug overdose following a concert in Miami, Florida.

DECEMBER 5

1835: Americans under Col. James Bowie begin a house-to-house search of San Antonio, flushing out Mexican troops.

1839: George Armstrong Custer born in New Rumley, Ohio. After a stellar career fighting for the Union in the Civil War, he will be directed to the western frontier, where he will be consumed by his own legend.

GEORGE ARMSTRONG CUSTER
Born: December 5, 1839
Died: June 25, 1876
Military leader

1856: Enters West Point.
1861: Graduates last in his class; fights in First Battle of Bull Run during the Civil War.
1863: Promoted to rank of brigadier general.
1864: Marries Elizabeth Bacon at Monroe, Michigan; returns to Civil War.
1865: Assigned to 7th Cavalry at Fort Riley, Kansas.
1867: Court-martialed for deserting command to visit his wife.
1868: Restored to command.
1868: Battle on the Washita; destroys a Cheyenne village in Indian Territory.
1872: Serves as a guide for the Grand Duke Alexis buffalo hunt.
1873: Battles Sioux Indians at Yellowstone.
1874: Publishes *My Life on the Plains*.
1876: Assigned to aid efforts to get Sioux and Cheyenne onto reservations.
1876: Removed from command after implicating President Grant's brother in a military scandal. Restored by public demand.
1876: Killed at the Battle of the Little Bighorn.

1848: President Polk informs Congress of the California gold discovery.

1871: Black rodeo star Bill Pickett, who will invent the sport of bulldogging and possess the ability to throw a cow by biting his own lip, flipping over, and inducing the cow to follow him, is born near Austin, Texas.

MESA VERDE RUINS

1901: Walter Elias Disney born in Chicago, Illinois. After a stint as a Kansas City commercial artist, Disney will migrate to California to set up his dream factory. His contributions to family entertainment will be unequalled, from Mickey Mouse to Disneyland, Epcot, and beyond, his "wish upon a star" outlook will charm millions.

1933: Prohibition is officially repealed as Utah becomes the 36th state to ratify the 21st Amendment.

DECEMBER 6

1862: Only 39 of the 303 Santee Sioux sentenced to die for a Minnesota uprising will actually face the gallows, as President Lincoln commutes the remaining sentences.

1866: Sioux chief Red Cloud attacks a wood train near Fort Phil Kearny in Wyoming. Soldiers coming to the rescue are met with stiff resistance.

1870: Actor William S. Hart born in New York City. He will carry the code of the West to the silent screen in films such as *Hells Hinges* (1917) and *Tumbleweeds* (1925).

1893: Actress/spy Pauline Cushman dies in San Francisco.

1901: Photographer Eliot Porter born. His stirring photographs of the western wilderness will make him one of the foremost nature photographers.

1949: Texas bluesman Huddie Ledbetter dies.

DECEMBER 7

1805: Lewis and Clark pitch winter camp at Fort Clatsop in Oregon.

1828: Lewis B. Dougherty is the third white child born in present Kansas, at Cantonment Leavenworth. He will live until 1925.

1850: The day the gambler hero of Bret Harte's *The Outcasts of Poker Flat* expires in the snow. On the back of a deuce of clubs is this messgae scrawled in pencil: *Beneath this tree lies the body of John Oakhurst, who struck a streak of bad luck on the 23d of November, 1850, and handed in his checks on the 7th December, 1850.*

1869: Frank and Jesse James and Cole Younger rob the Davies County Savings Bank of Gallatin, Missouri. Jesse kills cashier John Sheets, with whom the boys had shared a grudge since the Civil War. The gang gets away with $500.

1873: Author Willa Cather born in Virginia. As a child, she will move with her family to Nebraska. The rough change of scenery will be ever-present in her literature that will include *My Antonia, O Pioneers!* and *Death Comes for the Archbishop.*

1876: Texas Rangers John Armstrong and Leroy Deggs open fire on murderer John Mayfield at the latter's ranch in Wilson County, Texas. Mayfield is killed but the Rangers have to make a hasty exit when the deceased's relatives realize what has happened.

DECEMBER 8

> **1883: The Bisbee Massacre** ~ In Bisbee, near Tombstone, Arizona, a botched robbery results in several Christmas shoppers being slain. A posse forms, the bandits are caught and hanged in Tombstone in March of 1884.

1899: Navajo County, Arizona sheriff Francis Joseph Wattron issues the following statement: *You are hereby invited to attend the hanging of one George Smiley, Murderer. His soul will be swung into eternity on December 8, 1899, 2:00 P.M. sharp. The latest methods in the art of scientific strangulation will be done to make the surroundings cheerful and the execution a success.* The invitation draws a reprimand from President McKinley to Arizona's territorial governor.

1905: American Bison Society established to protect the buffalo.

1931: Premiere of *The Blonde Donna* in New York, a story based on an 1824 Indian uprising at a Santa Barbara mission.

1960: *Cimarron* with Glenn Ford released by MGM.

DECEMBER 9

1835: Texas forces under Ben Milam capture San Antonio from the Mexicans under Gen. Cos. The survivors of an earlier attack had taken refuge in the Alamo which now becomes an American fortress. Milam dies during the battle.

1867: The capital of Colorado territory is changed from Golden to Denver.

1876: Capt. Thomas B. Weir, the 38-year-old officer who led a futile rescue effort from Maj. Reno's beleaguered position at the Little Bighorn, dies in New York City of "congestion of the brain."

1898: J.C. Penney sells his first store, a Longmont, Colorado meat market. He will move north to Wyoming and try his hand in the dry goods business.

1917: Physicist L. James Rainwater, winner of the 1949 Nobel Prize for his work with atomic nuclei, born in Council, Idaho.

1924: Wupatki National Monument is established in Arizona.

1947: Nevada's Rocking F Ranch claims all the water in the clouds passing over it.

1962: Petrified Forest National Park established in Arizona. Petrified wood, Indian ruins and a part of the Painted Desert cover 94,189 acres.

DECEMBER 10

1805: Zebulon Pike leaves his Swan River stockade to continue his search for the source of the Mississippi.

1854: Texas cattle baron Richard King marries Henrietta Chamberlain.

1869: Wyoming Gov. John Campbell signs the measure passed by the territorial legislature authorizing the vote for women, as well as the right to hold office. This is a first for any American state or territory.

1878: Expressman Henry Wells, co-founder of Wells Fargo, dies at age 73.

RED CLOUD
Born: 1822
Died: December 10, 1909
Chief (Oglala Sioux)

1820s: Raised by his maternal uncle, Chief Smoke; joins war parties against the Crow and Pawnee.
1841: Kills rival chief, splitting Sioux alliances for 40 years.
1866: Storms out of peace negotiations at Fort Laramie; begins "Red Cloud War."
1866: Masterminds "Fetterman Massacre" near Fort Phil Kearny, followed by the "Wagon Box Fight."
1868: Agrees to end Bozeman Trail hostilities on the condition that Forts Phil Kearny, C.F. Smith, and Reno are abandoned. Occupies Powder River country.
1870: Meets President Grant in Washington.
1871: Installed at a temporary agency on the Platte River, near Fort Laramie.
1873: Moved to the Red Cloud Agency in northwestern Nebraska.
1874: Gold discovered in the Black Hills, sacred country to the Sioux.
1876: U.S. negotiations with the Indians turn tough in the wake of the Battle of the Little Bighorn in June, 1876. Signs treaty releasing the Black Hills.
1877: Moved to the Pine Ridge agency in Dakota Territory.
1881: Deposed as chief after demanding the ouster of an Indian agent.
1909: Dies at age 87 at the Pine Ridge Indian Reservation.

1946: Writer Damon Runyon dies of throat cancer in New York City.

DECEMBER 11

1872: Buffalo Bill Cody and Texas Jack Omohundro arrive in Chicago for their theatrical debut in *The Scouts of the Prairie*.

1879: Entrepreneur / art collector Amon Carter born in Crafton, Texas.

1909: The Denver Auditorium opens, the first municipal theatre in the United States.

1939: Author Thomas McGuane born.

1969: Chemical Warfare Test Center near Dugway, Utah is evacuated due to leaking nerve gas.

DECEMBER 12

1822: The United States recognizes independent Mexico.

1844: Anson Jones becomes the second president of Texas, succeeding Sam Houston.

1871: Wild Bill Hickok is relieved of his duties after eight months as marshal of Abilene, Kansas, the last of Abilene's days as a cowtown.

1874: Frank and Jesse James, Cole, Bob, and Jim Younger, Bud McDaniels, and Clell Miller make off with $25,000 after robbing a train at Muncie, Kansas.

1901: Wild Bunch member Ben Kilpatrick is sentenced to 15 years in Atlanta, Georgia for robbery.

1925: The first motel, the Motel Inn, opens at San Luis Obispo, California.

1927: Oklahoma Governor Henry

Johnston calls out troops to block the legislature from entering the state capitol to conduct his impeachment hearing.

1929: Cattle king Charles Goodnight dies at age 93.

1939: Actor Douglas Fairbanks dies in Santa Monica, California.

DECEMBER 13

1798: Mountain man Joseph R. Walker born in Roan County, Tennessee.

1806: The Pike expedition reaches the South Platte River in Colorado.

1844: The first wagon train reaches Sutter's Fort in California, having taken the Truckee-Donner Lake route.

1892: Henry Starr kills Deputy Floyd Wilson in Nowata, Oklahoma.

1901: Kid Curry goes berserk playing pool in Knoxville, Tennessee. He chokes one man, shoots another, then wounds two policemen before being subdued. Back at the jailhouse, they find out who he is and press charges for train robbery.

1901: The El Paso *Times* announces the new Collector of Customs, Pat Garrett.

1916: Stone City, Kansas, mine explosion kills 20.

1922: Humble, Texas, train wreck kills 22.

DECEMBER 14

1909: Biochemist and Nobel winner Edward L. Tatum who, with G.W. Beadle, will perform major rescarch into the chemical function of genes and enzyme production, born in Boulder, Colorado.

1924: Temperatures in Helena, Montana drop 79 degrees in 24 hours.

1932: Singer Charlie Rich ("Behind Closed Doors") born in Arkansas.

1949: Swift Packing Plant at Sioux City, Iowa explodes, killing 21.

1967: Biochemists at Stanford announce the development of a synthetic DNA, a molecule which can control heredity.

1976: Lame Deer, seeker of visions, dies.

DECEMBER 15

1835: Santa Anna introduces his constitution for Mexican territories.

1866: After establishing his literary career, Mark Twain leaves the West, sailing out of San Francisco Bay bound for New York.

1869: A posse of four surrounds the Samuel farmhouse in Clay County, Missouri, but Frank and Jesse James manage to escape. Deputy Sheriff John Thomason misses out on the $3,000 reward.

1881: America's second transcontinental railroad is completed when the tracks of the Texas and Pacific meet those of the Southern Pacific at Sierra Blanca, Texas.

1890: Sitting Bull is hauled from his bed and killed by U.S. Indian police who have become extremely suspicious and paranoid about the Ghost Dance movement. Authorities wrongly believe he is involved in the movement. Despite his innocence, when he resists the rude treatment he is put to death. The medicine man of the Little Bighorn was approximately 60 years old.

SITTING BULL
Born: March, 1831
Died: December 15, 1890
Chief (Hunkpapa Sioux)

1864: Camp attacked by Sully at Killdeer Mountain; first fight with whites.
1865: Raids Fort Rice.
1868: Remains at war with the whites after Red Cloud's surrender.
1874: Gold discovered in Black Hills, Sioux holy land.
1875: All Indians ordered onto reservations.
1876: Meets at huge gathering of Cheyenne, Sioux, and Arapaho Indians, perhaps as many as 11,000. Group attacked by Gen. Custer, resulting in the Battle of Little Bighorn.
1877: Leads his people into Canada in the wake of Little Bighorn reprisals.
1881: Surrenders at Fort Buford, Dakota Territory.
1883: Released from prison, assigned to Standing Rock agency.
1885: Tours briefly with Buffalo Bill's Wild West.
1890: Murdered by Indian police in the wake of the Ghost Dance hysteria.

1903: The date on the death sentence handed Wyoming outlaw Ernie Cashel in Canada for the murder of rancher Rufus Belt. Cashel, known to use the alias Nick Carter, escapes five days before the sentence is to be carried out.

1933: *Sagebrush Trail* with John Wayne released by Lone Star/Monogram.

1944: Major Glenn Miller is lost over the English Channel during World War II, en route to a special Christmas concert.

1966: Walt Disney dies at age 65.

1970: Forty-eight thousand acres of land in New Mexico are returned to the Taos Indians. It had been taken in 1906 by the Forest Service.

1978: Actor Chill Wills dies at age 76.

DECEMBER 16

1811: The worst earthquake in U.S. history, during a winter-long series of quakes, centers at New Madrid, Missouri. The Mississippi River flows north, grounds rise, and the tremor itself is felt over 30,000 square miles.

1826: Benjamin Edwards arrives in Nacogdoches, Texas, declaring himself the supreme potentate of his Republic of Fredonia. Stephen Austin will put down the revolt.

1841: Missouri Sen. Lewis Linn introduces legislation encouraging migration to Oregon.

1890: Gen. Alfred Terry, Custer's commanding officer during the 1876 campaign, dies of heart failure at age 64 in New Haven, Connecticut.

1908: The Moffat Road is completed to Steamboat Springs, Colorado.

1934: Construction begins on the All-American Canal from the Colorado River to west of Calexico.

1979: The sound barrier is broken on land for the first time, by Stan

December

Barrett driving a rocket car at Edwards AFB in California.

DECEMBER 17

1871: Denver Horse railroad, a horse-drawn trolley system, begins operation.

1872: Buffalo Bill has his stage debut in Chicago. *Scouts of the Prairie* is a terrible bit of doggerel penned by Ned Buntline. Neither Bill nor his co-star, Texas Jack Omohundro, are able to deliver a single line as written. The action and fight sequences thrill the audience though, and Cody is a sensation.

1889: Rosemary Echo Silver Dollar Tabor, second daughter of Silver King Horace Tabor and his wife Baby Doe, is born to opulent splendor in Denver.

1901: Pinkerton agents arrive in Knoxville to identify Kid Curry.

1912: Rose O'Neill copyrights an idea she had in Colorado, the Kewpie Doll.

1929: A lighted cigarette causes the Old Town Mine in McAlester, Oklahoma to explode, killing 61.

1983: A two-week cold snap begins in the west. Temperatures in 60 cities and 21 states will hit record lows ~ wind chills of -100 degrees will be recorded.

DECEMBER 18

1843: Lawyer / newspaper owner Charles Albert Franklin Banta born in Indiana. He will found five Arizona newspapers.

1922: A Federal Reserve truck is robbed of $200,000 during a fiery shoot out outside the U.S. Mint in Denver.

1971: Capitol Reef National Park is established in Utah. Sandstone cliffs and a great dome-shaped rock along the Fremont River, comprise 254,242 acres.

DECEMBER 19

1864: Nicholas P. Earp, father of Wyatt and six other children, arrives with his family in San Bernardino, California after a wagon trip from Iowa.

1866: In a prelude to the Fetterman Massacre, Red Cloud tries to draw troops out of Fort Phil Kearny. Col. Carrington does not follow.

1880: Billy the Kid avoids a trap set by Pat Garrett in Fort Sumner, New Mexico.

1905: Author Dorothy M. Johnson (*The Hanging Tree, Buffalo Woman*) born in Iowa. She will grow up in Montana, the setting for most of her stories.

1925: Singer Little Jimmy Dickens ("May the Bird of Paradise Fly Up Your Nose") born in Bolt, West Virginia.

1959: Last surviving veteran of the Civil War, Texan Walter Williams, dies at age 117. In 1956, he had been given a citation when the last Union soldier died.

1964: *Cheyenne Autumn* is released by Warner Brothers.

1977: Nellie Tayloe Ross, 101, dies in Cheyenne, Wyoming.

1984: Fire at the Utah Power and Light Co. mine near Orangeville, Utah kills 27.

DECEMBER 20

1798: Birthday of Bridey Murphy, the personality assumed by a Colorado woman during the 1950s. This supposed reincarnation will cause a wave of interest in the subject.

> **1803: Louisiana Purchase** ~ The United States takes title to Louisiana during formal ceremonies transferring the land from France at New Orleans.

1806: The Pike party camps near modern Buena Vista, Colorado.

1835: Cherokees cede their Georgia lands after gold is discovered on them. Their subsequent evacuation to present-day Oklahoma, the Trail of Tears, will kill 10 percent of the tribe.

1858: Working from his base in Kansas, John Brown storms into Missouri, frees 11 slaves, and kills one pro-slaver.

1865: The first oil is drilled in Texas by Lyne Barret, but backers refuse to believe that there can be much of the stuff in the Lone Star state.

1866: Fetterman and Capt. Fred Brown appeal to Col. Carrington to lead an offensive against Red Cloud.

1877: Sam Bass robs the Fort Worth-Cleburne stage of $11.25.

1951: Electricity is generated from an atomic testing station at Arco, Idaho.

1952: A U.S. Air Force C-124 crashes on takeoff at Moses Lake, Washington, killing 87.

DENVER MINT

1968: Nobel laureate John Steinbeck dies at age 66 in New York City.

1970: Fire at Tucson's Pioneer International Airport kills 28.

DECEMBER 21

1821: First white child born in Texas is Mary James Long.

> **1866: The Fetterman Massacre** ~ Outside Fort Phil Kearny in Wyoming, Red Cloud again attacks a group of men collecting lumber. Crazy Horse and a small decoy party charge their protectors Capt. William J. Fetterman and his eighty soldiers, alone, confusing the troops. They take the bait, and chase him into the valley behind Lodge Trail Ridge, where they are met by 2,000 Cheyenne, Arapaho, and Sioux warriors. The entire command is wiped out in this, the worst Army defeat so far in the Indian wars.

1876: Brothers John and Clay Allison raise hell at the Olympic Dance Hall in Las Animas, Colorado. When Deputy Charles Faber arrives to quiet matters, shooting erupts. John is wounded badly, Clay kills Faber.

1928: Congress approves the Hoover Dam construction act.

1936: The first luxury ski resort opens at Sun Valley, Idaho.

1967: LSD king Augustus Owsley Stanley III, 32, arrested by agents at his home in Orinda, California.

DECEMBER 22

1769: Daniel Boone and his party taken captive by Shawnee Indians. They will be released, then recaptured.

1878: Billy the Kid arrested by Lincoln County, New Mexico Sheriff John Kimball. After his release, he will ride toward Las Vegas, New Mexico.

1884: John Chisum, a central figure of the Lincoln County War, dies and is buried in Paris, Texas.

1912: Claudia Alta Taylor, future "Lady Bird" Johnson, born in Karnack, Texas.

1921: Singer Hawkshaw Hawkins ("Sunny Side of the Mountain") born in Huntingdon, West Virginia.

1964: Mother Nature goes on a rampage in California, Idaho, and Oregon, killing 40 and doing damage of over $1 billion with a combination of snow, rain, and wind.

DECEMBER 23

1806: Lt. James Wilkinson's party, practically frozen after three terrible weeks in Colorado, where they had been visiting the Pike expedition, arrives at the Osage winter camp near present Claremore, Oklahoma.

1829: Prince Paul of Wuerttemberg leads a small scientific expedition from St. Louis toward the Rockies.

1908: Rodeo great Bill Pickett attempts to bulldog a fighting bull in Mexico City. He will barely escape with his life.

DECEMBER 24

1809: Scout/mountain man/military leader Christopher Houston "Kit" Carson born in Madison County, Kentucky, the son of pioneers Lindsey and Rebecca Carson.

KIT CARSON
Born: December 24, 1809
Died: May 23, 1868
Scout, soldier

1809: Born in Madison County, Kentucky.
1824: Apprenticed as a saddler.
1829: Goes west with expedition to California.
1831: Begins a decade of trapping in the Rockies.
1842: Guides first John Charles Fremont expedition.
1843: Leads the second Fremont expedition through the Snake River Valley and on to California's San Joaquin Valley.
1847: Becomes famous when Fremont publishes his memoirs.
1850: Runs major sheep herding drive from Santa Fe to California.
1853: Becomes Indian Agent stationed in Taos.
1861-1865: Protects white settlements from Indian attack during the Civil War.
1864: Fights Kiowa and Comanche at the battle near Adobe Walls, Texas.
1868: Dies at age 59 at Fort Lyon, Colorado.

1813: Davy Crockett's 90-day enlistment runs out during the Creek War. He returns home for a Christmas break.

1849: Fire destroys a portion of San Francisco.

1853: Disaster on the high seas as the *San Francisco* sinks on its way to California, drowning 240 of the 700 passengers and crew on board.

1859: The entire population of Boulder, Colorado, 200 men and 17 women, attend a Christmas Dance at Bill Barney's dance hall.

1864: Boise becomes the capital of Idaho.

1905: Film maker / aviation pioneer and billionaire recluse Howard Robard Hughes, Jr. born in Houston, Texas. His fortune will begin with the inheritance of a certain type of oil drill with which he will found the Hughes Aircraft Co. A record-breaking pilot, he will go into seclusion in 1950. In 1966 he will sell his 78 percent share of TWA for $500 million.

1914: Naturalist John Muir dies at age 76 in Los Angeles.

1922: First column by Will Rogers appears in the *New York Times*.

1922: Giovanni Martini who, as a trumpeter in the 7th Cavalry was the last to hear George Armstrong Custer speak when he was dispatched just before the Battle of the Little Bighorn, dies of natural causes in Brooklyn, New York.

1924: A candle ignites a Christmas tree during a party at the Babb Switch School in Hobart, Oklahoma. People panic, clogging the only entry, and 36, mostly children, perish in the blaze.

1924: In Fairfield, Montana it is 84 degrees at noon. By midnight, it will reach -21 degrees.

1982: The "Christmas Blizzard" dumps 23.6 inches on Denver in 24 hours, a city record. It begins in the wee hours of December 23, and by December 25, the city is paralyzed. Owners of four-wheel drive vehicles are on alert for emergency driving. Mail delivery ceases for a week in many locations.

DECEMBER 25

1846: Col. Alexander Doniphan defeats the Mexicans at El Brazito during the Mexican War.

1858: Uncle Dick Wootten rolls into the mining camp that will become Denver. A 1900 *Denver Times* later reflected on his arrival, "The sun had just rubbed its sleepy eyes and peeped in on the little settlement...when Santa Claus made his appearance." In the back of Wootten's wagon are a couple of barrels of Taos Lightning, the first booze to hit camp.

1865: Chicago's Union Stockyards open.

1868: At the Battle of Soldier Spring on the North Fork of the Red River, U.S. troops under Maj. Andrew W. Evans defeat a band of Kiowa and Comanche Indians, destroying their village.

1869: Christmas goodwill be

damned! John Wesley Hardin, 16, kills James Bradley after a poker game in Towash, Texas.

1887: Hotel magnate Conrad Hilton born in San Antonio, New Mexico.

1889: Texas Rangers Ira Aten and John Hughes and Deputy Sheriff William Terry kill murderous brothers Will and Alvin Odle on a silent night in Vance, Texas.

1891: In Texas, Mexican revolutionary Catarino Garza tries to take Fort Ringgold. His attempt in unsuccessful, but he continues to harass U.S. troops in the area.

1902: The *Fort Bent River Press* reports that Kid Curry, in prison for over a year, is in failing health.

DECEMBER 26

1826: Moses Austin requests permission from the government of Mexico to bring 300 families into Texas.

1859: Denver is chosen as the name of the city at the junction of the Platte River and Cherry Creek. That name, in honor of the governor of Kansas, wins out over "Auraria" and "Highlands."

1862: Thirty-eight Sioux Indians are hanged for atrocities committed during a Minnesota uprising. President Lincoln had commuted the sentences of all but 39 of more than 300 Indians accused. One received a last-minute reprieve.

1874: The first commercial buffalo hunt in Texas begins.

1881: Texas Ranger James B. Gillett receives an honorable discharge.

1883: Eight miners are killed near Telluride, Colorado when an avalanche fills their mine with snow.

1908: The first black to win the heavyweight championship is Jack Johnson of Galveston, who pounds Tommy Burns at Rushcutter's Bay on the outskirts of Sydney, Australia.

1909: Western artist Frederic Remington, 48, dies in Connecticut.

1914: Actor Richard Widmark born in Sunrise, Minnesota. He will play Jim Bowie in *The Alamo* among his major performances.

1961: Actor/outlaw Al Jennings dies at age 98 on his chicken ranch in Tarzana, California.

1972: Thirty-third U.S. President Harry S Truman, 88, dies in Kansas City, Missouri.

DECEMBER 27

1836: Stephen F. Austin, 43, dies.

1846: Col. Doniphan occupies El Paso during the Mexican War.

1859: *The Western Mountaineer* by George West is the first newspaper published in Golden, Colorado.

1872: U.S. Army defeats the Apaches in a major conflict with that tribe in Arizona.

1894: Kid Curry murders Pike Landusky after a two-day Christmas blowout in Landusky, Montana. He beats the older man mercilessly in a saloon until Pike goes for his gun. The Kid is much quicker on the draw.

DECEMBER 28

1832: St. Louis University is chartered.

1841: Rev. Robert James marries Zerelda Cole in Stamping Ground, Kentucky. Their union will create the most dangerous brother act in the Old West, Frank and Jesse James.

1846: Iowa enters the Union as the 29th state. The capital is Iowa City,

the governor Ansel Briggs.

1854: William Russell, W.B. Waddell, and Alexander Majors obtain a government subsidy after they agree to provide freight service from Fort Leavenworth to California.

> **1872: The Battle of Skull Cave** – During his Tonto Basin Campaign, Gen. George Crook orders an action which will trap more than 100 Apaches in a cave in Arizona. About two-thirds of them will be killed by ricocheting bullets in the cave.

1872: Artist George Catlin dies a pauper at age 76 in Jersey City, New Jersey.

1878: The Old West's two most famous outlaws meet for the first and only time. Jesse James, traveling under the name of Thomas Howard, is introduced to William Bonney, Billy the Kid, in Las Vegas, New Mexico. Jesse asked the Kid to join him; the Kid politely declined. The two rode their separate ways.

1881: Virgil Earp is permanently crippled by a shotgun blast on the streets of Tombstone, Arizona, a reprisal for his part in the Gunfight at the OK Corral.

1886: John L. Sullivan boxes in a Denver exhibition.

1890: The last Northwestern stagecoach leaves Deadwood, South Dakota.

1900: Carry Nation smashes a mirror in a hotel bar in Wichita, Kansas, then tosses rocks at the painting *Cleopatra at the Bath*.

1930: Fire demolishes the state capitol building at Bismarck, North Dakota.

1934: *'Neath the Arizona Skies* with John Wayne released by Lone Star/Monogram.

DECEMBER 29

1829: Sen. Samuel Foot introduces a resolution calling for temporary restrictions on public land sales in the west.

1835: Cherokees surrender their eastern lands for $5 million and some land in Oklahoma with the signing of the Treaty of New Echota. Though most members of the tribe will disagree with the terms, the "Trail of Tears" is not far off.

1845: Texas enters the Union as the 28th state.

1846: U.S. forces march northward from San Diego toward Los Angeles, under Gen. Kearny and Commander Stockton.

1879: Stagecoach driver Charlie

Parkhurst is found dead in Watsonville, California. The big surprise was that cigar-smoking, rough-talking Charlie had a little secret he had been keeping from the boys. Charlie was really a woman. She had successfully carried off the charade throughout a long career in the Sierra Nevadas.

> **1890: The Battle of Wounded Knee** ~ The last major conflict between Native Americans and the U.S. Army finds 350 Miniconjou Sioux under Chief Big Foot camped at Wounded Knee Creek on the Pine Ridge Reservation in South Dakota. The 7th Cavalry under Col. James W. Forsyth orders them to turn over their weapons. A shot rings out, and the carnage unfolds. Rapid-firing Hotchkiss guns fire a shell a second. When it is over, Big Foot and 146 others, including 44 women and 18 children, are dead, 51 are wounded. Forsyth reports 25 dead soldiers, 39 wounded. Only minor skirmishes happen after this. Between the years 1866-1891, the U.S. Army records will show 1,065 combat actions against western Indians.

1916: Homesteads allowed up to 640 acres under the Stock Raising Homestead Act, revised today.

1951: Nineteen West Point cadets on Christmas break are among 28 killed when a USAF C-47 crashes into Armer Mountain near Phoenix.

DECEMBER 30

1853: The Gadsden Purchase of Arizona and New Mexico from Mexico is completed; 29,640 square miles comprise the southern borders of these future states, for which the United States pays $10 million. Three years later, gold and silver will be discovered there.

1900: Clarence Lewis Barnhart, future editor of the Thorndike-Barnhart dictionaries, is born near Plattsburg, Missouri.

1905: Former Idaho Gov. Frank Steunenberg is assassinated as a bomb goes off in his Caldwell home, revenge for his part in the 1899 labor problems in the Coeur d'Alene mining area. Western Federation of Miners leader William "Big Bill" Haywood will be charged in a famous murder conspiracy trial, defended by Clarence Darrow, and acquitted. The man who set the explosive, Harry Orchard, will serve a life sentence.

1915: Harry Houdini is suspended upside down in a strait jacket for a noontime crowd in front of *The Denver Post* building. In minutes, he writhes his way to freedom, tossing the jacket to the cheering throng.

1930: Actor Jack Lord ("Stoney Burke") born in New York City.

1931: Singer Skeeter Davis ("The End of the World") born Mary Frances Penick in Dry Ridge, Kentucky.

DECEMBER 31

1806: Pike becomes doubtful that he

is on the Red River. He is not. His party is on the Rio Grande, about a thousand miles distant.

1897: Greatest amount of precipitation in a calendar year in Colorado recorded at Ruby, 92.84 inches.

1907: Mine disaster in San Antonio, New Mexico kills 30.

1924: Actor/singer Rex Allen born in Wilcox, Arizona. He will earn a gold record in 1953 for "Crying in the Chapel."

1937: Least amount of precipitation in a calendar year in Colorado recorded at Buena Vista, 1.69 inches.

1943: John Henry Deutschendorf, future actor/singer John Denver, born in Roswell, New Mexico.

TV Westerns

The age of the television Western began with the medium itself, but it was not until the mid-fifties that the real boom hit. When television executives noted, in the summer of 1957, that of 60 shows cancelled from the previous season, not one had been a Western, the rush was on. By 1959, more than $50 million was being spent each year on 28 shows. This made for 570 hours of cowboy programming, the equivalent of 400 feature films a year. In 1961, the top three shows were "Wagon Train," "Bonanza," and "Gunsmoke." Popularity diminished in the early 1960s, as American viewing habits changed in favor of the situation comedy. What follows are the days of the TV Western, from the time they first hit the video pasture, until their last roundup came in the form of cancellation.

Alias Smith and Jones (ABC) 1/21/1971 ~ 1/13/1973
Bat Masterson (ABC/NBC) 10/8/1959 ~ 9/21/1961
Black Saddle (NBC) 1/10/1959 ~ 9/30/1960
Bonanza (NBC) 9/12/1959 ~ 1/16/1973
Branded (ABC) 1/24/1965 ~ 9/4/1966
Brave Eagle (CBS) 9/28/1955 ~ 6/6/1956
Broken Arrow (ABC) 9/25/1956 ~ 9/17/1960
Bronco (ABC) 9/23/1958 ~ 8/20/1962
Buckskin (NBC) 7/3/1958 ~ 8/29/1965
Cheyenne (ABC) 9/20/1955 ~ 9/13/1963
Cimarron City (NBC) 10/11/1958 ~ 9/16/1960
Cimarron Strip (CBS) 9/7/1967 ~ 9/7/1971
Colt .45 (ABC) 10/18/1957 ~ 9/27/1960
Cowtown Rodeo (ABC) 8/1/1957 ~ 9/8/1958
Custer (ABC) 9/6/1967 ~ 12/27/1967
Daniel Boone (NBC) 9/26/1964 ~ 8/27/1970
Damon Runyon Theatre with Dick Powell (CBS) 4/16/1955 ~ 6/30/1956
Destry (ABC) 2/14/1964 ~ 9/11/1964
Dick Powell's Zane Grey Theatre (CBS) 10/5/1956 ~ 9/20/1962
Dirty Sally (CBS) 1/11/1974 ~ 7/19/1974
Dundee and Culhane (CBS) 9/6/1967 ~ 12/13/1967
Empire (NBC) 9/25/1962 ~ 9/6/1964
F Troop (ABC) 9/14/1965 ~ 8/31/1967
Frontier Circus (CBS) 10/5/1961 ~ 9/20/1962
Frontier Justice (ABC) 7/7/1958 ~ 9/28/1961
Gunslinger (CBS) 2/9/1961 ~ 9/14/1961
Gunsmoke (CBS) 9/10/1955 ~ 9/1/1975
Have Gun Will Travel (CBS) 9/14/1957 ~ 9/21/1963
Hec Ramsey (NBC) 10/8/1972 ~ 8/25/1974
Hondo (ABC) 9/8/1967 ~ 12/29/1967
How the West Was Won (ABC) 2/12/1978 ~ 8/27/1978

Johnny Ringo (CBS) 10/1/1959 ~ 9/29/1960
Kung Fu (ABC) 10/14/1972 ~ 6/28/1975
Lancer (CBS) 9/24/1969 ~ 9/9/1971
Laramie (NBC) 9/15/1959 ~ 9/17/1963
Laredo (NBC) 9/16/1965 ~ 9/1/1967
Law of the Plainsman (NBC) 10/1/1959 ~ 9/24/1962
Little House on the Prairie (NBC) 9/11/1974 ~
Maverick (ABC) 9/22/1957 ~ 7/8/1962
Rawhide (CBS) 1/9/1959 ~ 1/4/1966
Redigo (NBC) 9/24/1963 ~ 12/31/1963
Sara (CBS) 2/13/1976 ~ 7/30/1976
Shane (ABC) 9/10/1966 ~ 12/31/1966
Stagecoach West (ABC) 10/4/1960 ~ 9/26/1961
Sugarfoot (ABC) 9/17/1957 ~ 7/3/1961
The Texas Rangers (ABC) 10/21/1956 ~ 5/25/1959
Tales of Wells Fargo (NBC) 3/18/1957 ~ 9/8/1962
Temple Houston (NBC) 9/19/1963 ~ 9/10/1964
The Adventures of Jim Bowie 9/7/1956 ~ 8/29/1958
The Adventures of Rin Tin Tin (ABC) 9/7/1956 ~ 8/28/1959
The Barbary Coast (ABC) 9/8/1975 ~ 1/9/1976
The Big Valley (ABC) 9/15/1965 ~ 5/19/1969
The Californians (NBC) 9/24/1957 ~ 8/27/1959
The Cowboys (ABC) 2/6/1974 ~ 8/14/1974
The Dakotas (ABC) 1/7/1963 ~ 9/9/1963
The Deputy (NBC) 9/12/1959 ~ 9/16/1961
The Gene Autry Show (CBS) 7/21/1950 ~ 8/7/1956
The Guns of Will Sonnett (ABC) 9/8/1967 ~ 9/15/1969
The Iron Horse (ABC) 9/12/1966 ~ 1/6/1968
The High Chaparral (NBC) 9/10/1967 ~ 9/10/1971
The Lawman (ABC) 10/5/1958 ~ 10/2/1962
The Legend of Jesse James (ABC) 9/13/1965 ~ 9/5/1966
The Life & Times of Grizzly Adams (NBC) 2/9/1977 ~ 7/26/1978
The Life and Legend of Wyatt Earp (ABC) 9/6/1955 ~ 9/26/1961
The Lone Ranger (ABC) 9/15/1949 ~ 9/12/1957
The Man From Blackhawk (ABC) 10/9/1959 ~ 9/23/1960
The Marshal of Gunsight Pass (ABC) 3/12/1950 ~ 9/30/1950
The Monroes (ABC) 9/7/1966 ~ 8/30/1967
The Outcasts (ABC) 9/23/1968 ~ 9/15/1969
The Oregon Trail (NBC) 9/21/1977 ~ 10/26/1977
The Outlaws (NBC) 9/29/1960 ~ 9/13/1962
The Overland Trail (NBC) 2/7/1960 ~ 9/11/1960
The Quest (NBC) 9/22/1976 ~ 12/29/1976
The Rebel (ABC) 10/4/1959 ~ 9/12/1962
The Restless Gun (NBC) 9/23/1957 ~ 9/14/1959
The Rifleman (ABC) 9/30/1958 ~ 7/1/1963
The Road West (NBC) 9/12/1966 ~ 8/28/1967
The Rounders (ABC) 9/6/1966 ~ 1/3/1967
The Roy Rogers Show (NBC) 12/30/1951 ~ 6/23/1957
The Tall Man (NBC) 9/10/1960 ~ 9/1/1962
The Texan (CBS) 9/29/1958 ~ 9/12/1960

The Travels of Jaimie McPheeters (ABC) 9/15/1963 ~ 3/15/1964
The Virginian (NBC) 9/19/1962 ~ 9/8/1971
The Wide Country (NBC) 9/20/1962 ~ 9/12/1963
The Wild Wild West (CBS) 9/17/1965 ~ 9/7/1970
Tombstone Territory (ABC) 10/16/1957 ~ 10/9/1959
Trackdown (CBS) 10/4/1957 ~ 9/23/1959
Wagon Train (ABC) 9/17/1957 ~ 9/5/1965
Wanted: Dead or Alive (CBS) 9/6/1958 ~ 3/29/1961
Whispering Smith (NBC) 5/15/1961 ~ 9/17/1961
Wichita Town (NBC) 9/30/1959 ~ 9/23/1960
Yancy Derringer (CBS) 10/2/1958 ~ 9/24/1959
Zorro (ABC) 10/10/1957 ~ 9/24/1959

Brigham Young's Wives

Certainly he was the most married man in the West. As head of the Church of Latter-day Saints, Brigham Young preached polygamy or, more properly, polygyny: the taking of plural wives. And he practiced what he preached. From 1824 when he took his first bride, until 1870, Young had more than 50 wives. What follows is a list of his anniversaries. Note, some of the entries are marriages, others are "sealings." Sometimes dates of sealings exist where marriage records do not. "Sealing" meant that the woman was bound to her husband on earth and in heaven.

1/8/1865: Brigham Young is sealed to Mary Van Cott, 20, his 50th bride.

1/14/1846: Brigham Young is sealed to Louisa Beaman, wife number seven, Emily Dow Partridge, wife number nine (both widows of Joseph Smith), and Margaret Maria Alley, his 14th bride. Partridge will bear him seven children, Alley two.

1/15/1846: Brigham Young is sealed to Emily Haws, 22, his 15th bride, and to Olive Andrews, 27, his 16th wife.

1/16/1847: Though it cannot be officially determined, it is believed that Brigham Young married two Sioux women on this date, brides numbers 55 and 56.

1/17/1846: Brigham Young is sealed to Mary Elizabeth Rollins, his 17th wife.

1/21/1846: Brigham Young is sealed to brides number 18, 19, 20, and 21. They are Ellen Ackland Rockwood, 16, Martha Bowker, 23, Maria Lawrence, 22, and Mary Ann Clark, 29.

1/22/1846: Margaret Pierce, 13th bride of Brigham Young is sealed to him on the day he marries his 22nd wife, Margaret Pierce.

1/24/1863: Brigham Young marries Harriet Amelia Folsom, 24, his 49th wife.

1/26/1846: Brigham Young is sealed to bride 23, 21-year-old Rebecca Greenlief Hollman.

1/28/1846: Brigham Young marries bride 24, 69-year-old Phoebe Ann Morton, and bride 25, Jemima Angell, 41, Phoebe's daughter. On the same day, he is sealed to bride 26, 62-year-old Cynthia Porter Weston, and bride 27, 64-year-old Abby Works.

1/30/1846: Brigham Young is sealed to his 28th wife, 17-year-old Elizabeth Fairchild.

1/31/1846: Brigham Young marries bride 29, 33-year-old Eliza Nelson Green and is sealed to bride 30, 61-year-old Rhoda Richards, his first cousin.

AN 1875 ILLUSTRATION FROM *HARPER'S WEEKLY* SHOWS A NUMBER OF BRIGHAM YOUNG'S WIVES AT THE MORMON TABERNACLE IN SALT LAKE

2/2/1846: Brigham Young is sealed to his 31st bride, Zina Diantha Huntington, who is 24 and pregnant with the second child of Henry B. Jacobs. (She had married Joseph Smith in 1841 when she was pregnant with Jacobs' first child.)

2/3/1846: Brigham Young marries wives 32-36. They are: Julia Foster, 35; Mary Ellen De La Montague, 42; Cecilia Cooper, 41; Abigail Hanks, 55; and Mary Ann Turley, 18. He is also sealed to number 37, 44-year-old Eliza Roxey Snow.

2/6/1846: Brigham Young is sealed to brides 38, 39, 40, and 41. They are Namah Kendel Jenkins Carter, 24; Nancy Cressy, 66; Clarissa Blake, 49; and Diora Chase, 18.

3/14/1856: Brigham Young is sealed to 25-year-old Emeline Barney, his 48th bride.

3/20/1847: Brigham Young marries Lucy Bigelow, 16, his 42nd wife. She in turn bears him three daughters. On the same day, he takes his 43rd wife, Mary Jane Bigelow, Lucy's 19-year-old sister.

3/31/1834: Brigham Young marries his second wife, Mary Ann Angell. She will bear him six children.

4/7/1868: Brigham Young, 67, is sealed to Anna Eliza Webb, 23, his 51st bride.

4/18/1848: Brigham Young is sealed to his 44th wife, 44-year-old Sarah Malin.

4/30/1845: Emmeline Free, at age 19 "the Light of the Harem" becomes Brigham Young's 12th wife, and his favorite for 20 years.

5/8/1844: Brigham Young marries his sixth wife, 14-year-old Clara Decker, sister of his third wife.

5/8/1870: Brigham Young is sealed to Lydia Farnsworth, 62, his 53rd bride.

6/15/1842: Brigham Young marries his third wife, Lucy Decker, his first plural wife, and the first of many married women he will take from their husbands. She will bear him seven children.

6/19/1855: Catherine Reeves, 51, is sealed to Brigham Young, becoming his 47th bride.

7/4/1869: Brigham Young is sealed to Elizabeth Jones, 56, his 52nd bride.

9/10/1844: Brigham Young marries his 8th wife, Clara Chase Ross. Dubbed "Clara the Maniac," she goes insane and dies in 1858 according to the New York *World*, "reproaching Brigham as the author of all her sorrows, and doubting the divine authority of polygamy."

10/3/1850: Brigham Young is sealed to his 45th wife, Eliza Burgess.

10/8/1824: Brigham Young marries his first wife, Miriam Works, in New York.

11/2/1843: Brigham Young marries his 4th wife, 19-year-old Harriet Elizabeth Cook (often called "Harriet the Neglected" because she had only one son, Oscar) and his 5th wife, Augusta Adams Cobb.

11/2/1844: Brigham Young marries his 10th wife, 29-year-old Susan Snively.

12/6/1852: Brigham Young is sealed to Mary Oldfield, 60, his 46th bride.

Selected Sources

American Headlines, Year by Year. Thomas Nelson, Inc., 1985.

Bancroft, Caroline. *Colorful Colorado.* Johnson Books, 1959.

Beal, Merrill D. *I Will Fight No More Forever: Chief Joseph and the Nez Perce War.* University of Washington Press, 1963.

Briehan, Carl W., *Great Gunfighters of the West.* The Naylor Company, 1962.

Connell, Evan S. *Son of the Morning Star.* North Point Press, 1984.

Cromie, Alice. *Tour Guide of the Old West.* Quadrangle/New York Times Book Company, 1977.

Custer, Elizabeth. *Boots and Saddles,* Harper and Brothers, 1885.

Dellar, Fred; Thompson, Roy; Green, Douglas B. *The Illustrated Encyclopedia of Country Music.* Harmony Books, 1977.

Gragg, Rod, *The Old West Quiz and Fact Book.* Harper & Row Publishers, Inc., 1986.

Idaho Blue Book, 1971-1972.

Jones, William C. and Forrest, Kenton. *Denver: A Pictorial History.* Pruett Publishing, 1973.

Lake, Stuart N. *Wyatt Earp: Frontier Marshal.* Houghton Mifflin Company, 1931.

Lamar, Howard R., ed. *The Reader's Encyclopedia of the America West.* Harper & Row Publishers, Inc., 1977.

Lavender, David. *The American Heritage History of the Great West,* American Heritage Publishing Company, 1965.

Lord, Walter. *A Time to Stand: The Epic of the Alamo.* Harper & Row Publishers, Inc. 1961.

McLoughlin, Denis. *Wild and Woolly: An Encyclopedia of the Old West.* Doubleday and Company, 1975.

Nash, Jay Robert. *Bloodletters and Bad Men.* Warner Books, 1973.

Newark, Peter. *The Illustrated Encyclopedia of the West.* Gallery Books, 1980.

The Old West. Time-Life Books

O'Neal, Bill. *Encyclopedia of Western Gunfighters.* University of Oklahoma Press, 1979.

Pointer, Larry. *In Search of Butch Cassidy.* University of Oklahoma Press, 1977.

The Random House Encyclopedia. Random House, Inc., 1977.

Sandoz, Mari. *Crazy Horse: The Strange Man of the Oglalas.* University of

Nebraska Press, 1961.

Stone, Ron. *Book of Texas Days*. Shearer Publishing, 1984.

Tuska, Jon. *The Filming of the West*. Doubleday and Company, 1976.

Waters, Frank. *The Earp Brothers of Tombstone*. Clarkson Potter, 1960.

The World Almanac of the American West. Newspaper Enterprise Association, Inc., 1986.

The World Almanac Book of Who. Newspaper Enterprise Association, Inc., 1980.

Photo Sources

The majority of the illustrations in *Days of the West* are period newspaper or magazine drawings. Unless noted below, the remainder are from the author's collection:

Buffalo Bill Museum: Pages 32, 46, 75
Colorado Historical Society: Pages 12, 16, 103, 104, 109
The Denver Post: Page 17
Denver Public Library: Page 31
Frederic Remington (Buffalo Bill Historical Center): Page 181
Hopalong Cassidy Productions, Inc.: Page 137
National Archives: Page 95
NBC Television: Page 124
Rocky Mountain News: Page 92

Index

Alamo ~
01/18/1836; 02/08/1836; 02/11/1836; 02/12/1836; 02/21/1836; 02/23/1836; 02/23/1955; 02/24/1836; 02/25/1836; 02/28/1836; 02/29/1836; 03/01/1836; 03/05/1836; 03/06/1836; 03/11/1836; 05/01/1718; 08/09/1809; 08/17/1786; 10/24/1960; 10/28/1835; 12/10/1835

Alaska ~
01/23/1974; 03/27/1964; 04/03/1929; 05/01/1891; 05/27/1975; 06/05/1922; 07/15/1923; 08/15/1935; 08/17/1896; 09/22/1784; 11/07/1960

Allison, Clay ~
01/07/1874; 07/01/1887; 10/07/1870; 10/30/1875; 11/01/1875; 12/21/1876

Apache ~
01/17/1863; 01/29/1881; 02/13/1861; 02/24/1855; 03/04/1930; 03/28/1883; 04/01/1877; 04/28/1880; 04/30/1871; 05/05/1871; 05/17/1885; 06/05/1859; 08/04/1706; 10/15/1880; 11/01/1889; 12/27/1872

Arapahoe ~
02/02/1865; 02/18/1861; 07/03/1865; 08/01/1867; 09/08/1865; 09/28/1864; 11/29/1864; 12/21/1866

Arizona ~
01/07/1971; 01/27/1870; 01/29/1905; 02/02/1848; 02/02/1952; 02/14/1912; 02/17/1904; 02/23/1945; 02/24/1863; 02/26/1919; 02/27/1907; 03/04/1930; 03/13/1930; 03/15/1881; 03/18/1911; 03/20/1909; 03/27/1886; 04/01/1877; 04/12/1886; 04/26/1882; 04/27/1930; 04/30/1867; 04/30/1871; 05/03/1882; 05/09/1916; 05/12/1947; 05/15/1882; 05/15/1926; 05/17/1885; 05/26/1930;
05/30/1899; 05/31/1923; 06/01/1829; 06/10/1833; 06/13/1966; 06/20/1910; 06/21/1924; 07/04/1888; 07/08/1892; 07/14/1882; 07/17/1964; 07/25/1939; 07/29/1776; 08/01/1861; 08/01/1941; 08/03/1918; 08/22/1911; 08/30/1869; 09/02/1887; 09/04/1886; 09/04/1970; 09/15/1908; 10/05/1917; 10/13/1936; 10/16/1931; 10/21/1972; 10/25/1939; 10/27/1972; 11/12/1916; 11/27/1952; 11/30/1951; 12/03/1939; 12/08/1883; 12/08/1899; 12/09/1924; 12/09/1962; 12/18/1843; 12/28/1934; 12/30/1853

Arkansas ~
02/18/1861; 03/02/1819; 03/04/1921; 03/08/1862; 03/29/1857; 05/08/1861; 06/15/1836; 11/10/1808; 12/14/1932

Ashley, William ~
02/13/1822; 03/20/1822

Astor, John Jacob ~
04/21/1811; 05/06/1812; 06/23/1810; 07/17/1763; 09/08/1810; 10/21/1810; 10/23/1813

Austin, Moses & Stephen ~
01/03/1834; 01/17/1821; 02/18/1823; 04/14/1823; 06/10/1821; 07/08/1833; 08/12/1821; 11/03/1793; 12/16/1826; 12/26/1826; 12/27/1836

Autry, Gene ~
02/23/1935; 04/18/1936; 07/21/1950; 08/07/1956; 09/29/1907

Bass, Sam ~
02/24/1878; 03/18/1878; 04/04/1878; 04/10/1878; 06/13/1878; 07/21/1851; 07/21/1878; 09/19/1877; 12/20/1877

Battles ~
01/01/1863; 01/08/1815; 01/09/1847; 02/22/1847; 02/24/1847; 02/28/1847; 03/06/1836; 03/08/1862; 04/03/1929; 04/06/1862; 04/21/1836; 04/27/1813; 05/08/1843; 05/09/1846; 05/14/1797; 05/23/1923; 06/17/1876; 06/25/1876; 06/26/1874; 06/27/1874; 06/29/1874; 07/05/1876; 07/07/1911; 07/11/1869; 07/12/1870; 07/14/1878; 07/15/1878; 07/17/1878; 07/20/1878; 07/24/1865; 07/27/1894; 08/11/1873; 08/12/1840; 08/30/1874; 09/03/1855; 09/08/1865; 09/14/1905; 09/17/1868; 09/25/1867; 09/27/1868; 10/02/1835; 10/05/1813; 10/07/1894; 10/08/1838; 10/21/1876; 11/06/1891; 11/07/1811; 11/26/1855; 11/27/1868; 12/10/1835; 12/29/1890

Bean, Judge Roy ~
02/21/1896; 03/16/1903; 07/25/1882; 08/02/1882; 10/28/1866; 11/06/1882

Billy the Kid ~
01/26/1925; 02/07/1908; 03/01/1873; 03/06/1878; 03/09/1878; 03/17/1879; 04/01/1878; 04/04/1878; 04/09/1881; 04/17/1882; 04/28/1881; 05/01/1878; 05/13/1881; 05/14/1878; 05/17/1958; 06/05/1850; 06/14/1918; 06/22/1936; 07/03/1878; 07/04/1878; 07/14/1878; 07/14/1881; 08/05/1878; 08/10/1870; 08/13/1878; 08/17/1877; 08/18/1877; 08/29/1881; 09/01/1962; 09/14/1869; 09/16/1874; 09/23/1875; 09/25/1875; 09/26/1862; 10/16/1938; 10/18/1930; 11/02/1880; 11/12/1880; 11/13/1878; 11/23/1828; 11/23/1859; 11/29/1880; 12/01/1842; 12/19/1880; 12/22/1878; 12/28/1878

Boone, Daniel ~
03/16/1775; 05/01/1769;
06/07/1769; 08/22/1828;
08/27/1970; 11/02/1734;
12/22/1769

Bowie, Jim ~
01/18/1836; 03/06/1836;
04/22/1830; 09/07/1956;
09/19/1827; 09/30/1830;
10/24/1960; 10/28/1835

Bridger, Jim ~
02/13/1822; 03/17/1804;
05/12/1825; 07/17/1881

Calamity Jane ~
05/01/1852; 05/11/1941;
08/01/1903; 09/01/1870;
09/25/1873

California ~
01/05/1850; 01/06/1799;
01/08/1856; 01/09/1847;
01/10/1847; 01/18/1969;
01/20/1981; 01/21/1813;
01/22/1850; 01/24/1848;
01/28/1969; 01/29/1850;
02/01/1935; 02/02/1848;
02/03/1923; 02/09/1971;
02/10/1879; 02/13/1847;
02/14/1983; 02/18/1849;
02/18/1960; 02/19/1959;
02/27/1937; 02/28/1849;
02/28/1960; 03/04/1940;
03/05/1980; 03/12/1850;
03/14/1961; 03/15/1848;
03/18/1852; 03/26/1825;
03/26/1872; 03/29/1857;
04/03/1900; 04/11/1873;
04/13/1984; 04/14/1981;
04/19/1852; 04/26/1858;
04/30/1598; 05/01/1843;
05/06/1979; 05/14/1901;
05/17/1891; 05/19/1853;
05/19/1913; 05/27/1831;
05/29/1843; 05/30/1914;
06/03/1846; 06/04/1968;
06/14/1846; 06/15/1579;
06/18/1880; 06/25/1900;
07/01/1839; 07/07/1846;
07/10/1851; 07/18/1938;
07/24/1846; 07/24/1898;
08/03/1877; 08/15/1846;
08/17/1846; 08/19/1848;
08/22/1826; 08/25/1540;
08/28/1934; 08/31/1964;
09/02/1846; 09/03/1851;
09/06/1939; 09/08/1965;
09/09/1850; 09/11/1857;
09/13/1859; 09/22/1975;
09/25/1846; 10/01/1890;
10/02/1968; 10/06/1846;
10/14/1913; 10/25/1926;
10/26/1984; 10/27/1972;
10/29/1796; 11/03/1853;
11/03/1883; 11/03/1954;
11/05/1846; 11/05/1911;
11/10/1934; 11/18/1805;
11/18/1966; 11/22/1924;
11/23/1852; 11/27/1826;
11/28/1872; 11/29/1777;
11/29/1831; 12/05/1848;
12/12/1844; 12/13/1844;
12/16/1979; 12/22/1964;
12/24/1853; 12/28/1854

Carson, Kit ~
01/28/1842; 05/14/1870;
05/23/1868; 05/29/1843;
10/06/1846; 11/24/1864;
11/25/1864; 12/24/1809

Cassidy, Butch ~
01/26/1925; 04/13/1866;
04/21/1897; 06/02/1899;
06/24/1889; 06/29/1903;
07/03/1901; 07/15/1879;
07/20/1937; 08/18/1937;
11/10/1934

Catlin, George ~
03/26/1832; 04/21/1844;
07/26/1796; 10/26/1832;
12/28/1872

Cherokee ~
02/21/1828; 03/17/1775;
04/26/1791; 05/26/1928;
06/12/1858; 06/22/1850;
06/23/1865; 07/26/1827;
08/05/1893; 09/01/1893;
09/16/1893; 12/02/1832;
12/20/1835; 12/29/1835

Cheyenne ~
01/01/1877; 01/05/1879;
01/07/1865; 01/09/1879;
02/02/1865; 02/10/1876;
02/18/1861; 02/26/1875;
03/17/1876; 04/04/1894;
04/29/1868; 06/17/1876;
06/25/1876; 06/26/1874;
07/11/1869; 08/01/1867;
08/07/1877; 08/30/1874;
09/08/1865; 09/09/1878;
09/17/1868; 09/23/1878;
09/28/1864; 11/27/1868;
11/29/1864; 12/21/1866

Chief Joseph ~
09/21/1904; 10/05/1877

Chinese ~
02/02/1848; 02/07/1886;
03/12/1888; 04/26/1858;
04/28/1869; 05/06/1882;
07/04/1864; 07/13/1869;
07/23/1877; 07/25/1877;
09/02/1885; 10/24/1871;
11/03/1885

Clark, William ~
01/10/1807; 01/11/1897;
02/11/1805; 02/19/1806;
02/28/1803; 03/23/1806;
04/07/1805; 04/25/1805;
04/26/1805; 05/14/1804;
06/01/1905; 06/13/1805;
06/15/1806; 06/26/1804;
07/03/1804; 07/04/1804;
07/16/1808; 07/25/1806;
08/01/1770; 08/15/1805;
08/15/1806; 08/17/1805;
08/18/1774; 08/19/1804;
08/31/1803; 09/01/1838;
09/04/1877; 09/15/1806;
09/20/1806; 09/23/1806;
10/15/1905; 10/26/1804;
10/26/1832; 10/27/1804;
11/02/1805; 11/07/1805;
11/18/1805; 12/07/1805

Cochise ~
01/27/1870; 05/05/1871;
09/09/1899

Cody, William F. ~
01/10/1917; 01/14/1872;
02/26/1846; 03/03/1890;
03/03/1890; 03/20/1823;
03/28/1868; 05/09/1887;
05/09/1987; 06/13/1893;
07/04/1883; 08/13/1860;
10/28/1901; 11/05/1905;
12/11/1872; 12/17/1872

Colorado ~
01/01/1916; 01/19/1897;
01/25/1971; 01/26/1915;
01/29/1861; 02/01/1935;
02/01/1951; 02/01/1985;
02/02/1848; 02/03/1965;
02/04/1847; 02/10/1907;
02/18/1861; 02/25/1510;
02/26/1892; 02/26/1928;
02/28/1861; 02/28/1897;
03/02/1923; 03/03/1831;
03/04/1878; 03/07/1935;
03/13/1895; 03/16/1905;
03/17/1932; 04/01/1883;
04/19/1859; 04/20/1914;
04/25/1967; 04/29/1925;
04/29/1931; 05/10/1929;
05/13/1902; 05/14/1901;
05/15/1950; 05/22/1871;
05/24/1869; 05/24/1911;
05/31/1894; 06/05/1929;
06/08/1904; 06/16/1965;
06/18/1859; 06/21/1851;
06/24/1858; 06/24/1864;
06/24/1954; 06/27/1893;
06/29/1906; 07/04/1890;
07/04/1919; 07/07/1927;
07/08/1898; 07/11/1869;
07/11/1888; 07/13/1950;
07/15/1982; 07/18/1963;
07/20/1860; 07/22/1839;

07/22/1893; 07/25/1902;
07/29/1776; 07/29/1958;
08/01/1876; 08/01/1941;
08/01/1976; 08/02/1846;
08/03/1933; 08/09/1936;
08/10/1903; 08/10/1972;
08/12/1842; 08/14/1846;
08/14/1862; 08/16/1986;
08/20/1846; 08/24/1873;
08/28/1869; 08/30/1869;
09/10/1873; 09/12/1964;
09/24/1870; 09/26/1935;
09/27/1868; 09/28/1864;
09/29/1879; 10/02/1877;
10/03/1859; 10/04/1915;
10/12/1907; 10/17/1893;
11/07/1893; 11/10/1806;
12/04/1976; 12/09/1867;
12/13/1806; 12/16/1934;
12/17/1912; 12/20/1798;
12/31/1897; 12/31/1937

Comanche ~
02/22/1911; 03/19/1840;
05/19/1836; 05/27/1831;
06/02/1875; 06/04/1860;
06/05/1859; 06/26/1874;
07/05/1739; 07/24/1977;
08/03/1859; 08/12/1840;
08/30/1874; 09/28/1874;
11/24/1864

Coronado ~
02/23/1540; 02/25/1510;
06/29/1541; 07/07/1540;
09/26/1888

Crazy Horse ~
01/08/1877; 03/19/1868;
05/06/1877; 05/11/1896;
06/13/1865; 06/14/1865;
06/17/1876; 06/25/1876;
07/24/1865; 07/25/1865;
08/02/1867; 09/01/1877;
09/03/1855; 09/04/1877;
09/05/1877; 09/06/1877;
12/04/1842; 12/21/1866

Crockett, Davy ~
01/01/1821; 01/05/1833;
01/26/1955; 02/08/1836;
02/23/1955; 03/06/1836;
04/01/1818; 04/25/1831;
04/25/1834; 05/22/1816;
05/28/1955; 08/14/1806;
08/16/1925; 08/17/1786;
09/28/1814; 10/21/1805;
10/22/1824; 10/24/1960;
11/03/1813; 11/16/1955;
11/17/1817; 11/17/1821;
12/14/1955; 12/15/1954;
12/24/1813

Custer ~
01/05/1852; 01/12/1872;
01/13/1879; 02/09/1864;
02/28/1864; 03/15/1845;
03/20/1842; 04/06/1933;
04/08/1842; 04/10/1865;
04/30/1885; 05/17/1876;
05/23/1923; 05/27/1856;
06/01/1876; 06/05/1862;
06/21/1876; 06/22/1876;
06/22/1890; 06/25/1876;
06/26/1876; 06/27/1876;
07/03/1876; 07/04/1876;
07/05/1876; 07/06/1876;
07/29/1842; 08/04/1863;
08/11/1873; 09/06/1967;
09/14/1905; 09/21/1873;
10/10/1877; 10/31/1848;
11/18/1856; 11/27/1862;
11/27/1868; 11/27/1892;
12/05/1839; 12/16/1890;
12/24/1890; 12/27/1967

Dakota, North/South ~
01/07/1963; 01/23;1964;
01/26/1982; 02/10/1876;
02/15/1936; 02/20/1936;
02/22/1889; 03/01/1877;
03/02/1861; 03/12/1802;
03/15/1941; 03/25/1867;
04/15/1892; 04/17/1923;
04/29/1868; 06/04/1968;
06/13/1979; 07/02/1939;
07/04/1838; 07/19/1881;
07/25/1868; 07/27/1931;
08/03/1876; 08/10/1927;
08/28/1857; 09/09/1963;
09/17/1937; 10/01/1925;
11/02/1889; 11/10/1978;
11/10/1933; 11/27/1876;
12/29/1890

Dalton Gang ~
02/06/1891; 02/06/1897;
03/08/1893; 06/02/1892;
07/13/1937; 07/15/1892;
08/06/1924; 10/05/1892;
11/06/1910; 11/10/1921

Deadwood ~
01/20/1943; 08/01/1903;
08/02/1876; 08/03/1876;
12/28/1890

Denver ~
01/01/1913; 01/06/1923;
01/07/1901; 01/07/1929;
01/10/1901; 01/10/1917;
01/15/1978; 01/22/1822;
01/24/1931; 01/25/1987;
01/27/1955; 01/29/1906;
02/01/1859; 02/01/1910;
02/02/1933; 02/04/1920;
02/08/1936; 02/12/1904;
02/12/1933; 02/17/1927;
02/25/1906; 02/25/1950;
02/27/1963; 03/03/1859;
03/08/1890; 03/10/1910;
03/10/1922; 03/12/1922;
03/14/1894; 03/23/1823;
03/23/1895; 03/27/1877;
03/28/1890; 04/03/1898;
04/06/1983; 04/11/1900;
04/12/1882; 04/19/1863;
04/19/1864; 04/23/1859;
04/29/1907; 04/29/1978;
05/01/1890; 05/05/1917;
05/06/1859; 05/07/1880;
05/08/1911; 05/09/1859;
05/10/1899; 05/11/1954;
05/13/1902; 05/17/1877;
05/17/1879; 05/19/1864;
05/20/1954; 05/22/1876;
05/22/1878; 05/23/1883;
05/25/1934; 05/30/1908;
06/01/1881; 06/02/1931;
06/03/1865; 06/06/1859;
06/12/1858; 06/14/1984;
06/15/1941; 06/15/1952;
06/19/1947; 06/22/1870;
06/28/1946; 07/03/1950;
07/04/1890; 07/10/1908;
07/11/1954; 07/13/1953;
07/14/1912; 07/15/1983;
07/16/1936; 07/16/1938;
07/17/1893; 07/18/1952;
07/18/1963; 07/23/1911;
07/25/1878; 07/26/1885;
07/28/1922; 07/29/1986;
08/06/1877; 08/06/1934;
08/08/1878; 08/12/1890;
08/12/1919; 08/14/1959;
08/15/1870; 08/16/1986;
08/18/1870; 08/18/1895;
08/25/1877; 08/30/1870;
09/02/1919; 09/04/1917;
09/05/1881; 09/13/1954;
09/21/1950; 09/24/1870;
09/24/1955; 09/27/1936;
10/03/1880; 10/17/1909;
10/18/1895; 10/20/1859;
10/20/1981; 10/24/1859;
10/28/1895; 10/29/1858;
10/31/1880; 11/01/1955;
11/06/1960; 11/10/1926;
11/10/1955; 11/17/1929;
11/19/1943; 11/21/1934;
11/22/1931; 11/25/1983;
12/01/1913; 12/02/1952;
12/09/1867; 12/11/1909;
12/17/1871; 12/17/1889;
12/18/1922; 12/24/1982;
12/26/1859; 12/28/1886;
12/30/1915

Dodge City ~
04/09/1878; 04/16/1881;
05/17/1936; 07/26/1878;
08/21/1877; 09/23/1878;
11/05/1905

Donner Party ~

02/19/1847; 05/17/1891;
09/02/1846; 09/17/1846;
10/18/1846; 10/19/1846;
12/13/1844

Earhart, Amelia ~
01/11/1935; 02/08/1931;
04/19/1937; 05/08/1937;
05/20/1932; 07/02/1937;
07/24/1907

Earp ~
01/03/1929; 01/13/1929;
01/16/1929; 03/09/1855;
03/18/1882; 03/19/1848;
03/20/1882; 03/22/1882;
04/19/1876; 04/19/1930;
04/21/1875; 04/24/1851;
05/08/1871; 07/03/1888;
07/06/1957; 07/26/1878;
08/21/1877; 09/06/1955;
09/26/1961; 10/26/1881;
10/28/1880; 12/01/1879;
12/19/1864; 12/28/1881

El Paso ~
01/11/1854; 03/26/1930;
04/01/1932; 08/19/1895;
09/01/1972; 09/16/1921;
09/26/1925; 10/15/1880;
11/30/1944; 12/13/1901;
12/27/1846

Fall, Albert Bacon ~
01/02/1923; 01/24/1924;
02/28/1927; 03/04/1923;
04/07/1922; 05/31/1921;
06/30/1924; 10/25/1929;
11/01/1929; 11/26/1861;
11/30/1944

Films ~
01/01/1955; 01/05/1930;
01/13/1937; 01/13/1939;
01/18/1931; 01/20/1929;
01/20/1932; 01/22/1934;
02/01/1935; 02/02/1934;
02/04/1961; 02/09/1931;
02/12/1933; 02/14/1931;
02/20/1963; 02/21/1959;
02/23/1935; 02/25/1956;
03/01/1933; 03/01/1935;
03/01/1952; 03/03/1930;
03/12/1935; 03/20/1930;
03/21/1947; 04/01/1930;
04/02/1959; 04/04/1959;
04/05/1946; 04/11/1962;
04/22/1935; 04/27/1930;
04/30/1935; 05/01/1934;
05/04/1952; 05/17/1932;
05/17/1958; 05/23/1950;
05/27/1957; 06/01/1958;
06/15/1934; 06/15/1958;
06/28/1930; 06/29/1930;
06/30/1965; 07/01/1965;
07/06/1956; 07/07/1933;

07/13/1930; 07/15/1933;
07/27/1932; 07/27/1959;
07/30/1934; 07/30/1952;
08/01/1947; 08/01/1953;
08/24/1930; 08/25/1933;
09/01/1957; 09/01/1959;
09/15/1934; 09/17/1948;
09/27/1930; 09/28/1930;
09/29/1934; 09/30/1932;
10/03/1956; 10/08/1932;
10/12/1930; 10/15/1955;
10/18/1930; 10/22/1934;
10/22/1949; 10/24/1930;
10/24/1960; 10/27/1929;
10/28/1931; 10/30/1961;
11/07/1960; 11/09/1929;
11/10/1921; 11/13/1963;
11/14/1931; 11/15/1934;
11/22/1934; 11/24/1956;
11/27/1953; 12/01/1934;
12/03/1932; 12/08/1960;
12/15/1933; 12/19/1964;
12/28/1934

Fremont, John Charles ~
01/13/1847; 01/16/1847;
01/21/1813; 01/27/1846;
01/31/1848; 02/14/1844;
03/06/1844; 03/06/1846;
05/29/1843; 05/31/1847;
06/06/1842; 06/14/1846;
07/13/1890; 07/24/1846;
08/07/1844; 08/30/1861;
09/06/1844; 11/04/1856

Garrett, Pat ~
01/04/1880; 01/14/1880;
01/25/1869; 01/31/1896;
02/29/1908; 03/25/1867;
04/17/1882; 06/05/1850;
06/22/1936; 07/14/1881;
09/01/1962; 11/02/1880;
11/23/1828; 12/13/1901;
12/19/1880

Geronimo ~
02/17/1909; 03/27/1886;
04/12/1886; 04/30/1871;
05/17/1855; 05/17/1885;
06/01/1829; 09/04/1886

Gold ~
01/24/1848; 01/26/1982;
02/12/1873; 02/28/1849;
03/09/1842; 03/15/1848;
04/18/1859; 05/06/1859;
05/10/1869; 05/20/1863;
05/26/1863; 06/05/1922;
06/12/1858; 06/15/1958;
06/18/1859; 06/18/1880;
06/22/1850; 07/04/1891;
07/15/1923; 07/17/1893;
07/20/1860; 07/28/1862;
08/02/1862; 08/06/1934;
08/12/1896; 08/14/1862;

08/16/1896; 08/17/1896;
08/19/1848; 09/02/1919;
09/11/1847; 09/19/1877;
09/30/1860; 11/04/1870;
11/27/1907; 11/30/1835;
12/04/1902; 12/05/1848;
12/09/1867; 12/20/1835;
12/27/1859

Greeley, Horace ~
02/03/1811; 05/06/1859;
05/10/1859; 06/06/1859;
07/13/1859; 11/29/1872

Grey, Zane ~
01/31/1872; 02/01/1935;
02/27/1907; 03/01/1933;
03/01/1935; 03/03/1930;
03/27/1907; 05/01/1934;
06/28/1930; 07/07/1933;
08/01/1947; 08/25/1933;
09/15/1934; 09/20/1962;
09/29/1934; 09/30/1932;
10/05/1956; 10/21/1939;
10/28/1931; 12/03/1932

Guthrie, Woody ~
01/09/1944; 01/13/1901;
02/23/1940; 04/14/1935;
07/14/1912; 10/03/1967;
10/25/1933; 10/28/1934;
11/20/1906

Hardin, John Wesley ~
02/17/1894; 03/16/1894;
05/26/1853; 06/01/1871;
08/19/1895; 08/23/1877;
12/25/1869

Hickok, Wild Bill ~
01/13/1937; 01/19/1922;
03/01/1877; 03/08/1862;
03/13/1868; 03/22/1858;
03/28/1868; 04/15/1871;
05/05/1852; 05/11/1941;
05/27/1837; 06/01/1871;
06/04/1870; 07/12/1861;
07/17/1870; 07/21/1865;
08/01/1903; 08/02/1876;
08/03/1876; 08/03/1879;
08/24/1869; 08/28/1872;
09/01/1870; 09/25/1873;
09/27/1867; 09/27/1869;
09/27/1872; 10/05/1871;
10/07/1905; 10/10/1869;
11/02/1869; 11/05/1867;
11/27/1876; 12/12/1871;
12/13/1871

Holliday, Doc ~
03/20/1882; 03/21/1852;
03/22/1882; 07/19/1879;
07/25/1878; 10/26/1881;
11/08/1887

Hopi ~
05/15/1926; 07/25/1902

Horn, Tom ~
07/08/1900; 07/18/1901;
08/09/1903; 09/29/1912;
10/03/1900; 11/20/1903;
11/21/1860

Houston, Sam & Temple
01/21/1861; 02/29/1836;
03/02/1793; 03/02/1836;
03/11/1836; 03/13/1836;
04/11/1819; 04/21/1836;
05/09/1840; 07/26/1863;
08/12/1860; 10/07/1894;
10/22/1836; 11/19/1854;
12/02/1832; 12/12/1844;
12/24/1809

Houston, Texas ~
01/16/1935; 01/18/1935;
02/07/1984; 02/21/1936;
02/22/1984; 04/01/1912;
04/05/1976; 04/09/1965;
04/10/1962; 06/29/1928;
07/18/1963; 07/25/1974;
08/03/1940; 08/14/1959;
08/16/1915; 08/18/1983;
09/07/1943; 11/17/1981;
12/24/1905

Houston & Texas Central RR ~
02/24/1878; 03/18/1878

Idaho ~
01/03/1961; 01/04/1915;
01/08/1894; 01/19/1922;
01/19/1940; 02/22/1897;
03/01/1872; 03/04/1863;
03/06/1893; 03/09/1895;
03/12/1934; 04/01/1892;
04/14/1860; 04/29/1899;
05/02/1924; 05/19/1887;
05/19/1898; 05/22/1909;
05/26/1863; 05/26/1892;
06/05/1976; 06/22/1900;
07/03/1890; 07/08/1950;
07/10/1863; 07/11/1892;
07/14/1892; 07/28/1862;
07/28/1934; 08/02/1862;
08/20/1910; 08/30/1931;
09/12/1893; 09/30/1860;
10/01/1922; 10/03/1892;
10/09/1891; 12/22/1964;
12/24/1864; 12/30/1905

Iowa ~
01/24/1922; 02/26/1846;
02/27/1934; 04/21/1844;
05/11/1954; 05/18/1871;
05/19/1836; 06/04/1860;
06/04/1923; 06/09/1856;
06/12/1838; 06/17/1882;
06/26/1874; 07/03/1958;
07/04/1838; 07/05/1843;
07/10/1881; 07/12/1870;
07/15/1830; 07/23/1851;
07/27/1931; 08/18/1925;
08/30/1874; 09/19/1959;
10/25/1949; 11/01/1844;
11/21/1921; 11/24/1864;
12/19/1864; 12/19/1905;
12/28/1846

Jackson, Andrew ~
01/08/1815; 03/03/1837;
03/04/1829; 03/04/1833;
03/15/1767; 05/28/1830;
07/01/1836; 08/17/1786;
08/25/1829; 11/03/1813

Jackson, William Henry
04/04/1843; 08/24/1873

James, Frank ~
01/10/1843; 01/15/1844;
01/15/1874; 02/06/1878;
02/11/1911; 02/18/1915;
03/21/1868; 04/29/1872;
06/03/1871; 07/01/1882;
07/06/1944; 07/19/1845;
07/28/1881; 08/21/1863;
08/21/1883; 09/23/1872;
10/05/1882; 10/07/1879;
11/18/1959; 11/26/1849;
12/07/1869; 12/12/1874;
12/15/1869; 12/28/1841

James, Jesse ~
01/13/1939; 01/15/1844;
01/15/1874; 01/26/1875;
01/31/1874; 02/07/1902;
02/11/1911; 02/13/1866;
02/21/1916; 03/08/1948;
03/21/1868; 03/21/1947;
03/26/1951; 04/02/1959;
04/03/1882; 04/12/1875;
04/24/1874; 04/29/1872;
05/12/1875; 05/20/1868;
05/22/1867; 05/23/1872;
06/03/1871; 06/08/1892;
06/21/1877; 07/06/1944;
07/07/1875; 07/07/1876;
07/10/1881; 07/14/1901;
07/15/1881; 07/19/1845;
07/21/1873; 07/28/1881;
08/07/1881; 09/05/1847;
09/05/1966; 09/06/1950;
09/07/1876; 09/13/1965;
09/21/1876; 09/23/1872;
09/27/1864; 10/05/1882;
10/07/1879; 10/30/1866;
11/24/1870; 11/26/1849;
12/07/1869; 12/12/1874;
12/15/1869; 12/28/1841;
12/28/1878

Jefferson, Thomas ~
01/10/1807; 01/18/1803;
01/22/1807; 02/19/1806;
03/01/1784; 03/03/1807;
03/04/1801; 03/04/1805;
03/11/1805; 07/17/1804;
08/30/1936; 10/21/1806

Kansas ~
01/11/1970; 01/15/1856;
01/15/1967; 01/20/1874;
01/23/1907; 01/27/1825;
01/29/1861; 02/02/1858;
02/08/1936; 02/16/1900;
02/18/1861; 02/19/1881;
02/24/1835; 02/25/1510;
02/28/1861; 03/02/1819;
03/03/1911; 03/04/1856;
03/04/1921; 03/07/1885;
03/08/1862; 03/08/1893;
03/28/1904; 03/29/1857;
04/05/1915; 04/18/1859;
04/21/1833; 04/26/1854;
05/08/1827; 05/08/1861;
05/12/1846; 05/14/1870;
05/16/1914; 05/17/1673;
05/25/1917; 05/30/1854;
06/02/1921; 06/03/1921;
06/13/1878; 06/15/1836;
06/29/1541; 06/29/1854;
06/30/1956; 07/02/1855;
07/04/1804; 07/04/1919;
07/12/1951; 07/15/1892;
07/17/1981; 07/18/1857;
07/21/1931; 07/31/1855;
08/05/1914; 08/06/1924;
08/15/1870; 08/18/1856;
08/20/1846; 08/22/1828;
08/25/1863; 08/30/1856;
09/03/1806; 09/04/1917;
09/15/1806; 09/15/1896;
09/23/1872; 09/23/1878;
09/25/1806; 09/27/1872;
09/29/1912; 10/03/1880;
10/04/1859; 10/07/1854;
10/18/1806; 10/23/1855;
10/29/1831; 11/06/1874;
11/06/1910; 11/10/1808;
11/10/1921; 11/21/1922;
11/26/1855; 11/30/1806;
12/05/1901; 12/07/1828;
12/14/1932; 12/20/1858;
12/26/1859; 12/26/1972

Kearny, Stephen ~
01/10/1847; 02/13/1847;
04/18/1846; 05/31/1847;
06/03/1846; 07/22/1846;
08/02/1846; 08/15/1846;
08/18/1846; 09/22/1846;
09/25/1846; 10/06/1846;
11/05/1846; 12/29/1846

Leadville, Colorado ~
01/01/1896; 01/25/1899;
03/04/1899; 03/07/1935;
04/28/1896; 06/28/1880;
08/24/1873; 11/25/1895

Lewis, Meriwether ~
01/10/1807; 01/11/1897;

02/11/1805; 02/19/1806;
02/28/1803; 03/03/1807;
03/09/1804; 03/23/1806;
04/07/1805; 04/25/1805;
04/26/1805; 05/14/1804;
06/01/1905; 06/13/1805;
06/15/1806; 06/26/1804;
07/03/1804; 07/04/1804;
07/25/1806; 08/01/1770;
08/15/1805; 08/15/1806;
08/17/1805; 08/18/1774;
08/19/1804; 08/31/1803;
09/15/1806; 09/20/1806;
09/23/1806; 10/11/1809;
10/15/1905; 10/26/1804;
10/27/1804; 11/02/1805;
11/07/1805; 11/18/1805;
12/07/1805

Lincoln County War ~
01/16/1869; 02/18/1878;
02/26/1898; 03/06/1853;
03/06/1878; 03/09/1878;
03/13/1878; 04/01/1878;
04/04/1878; 04/28/1881;
05/01/1878; 05/13/1881;
05/14/1878; 05/22/1848;
07/04/1878; 07/11/1878;
07/14/1878; 07/15/1878;
07/17/1878; 08/15/1824;
08/26/1879; 08/29/1877;
09/30/1878; 10/07/1878;
11/02/1880; 11/12/1880;
11/13/1878; 11/23/1859;
12/22/1878

Lincoln, Abraham ~
03/02/1864; 07/01/1862;
07/22/1920; 09/17/1937;
09/30/1878; 10/07/1878;
10/31/1864; 11/05/1862;
12/06/1862; 06/03/1865

Little Bighorn ~
01/13/1879; 03/05/1879;
03/11/1950; 05/23/1923;
05/25/1840; 06/17/1876;
06/21/1876; 06/22/1890;
06/25/1876; 06/27/1876;
07/02/1877; 07/05/1876;
07/06/1876; 09/14/1905;
11/06/1891; 11/25/1876;
12/09/1876; 12/24/1922

Los Angeles ~
01/01/1923; 01/03/1929;
01/03/1979; 01/10/1847;
01/13/1929; 01/15/1932;
01/15/1967; 01/20/1980;
01/22/1984; 01/26/1969;
02/01/1958; 02/09/1971;
02/14/1886; 02/16/1914;
02/22/1923; 02/25/1921;
03/04/1928; 03/13/1928;
05/18/1926; 05/26/1928;

05/29/1973; 06/04/1968;
06/05/1943; 06/11/1979;
06/23/1946; 06/25/1965;
06/30/1956; 07/28/1984;
08/01/1941; 08/08/1922;
08/09/1969; 08/11/1965;
08/12/1984; 08/13/1846;
08/14/1959; 08/22/1923;
08/26/1930; 09/04/1781;
09/07/1971; 09/11/1928;
10/01/1910; 10/08/1860;
10/09/1936; 10/16/1931;
10/24/1871; 10/25/1926;
11/01/1966; 11/05/1905;
11/10/1934; 12/24/1914;
12/29/1846

Louisiana ~
01/18/1803; 01/25/1869;
03/03/1805; 03/03/1807;
03/05/1766; 03/09/1804;
03/11/1805; 04/11/1803;
04/30/1803; 04/30/1812;
04/30/1904; 05/02/1803;
05/20/1770; 05/23/1934;
05/26/1804; 06/04/1812;
07/17/1804; 08/09/1936;
09/11/1902; 10/01/1800;
11/03/1762; 12/01/1904;
12/20/1803

Marriages ~
01/04/1880; 01/14/1880;
01/16/1847; 02/09/1864;
02/09/1931; 03/01/1873;
03/06/1866; 03/20/1932;
04/12/1879; 04/22/1830;
04/24/1874; 05/08/1844;
05/22/1816; 05/30/1893;
06/20/1882; 08/01/1927;
08/14/1806; 08/15/1887;
09/01/1870; 09/07/1967;
09/07/1971; 09/16/1960;
09/24/1890; 10/08/1824;
10/11/1958; 10/20/1859;
10/21/1805; 10/25/1933;
10/28/1866; 11/24/1870;
12/08/1960; 12/10/1854;
12/28/1841

Massacres ~
01/06/1891; 01/07/1865;
01/14/1891; 01/23/1870;
03/07/1782; 03/26/1836;
03/29/1857; 04/20/1914;
04/30/1871; 05/18/1871;
05/21/1856; 05/24/1856;
06/04/1782; 08/19/1854;
09/11/1857; 09/22/1711;
09/29/1879; 10/30/1838;
11/25/1876; 11/29/1847;
11/29/1864; 12/08/1883;
12/21/1866

Masterson, Bat ~

01/24/1876; 01/28/1878;
04/09/1878; 04/16/1881;
06/26/1874; 10/25/1921;
11/26/1853

Mexican War ~
01/10/1847; 02/02/1848;
02/03/1846; 02/22/1847;
02/28/1847; 03/28/1845;
04/18/1846; 04/25/1846;
05/18/1846; 07/04/1854;
09/13/1847; 09/14/1847;
09/17/1846; 11/16/1846;
12/25/1846; 12/27/1846

Minnesota ~
01/09/1977; 01/11/1970;
03/03/1849; 03/15/1941;
05/11/1858; 07/04/1838;
07/14/1901; 07/15/1830;
07/23/1851; 08/16/1889;
08/18/1862; 09/07/1876;
09/14/1889; 09/17/1900;
09/21/1805; 10/19/1901;
11/05/1862; 12/26/1862

Mississippi ~
02/12/1806; 03/02/1819;
03/03/1817; 03/03/1853;
03/08/1862; 04/13/1893;
04/21/1856; 04/30/1806;
05/17/1673; 05/25/1892;
06/27/1831; 06/30/1831;
07/12/1808; 08/09/1805;
09/21/1832; 09/30/1830;
10/14/1832; 10/28/1806;
11/03/1762; 12/10/1806;
12/16/1811

Missouri ~
01/08/1818; 01/12/1838;
02/11/1839; 02/11/1911;
02/13/1819; 02/13/1822;
02/14/1682; 02/18/1915;
03/03/1857; 03/06/1820;
03/09/1914; 03/19/1743;
03/20/1822; 03/26/1832;
03/26/1951; 04/03/1882;
04/03/1924; 04/07/1805;
04/21/1833; 04/25/1805;
05/01/1832; 05/12/1794;
05/14/1804; 05/22/1822;
06/04/1812; 06/05/1813;
06/13/1805; 07/07/1875;
07/10/1700; 07/12/1808;
07/15/1830; 07/15/1892;
07/16/1808; 07/17/1881;
07/28/1881; 08/07/1904;
08/10/1821; 08/25/1863;
08/30/1861; 08/30/1984;
09/05/1847; 09/13/1982;
09/15/1806; 09/15/1896;
10/21/1810; 10/26/1804;
10/30/1838; 11/01/1855;
11/02/1734; 11/10/1808;

Days of the West   207

11/20/1809; 11/20/1843;
11/26/1855; 12/16/1841;
12/20/1858
Montana ~
01/11/1922; 01/17/1972;
01/28/1888; 02/22/1889;
03/01/1872; 03/04/1917;
03/05/1925; 03/20/1930;
04/29/1868; 05/07/1901;
05/11/1933; 05/20/1863;
05/22/1909; 05/23/1923;
05/26/1864; 06/10/1962;
06/19/1921; 07/07/1981;
07/28/1862; 08/01/1867;
08/27/1872; 08/30/1984;
10/15/1892; 10/22/1903;
11/03/1899; 11/04/1891;
11/08/1889
Mormons ~
01/01/1917; 01/12/1838;
02/01/1885; 02/10/1846;
02/25/1858; 03/10/1849;
03/22/1882; 04/12/1858;
05/03/1833; 05/07/1838;
05/19/1890; 06/01/1801;
06/09/1856; 06/11/1978;
06/26/1858; 06/27/1844;
07/01/1858; 07/01/1862;
07/04/1858; 07/18/1857;
07/20/1856; 07/22/1847;
07/24/1847; 07/25/1887;
08/17/1854; 08/19/1854;
08/23/1877; 09/11/1857;
09/24/1890; 10/02/1871;
10/30/1838
Muir, John ~
01/09/1908; 04/21/1838;
05/14/1903; 05/28/1892;
12/24/1914
Nation, Carry ~
02/16/1900; 06/09/1911;
11/25/1846; 12/28/1900
National Monuments ~
01/09/1908; 01/11/1908;
01/16/1908; 01/18/1933;
01/24/1922; 01/24/1923;
02/11/1916; 03/01/1933;
03/02/1923; 03/02/1933;
03/17/1932; 03/20/1909;
04/14/1924; 04/16/1908;
05/02/1924; 05/10/1929;
05/15/1950; 05/24/1911;
05/26/1930; 05/30/1910;
05/31/1923; 06/28/1965;
07/25/1939; 08/03/1918;
08/23/1933; 08/31/1965;
09/15/1908; 09/24/1906;
10/04/1915; 10/14/1913;
10/14/1922; 10/21/1972;
10/23/1972; 10/25/1923;
10/25/1949; 10/26/1974;

11/01/1925; 12/09/1924
National Parks ~
01/09/1903; 01/26/1915;
02/26/1919; 02/26/1929;
03/01/1872; 03/02/1899;
03/04/1921; 03/04/1940;
03/05/1980; 04/04/1843;
04/21/1838; 05/14/1930;
05/22/1902; 06/08/1923;
06/20/1935; 06/25/1900;
06/29/1906; 06/29/1938;
07/07/1981; 09/12/1964;
10/01/1890; 10/02/1968;
10/15/1966; 11/10/1978;
11/12/1971; 11/19/1919;
12/09/1962; 12/18/1971
Navajo ~
06/03/1846; 11/02/1982;
11/10/1970
Nebraska ~
01/05/1879; 01/09/1879;
01/16/1919; 01/29/1861;
02/12/1899; 02/27/1895;
02/28/1861; 03/01/1867;
04/07/1891; 04/09/1905;
05/06/1877; 05/11/1896;
05/15/1948; 05/23/1958;
05/30/1854; 06/04/1923;
07/08/1950; 07/27/1931;
08/30/1919; 09/05/1877;
09/20/1921; 12/01/1917
Nevada ~
01/24/1922; 02/01/1864;
02/02/1848; 03/02/1861;
03/02/1864; 03/05/1925;
03/10/1933; 03/18/1919;
03/19/1931; 04/22/1952;
06/03/1865; 07/02/1859;
09/30/1935; 10/10/1961;
10/13/1936; 10/31/1864;
11/29/1951; 11/30/1835;
12/04/1902; 12/09/1947;
12/29/1879
New Mexico ~
01/02/1777; 01/04/1847;
01/05/1848; 01/06/1912;
01/07/1874; 01/08/1981;
01/10/1914; 01/11/1892;
01/14/1880; 01/16/1869;
01/18/1933; 01/19/1847;
01/23/1974; 01/24/1923;
01/28/1890; 01/29/1850;
01/29/1861; 01/31/1896;
02/02/1848; 02/03/1845;
02/05/1883; 02/08/1923;
02/11/1916; 02/13/1861;
02/15/1905; 02/18/1878;
02/19/1846; 02/24/1855;
02/24/1949; 02/27/1895;
02/28/1861; 03/08/1881;
03/09/1916; 03/19/1848;

03/19/1954; 04/01/1878;
04/02/1880; 04/07/1959;
04/09/1881; 04/18/1969;
04/22/1904; 04/28/1880;
04/30/1598; 05/01/1878;
05/06/1951; 05/08/1827;
05/09/1916; 05/14/1930;
05/19/1853; 05/19/1955;
05/22/1957; 05/25/1850;
05/27/1957; 05/28/1892;
06/05/1878; 06/06/1819;
06/14/1740; 06/20/1910;
06/21/1978; 06/27/1893;
06/27/1950; 06/28/1965;
07/11/1878; 07/12/1899;
07/14/1881; 07/16/1945;
07/19/1879; 07/25/1861;
07/26/1878; 07/28/1933;
07/29/1776; 07/30/1946;
07/31/1850; 08/01/1861;
08/02/1846; 08/09/1850;
08/09/1945; 08/12/1821;
08/15/1824; 08/15/1846;
08/15/1850; 08/16/1878;
08/17/1846; 08/18/1937;
08/23/1945; 08/24/1821;
08/26/1879; 09/01/1821;
09/04/1878; 09/04/1972;
09/09/1850; 09/14/1712;
09/16/1857; 09/16/1874;
09/22/1846; 09/23/1875;
09/25/1867; 09/25/1875;
09/30/1878; 10/01/1804;
10/07/1870; 10/07/1878;
10/10/1867; 10/25/1923;
10/30/1875; 11/01/1875;
11/04/1862; 11/12/1880;
11/13/1878; 11/20/1809;
11/23/1859; 11/24/1835;
11/27/1886; 11/29/1880;
11/29/1975; 11/30/1884;
12/07/1828; 12/15/1970;
12/19/1880; 12/22/1878;
12/25/1887; 12/26/1826;
12/28/1854; 12/28/1878;
12/30/1853; 12/31/1907;
12/31/1943; 01/02/1777
Oakley, Annie ~
02/11/1866; 04/16/1884;
05/16/1946; 06/20/1882;
08/13/1860; 10/28/1901;
11/03/1926; 11/23/1926
Oil ~
01/04/1948; 01/06/1905;
01/10/1901; 01/24/1924;
01/28/1969; 02/17/1889;
03/04/1923; 05/31/1921;
06/06/1976; 06/25/1921;
08/04/1931; 11/01/1832;
11/28/1873; 11/29/1974;
12/20/1865
Oklahoma ~

01/27/1825; 01/30/1885;
02/03/1904; 02/22/1911;
02/25/1510; 02/27/1934;
02/29/1932; 03/02/1889;
03/04/1868; 03/22/1896;
03/23/1889; 03/31/1943;
04/04/1934; 04/07/1959;
04/11/1971; 04/13/1918;
04/22/1889; 05/02/1890;
05/15/1963; 05/26/1928;
05/30/1893; 06/13/1918;
06/16/1906; 06/20/1921;
07/14/1912; 07/14/1923;
07/15/1892; 07/26/1931;
07/26/1943; 07/27/1931;
08/04/1931; 08/07/1877;
08/18/1939; 08/25/1896;
09/01/1893; 09/04/1886;
09/15/1923; 09/16/1893;
09/22/1891; 09/30/1830;
10/09/1832; 10/10/1973;
10/13/1832; 10/15/1955;
10/15/1956; 10/22/1934;
11/10/1808; 11/10/1832;
11/10/1955; 11/13/1974;
11/16/1907; 11/20/1906;
11/21/1869; 12/02/1832;
12/12/1927; 12/29/1835

Omaha, Nebraska ~
01/05/1886; 01/12/1872;
01/16/1855; 02/11/1909;
03/23/1913; 04/03/1924;
07/10/1865; 07/13/1921;
10/17/1920; 12/01/1863

Oregon ~
01/21/1813; 01/21/1924;
02/03/1843; 02/03/1845;
02/14/1859; 02/28/1901;
03/16/1975; 03/17/1859;
03/19/1950; 04/21/1811;
05/01/1832; 05/06/1812;
05/09/1846; 05/16/1846;
05/22/1843; 05/22/1902;
06/16/1975; 07/05/1843;
07/08/1828; 07/14/1828;
07/28/1862; 08/14/1848;
08/17/1854; 09/01/1959;
09/08/1810; 09/21/1977;
09/26/1823; 09/28/1937;
10/03/1842; 10/03/1873;
10/26/1974; 12/07/1805;
12/12/1844; 12/16/1841;
12/22/1964

Overland Mail ~
07/01/1850; 07/03/1865;
09/16/1857; 09/16/1858;
10/09/1958

Packer Alfred ~
01/07/1901; 01/10/1901;
01/21/1874; 02/09/1874;
04/23/1907; 07/16/1938;

07/30/1934

Parker, Cynthia & Quanah ~
02/22/1911; 05/29/1836;
06/02/1875; 06/26/1874

Phoenix ~
01/01/1909; 02/11/1881;
02/21/1828; 04/22/1936;
06/11/1972; 07/29/1986;
12/29/1951

Pike, Zebulon ~
01/04/1806; 01/05/1779;
01/05/1807; 01/27/1807;
01/30/1807; 02/12/1806;
02/26/1807; 04/01/1807;
04/02/1806; 04/27/1813;
04/30/1806; 06/06/1819;
06/30/1891; 07/01/1807;
07/15/1806; 07/15/1820;
07/22/1893; 08/05/1858;
08/09/1805; 08/12/1859;
08/26/1806; 09/03/1806;
09/21/1805; 09/25/1806;
10/18/1806; 10/20/1890;
10/28/1806; 11/10/1806;
11/15/1806; 11/24/1806;
11/27/1806; 11/30/1806;
12/03/1806; 12/10/1806;
12/13/1806; 12/20/1806;
12/31/1806

Pinkertons ~
01/26/1875; 02/15/1922;
02/28/1900; 06/29/1903;
12/17/1901

Pony Express ~
03/02/1861; 04/03/1860;
04/13/1860; 07/03/1861;
09/10/1923; 10/24/1861

Powell, John Wesley ~
03/24/1834; 04/06/1862;
05/22/1871; 05/24/1869;
06/30/1894; 07/28/1869;
08/28/1869; 08/30/1869;
09/23/1902

Railroads ~
01/02/1907; 01/15/1909;
01/28/1878; 01/31/1874;
02/06/1891; 02/14/1886;
02/16/1877; 02/26/1928;
03/01/1910; 03/16/1906;
03/18/1878; 03/18/1912;
03/21/1910; 04/04/1878;
04/13/1866; 04/21/1856;
04/26/1901; 05/12/1870;
05/18/1871; 05/25/1934;
06/02/1899; 06/22/1870;
06/29/1903; 06/30/1891;
07/03/1901; 07/07/1875;
07/07/1903; 07/12/1899;
07/15/1892; 07/21/1873;

08/05/1914; 08/05/1922;
08/07/1904; 08/31/1901;
09/09/1899; 09/15/1896;
09/19/1877; 09/24/1870;
09/25/1908; 09/28/1917;
10/01/1897; 10/10/1904;
10/22/1902; 10/28/1901;
11/01/1855; 11/01/1887;
11/04/1870; 11/30/1902;
12/02/1873; 12/12/1874;
12/13/1844; 12/13/1922

Remington, Frederic ~
02/26/1882; 10/04/1861;
12/26/1909

Robberies ~
01/06/1923; 01/28/1878;
01/31/1874; 02/06/1891;
02/17/1904; 02/22/1921;
02/24/1878; 03/15/1881;
03/18/1878; 03/21/1868;
04/04/1878; 04/10/1878;
04/29/1872; 05/12/1875;
05/22/1867; 05/23/1872;
05/30/1899; 06/02/1895;
06/02/1899; 06/03/1871;
06/28/1897; 06/29/1903;
07/03/1901; 07/07/1903;
07/10/1881; 07/12/1899;
07/14/1901; 07/15/1881;
07/21/1873; 07/21/1878;
08/03/1877; 08/07/1881;
09/07/1876; 09/19/1877;
09/21/1876; 09/23/1872;
09/24/1976; 10/01/1897;
10/07/1879; 10/22/1902;
10/30/1866; 11/01/1932;
11/03/1883; 11/03/1899;
11/04/1870; 11/10/1921;
11/30/1902; 12/02/1873;
12/12/1874; 12/12/1901;
12/18/1922; 12/20/1877

Rodeo ~
02/28/1945; 04/02/1932;
04/10/1891; 06/10/1962;
06/14/1913; 07/04/1883;
07/04/1888; 07/04/1917;
08/01/1957; 09/08/1958;
09/12/1912; 11/12/1916;
11/27/1886; 12/05/1871;
12/23/1908

Roosevelt, Theodore ~
03/18/1911; 05/14/1903;
05/28/1902; 06/16/1906;
07/01/1898; 07/02/1939;
07/04/1903; 09/14/1901;
09/24/1906; 11/08/1904

Russell, Charles M. ~
03/19/1864; 10/24/1926

Salt Lake City ~
01/06/1913; 01/10/1914;

02/01/1885; 03/14/1944; 04/12/1858; 06/09/1856; 06/26/1858; 07/01/1850; 07/01/1858; 07/02/1859; 07/04/1858; 07/04/1885; 07/18/1857; 07/18/1914; 10/24/1861

San Antonio, Texas ~
01/13/1985; 02/11/1842; 02/28/1836; 03/11/1884; 03/14/1924; 03/18/1912; 03/19/1840; 03/23/1908; 04/22/1830; 04/26/1934; 05/01/1718; 06/30/1930; 07/09/1857; 07/25/1882; 08/12/1821; 09/11/1842; 09/11/1921; 10/22/1902; 10/23/1914; 10/28/1835; 10/28/1866; 11/14/1896; 12/09/1835; 12/25/1887; 12/31/1907

San Francisco ~
01/02/1850; 01/02/1853; 01/05/1874; 01/05/1933; 01/07/1860; 01/07/1961; 01/09/1847; 01/09/1848; 01/12/1876; 01/14/1967; 01/15/1852; 01/16/1850; 01/17/1859; 01/17/1871; 01/20/1891; 01/20/1985; 01/22/1850; 01/24/1982; 01/25/1915; 01/30/1847; 02/02/1811; 02/02/1848; 02/05/1887; 02/06/1915; 02/10/1879; 02/13/1945; 02/15/1922; 02/16/1914; 02/18/1939; 02/20/1902; 02/20/1915; 02/20/1954; 02/28/1849; 03/03/1857; 03/04/1936; 03/15/1848; 03/24/1860; 03/28/1776; 03/28/1882; 04/03/1848; 04/03/1860; 04/13/1860; 04/15/1850; 04/16/1866; 04/18/1906; 04/19/1874; 04/19/1906; 04/29/1863; 05/01/1860; 05/03/1851; 05/04/1850; 05/04/1851; 05/14/1852; 05/22/1856; 05/23/1873; 05/23/1908; 05/25/1948; 05/31/1930; 06/01/1850; 06/02/1873; 06/04/1863; 06/04/1876; 06/05/1875; 06/13/1911; 06/14/1850; 06/26/1927; 06/28/1982; 07/01/1839; 07/01/1895; 07/03/1852; 07/03/1861; 07/04/1876; 07/04/1903; 07/05/1920; 07/09/1846; 07/09/1907; 07/13/1869; 07/17/1944; 07/17/1964; 07/22/1916; 07/23/1877; 07/25/1877; 07/28/1849; 07/29/1920; 08/01/1903; 08/02/1873; 08/06/1934; 08/08/1923; 08/12/1853; 08/14/1903; 08/23/1836; 08/23/1872; 08/23/1899; 08/26/1907; 08/27/1875; 08/29/1966; 08/30/1869; 08/31/1903; 09/04/1951; 09/05/1925; 09/08/1951; 09/10/1923; 09/11/1853; 09/15/1850; 09/16/1857; 09/16/1858; 09/17/1776; 09/17/1975; 09/19/1900; 09/22/1869; 09/22/1975; 09/24/1930; 10/01/1922; 10/08/1860; 10/09/1776; 10/09/1858; 10/10/1858; 10/15/1863; 10/21/1868; 10/22/1812; 10/23/1908; 10/23/1962; 10/24/1861; 10/29/1953; 11/02/1856; 11/03/1883; 11/04/1867; 11/06/1862; 11/09/1848; 11/12/1936; 11/15/1869; 11/15/1872; 11/18/1846; 11/20/1969; 11/23/1852; 11/24/1852; 11/26/1868; 11/26/1872; 11/27/1978; 11/30/1884; 12/02/1863; 12/06/1893; 12/15/1866; 12/24/1849; 12/24/1853

Santa Fe ~
01/02/1777; 01/05/1848; 02/03/1980; 03/01/1873; 03/06/1986; 03/08/1881; 03/09/1842; 04/18/1846; 04/26/1869; 05/08/1827; 05/22/1822; 05/27/1831; 05/28/1848; 06/02/1892; 07/22/1739; 08/04/1706; 08/18/1846; 09/01/1821; 09/17/1848; 09/23/1878; 09/25/1846; 09/27/1930; 10/06/1846; 10/30/1868; 11/15/1934; 11/16/1821; 11/16/1934

Silver ~
02/16/1878; 02/26/1892; 04/10/1899; 05/02/1972; 06/27/1893; 07/17/1893; 12/17/1889

Sioux ~
01/01/1877; 01/06/1891; 01/07/1865; 01/14/1891; 01/16/1847; 01/26/1982; 01/31/1876; 02/01/1876; 02/02/1865; 02/03/1876; 02/10/1876; 02/11/1890; 03/17/1876; 04/29/1868; 05/08/1973; 05/23/1923; 06/11/1865; 06/12/1867; 06/13/1865; 06/13/1979; 06/14/1865; 06/17/1876; 06/25/1876; 06/30/1918; 07/08/1864; 07/15/1830; 07/16/1866; 07/19/1881; 07/23/1851; 08/01/1867; 08/02/1867; 08/04/1846; 08/05/1863; 08/11/1873; 08/17/1854; 08/18/1862; 08/19/1854; 09/03/1855; 09/03/1868; 09/08/1865; 09/09/1876; 09/17/1868; 09/28/1864; 11/05/1862; 12/06/1862; 12/14/1949; 12/21/1866; 12/26/1862; 12/29/1890

Sitting Bull ~
02/01/1876; 02/03/1876; 03/01/1831; 05/05/1877; 05/10/1883; 07/19/1881; 07/28/1864; 10/21/1876; 12/15/1890

Slaughter, John ~
02/08/1945; 02/15/1922; 06/07/1888; 10/02/1841

Smith, Jedediah ~
02/13/1822; 07/03/1827; 07/08/1828; 07/14/1828; 08/22/1826

Smith, Joseph ~
01/12/1838; 04/06/1830; 06/27/1844

Starr, Belle ~
02/03/1889; 02/05/1848; 08/06/1874

St. Louis, Missouri ~
01/11/1872; 02/12/1926; 03/06/1866; 03/09/1804; 03/09/1914; 03/26/1832; 04/03/1860; 04/07/1805; 04/10/1830; 04/13/1860; 04/13/1893; 04/21/1811; 04/30/1806; 04/30/1904; 05/12/1794; 05/14/1797; 05/14/1804; 05/17/1849; 05/20/1770; 05/22/1843; 05/25/1892; 05/27/1896; 06/05/1813; 07/12/1808; 07/15/1806; 07/17/1804; 07/17/1822; 07/29/1986; 08/07/1844; 08/12/1820; 08/30/1870; 09/01/1821; 09/16/1857; 09/16/1858; 09/23/1806; 10/09/1858; 10/10/1858; 10/26/1832; 10/28/1965; 12/01/1904; 12/23/1829; 12/28/1832

Tabor ~
03/07/1935; 04/10/1899;

04/12/1882; 09/05/1881;
09/17/1925; 12/17/1889

Taylor, Zachary ~
01/13/1846; 02/03/1846;
02/22/1847; 02/24/1847;
04/25/1846; 05/08/1846;
05/09/1846; 05/18/1846;
06/11/1845; 07/09/1850;
08/19/1846; 11/07/1848

Teapot Dome ~
01/02/1923; 01/24/1924;
02/28/1927; 03/04/1923;
04/07/1922; 05/31/1921;
06/30/1924; 09/27/1909;
10/25/1923; 10/25/1929;
11/01/1929; 11/26/1861;
11/30/1944

Texas ~
01/03/1823; 01/06/1882;
01/08/1884; 01/09/1858;
01/10/1901; 01/10/1925;
01/12/1884; 01/13/1985;
01/21/1861; 01/23/1875;
01/25/1839; 01/25/1845;
01/29/1850; 01/31/1927;
02/01/1845; 02/01/1861;
02/01/1935; 02/03/1959;
02/06/1897; 02/07/1855;
02/08/1945; 02/09/1914;
02/10/1850; 02/11/1842;
02/13/1913; 02/15/1876;
02/16/1877; 02/17/1889;
02/19/1846; 02/21/1936;
02/22/1894; 02/23/1861;
02/24/1878; 02/25/1510;
02/27/1917; 02/28/1918;
03/01/1845; 03/02/1793;
03/02/1836; 03/03/1837;
03/05/1918; 03/06/1836;
03/07/1885; 03/10/1925;
03/17/1949; 03/18/1878;
03/19/1836; 03/24/1825;
03/26/1836; 03/28/1846;
03/30/1870; 03/31/1861;
04/01/1930; 04/03/1817;
04/04/1878; 04/06/1830;
04/10/1878; 04/10/1962;
04/12/1844; 04/14/1823;
04/16/1947; 04/26/1837;
04/26/1901; 04/30/1598;
05/01/1846; 05/06/1930;
05/07/1824; 05/08/1843;
05/09/1916; 05/13/1975;
05/14/1836; 05/19/1853;
06/01/1958; 06/06/1976;
06/10/1821; 06/11/1845;
06/13/1875; 06/15/1843;
06/15/1845; 06/19/1865;
06/20/1899; 06/20/1935;
06/23/1845; 06/23/1931;
06/24/1716; 06/26/1874;
06/28/1880; 06/30/1835;
07/01/1836; 07/04/1883;
07/05/1899; 07/08/1833;
07/10/1824; 07/12/1926;
07/15/1892; 07/18/1902;
07/18/1938; 07/21/1878;
07/21/1832; 07/23/1921;
07/24/1958; 07/26/1863;
07/26/1878; 07/26/1931;
07/27/1931; 07/28/1933;
07/30/1923; 08/01/1966;
08/02/1973; 08/03/1859;
08/04/1837; 08/07/1913;
08/09/1850; 08/12/1821;
08/12/1936; 08/18/1983;
08/20/1971; 08/25/1829;
08/30/1874; 08/31/1965;
09/11/1842; 09/12/1958;
09/15/1896; 09/20/1967;
09/23/1839; 09/28/1874;
09/30/1830; 10/02/1835;
10/02/1841; 10/05/1871;
10/05/1899; 10/08/1838;
10/11/1878; 10/12/1974;
10/15/1955; 10/15/1966;
10/22/1836; 11/01/1832;
11/02/1912; 11/03/1793;
11/04/1958; 11/05/1960;
11/06/1528; 11/07/1876;
11/13/1863; 11/15/1887;
11/17/1882; 11/17/1981;
11/19/1985; 11/22/1963;
11/24/1835; 11/25/1835;
11/25/1864; 11/30/1837;
12/02/1832; 12/06/1949;
12/07/1876; 12/09/1835;
12/10/1854; 12/11/1872;
12/12/1844; 12/15/1881;
12/20/1865; 12/21/1821;
12/25/1891; 12/26/1826;
12/26/1874; 12/29/1845

Texas Rangers ~
01/06/1899; 01/07/1899;
01/29/1881; 02/02/1927;
04/03/1817; 05/01/1913;
05/25/1959; 06/13/1878;
07/21/1878; 08/02/1882;
08/05/1953; 10/01/1876;
10/17/1835; 10/21/1956;
11/04/1856; 11/24/1835;
12/07/1876; 12/25/1889;
12/26/1881

Tombstone, Arizona ~
01/06/1882; 01/31/1931;
02/05/1918; 02/08/1945;
04/01/1877; 05/03/1882;
06/22/1880; 07/10/1889;
08/06/1880; 10/09/1959;
10/16/1957; 10/26/1881;
10/27/1881; 10/28/1880;
11/14/1882; 12/01/1879;
12/08/1883; 12/28/1881

Tucson, Arizona ~
01/25/1934; 01/31/1931;
02/15/1955; 09/06/1966;
11/16/1958; 12/20/1970

Twain, Mark ~
04/20/1910; 07/06/1862;
11/18/1865; 11/30/1835;
12/15/1866

Union Pacific Railroad ~
03/28/1908; 05/10/1869;
06/02/1895; 06/30/1905;
07/01/1862; 07/10/1865;
09/13/1982; 09/19/1877;
11/02/1897; 11/17/1889;
12/01/1863

Utah ~
01/01/1917; 01/04/1896;
01/17/1977; 01/18/1987;
01/25/1965; 01/29/1850;
01/29/1861; 02/02/1848;
02/02/1870; 02/06/1899;
02/12/1870; 02/22/1880;
02/28/1861; 02/28/1898;
03/02/1923; 03/10/1849;
03/12/1934; 04/13/1866;
04/14/1860; 04/21/1897;
04/28/1869; 05/08/1895;
05/12/1825; 05/30/1910;
06/08/1923; 06/12/1983;
07/01/1862; 07/13/1857;
07/13/1950; 07/18/1857;
07/22/1918; 07/24/1847;
07/28/1872; 07/29/1776;
07/31/1850; 08/22/1826;
08/23/1877; 08/23/1933;
09/09/1850; 09/11/1857;
09/12/1964; 09/15/1857;
09/24/1890; 09/30/1855;
10/02/1919; 10/04/1915;
10/14/1922; 10/23/1970;
10/27/1972; 11/12/1971;
11/19/1915; 11/19/1919;
12/05/1933; 12/18/1971;
12/19/1984

Virginia City ~
03/10/1864; 05/26/1863;
06/07/1873; 07/06/1862;
09/17/1864

Wells Fargo ~
03/18/1852; 03/18/1957;
04/16/1866; 07/14/1923;
09/08/1962

Whitman, Marcus ~
09/04/1802; 10/03/1842;
11/29/1847

Wyoming ~
01/05/1925; 02/02/1870;
02/04/1889; 02/09/1933;
02/26/1929; 03/01/1872;
03/03/1905; 03/04/1881;
03/04/1886; 03/12/1922;

Days of the West 211

03/29/1879; 04/07/1922;
04/10/1905; 04/13/1892;
04/14/1902; 05/11/1933;
05/28/1902; 05/31/1921;
06/06/1938; 06/15/1846;
07/03/1865; 07/10/1890;
07/20/1889; 07/24/1865;
07/25/1868; 08/01/1985;
08/02/1867; 08/08/1814;
08/19/1872; 08/23/1897;
09/08/1865; 09/24/1906;
09/27/1909; 09/30/1889;
10/02/1924; 10/23/1972;
10/26/1901; 11/09/1924;
11/29/1976; 12/02/1905;
12/09/1898; 12/10/1869;
12/21/1866

Young, Brigham ~
01/08/1865; 01/14/1846;
01/15/1846; 01/16/1847;
01/17/1846; 01/21/1846;
01/22/1846; 01/24/1863;
01/26/1846; 01/28/1846;
01/30/1846; 01/31/1846;
02/02/1846; 02/03/1846;
02/06/1846; 02/10/1846;
02/25/1858; 03/14/1856;
03/17/1804; 03/20/1847;
03/31/1834; 04/06/1830;
04/07/1868; 04/16/1847;
04/18/1848; 04/30/1845;
05/08/1844; 05/08/1870;
06/01/1801; 06/10/1857;
06/15/1842; 06/19/1845;
06/19/1855; 07/03/1869;
07/13/1857; 07/13/1859;
07/18/1857; 07/22/1847;
07/31/1850; 08/23/1877;
09/08/1832; 09/10/1844;
09/15/1857; 09/30/1855;
10/02/1871; 10/03/1850;
10/06/1845; 10/08/1824;
11/02/1843; 11/02/1844;
12/06/1852

Yellowstone ~
03/01/1872; 03/26/1832;
04/04/1843; 04/21/1833;
04/25/1805; 04/26/1805;
05/17/1876; 06/21/1876;
07/19/1871; 08/11/1873;
08/15/1806; 08/23/1883;
09/25/1926

Youngers ~
01/15/1844; 01/15/1848;
01/15/1874; 02/21/1916;
03/16/1874; 03/21/1868;
03/21/1916; 04/29/1872;
05/12/1875; 05/23/1872;
06/03/1871; 07/07/1875;
07/14/1901; 07/21/1873;
08/16/1889; 08/21/1863;
09/07/1876; 09/14/1889;
09/21/1876; 09/23/1872;
10/19/1901; 10/30/1866;
12/07/1869; 12/12/1874

Mike Flanagan

Mike Flanagan was born in Oklahoma in 1950. Since 1982 he has been writing the weekly historical column "Out West" for *The Denver Post*. His features on a variety of subjects have been syndicated internationally. He lives in Denver with his wife and their daughter, Sarah, who tells him the future is the past, it just hasn't happened yet. *Days of the West* is his second book.